O. T., A Danish Romance

by

H. C. Andersen

Double 9
BOOKS

O. T., A Danish Romance
by H. C. Andersen

ISBN: 978-93-64282-09-3

Published by

DOUBLE 9 BOOKS

2/13-B, Ansari Road
Daryaganj, New Delhi – 110002
info@double9books.com
www.double9books.com
Tel. 011-40042856

ABOUT THE AUTHOR

Hans Christian Andersen (1805–1875) was a Danish author and poet renowned for his fairy tales and literary contributions that have captivated readers worldwide. Born in Odense, Denmark, Andersen grew up in humble beginnings, marked by poverty and early struggles. Despite these challenges, his creative talents began to flourish at a young age, and he developed a love for storytelling and theater. As a writer, Andersen embraced Romanticism, infusing his tales with themes of love, fate, transformation, and the struggle for personal fulfillment. His narratives often featured protagonists who overcome adversity and discover their true selves through courage, kindness, and perseverance. Andersen's stories also reflected his keen observations of human nature and society, addressing themes of social class, identity, and the pursuit of dreams. Beyond fairy tales, Andersen wrote plays, travelogues, poetry, and novels, showcasing his versatility and literary craftsmanship. His works were influenced by his travels across Europe, where he met and befriended prominent figures such as Charles Dickens and Alexandre Dumas. Hans Christian Andersen's contributions to literature earned him admiration and recognition during his lifetime, and his legacy continues to endure today. His fairy tales have been translated into numerous languages and adapted into various forms of media, cementing his status as one of the most beloved storytellers in history. Andersen's ability to blend imagination with profound insight into the human condition remains a source of inspiration for readers of all ages around the world.

CONTENTS

CHAPTER I

"Quod felix faustumque sit!"

There is a happiness which no poet has yet properly sung, which no lady-reader, let her be ever so amiable, has experienced or ever will experience in this world. This is a condition of happiness which alone belongs to the male sex, and even then alone to the elect. It is a moment of life which seizes upon our feelings, our minds, our whole being. Tears have been shed by the innocent, sleepless nights been passed, during which the pious mother, the loving sister, have put up prayers to God for this critical moment in the life of the son or the brother.

Happy moment, which no woman, let her be ever so good, so beautiful, or intellectual, can experience—that of becoming a student, or, to describe it by a more usual term, the passing of the first examination!

The cadet who becomes an officer, the scholar who becomes an academical burgher, the apprentice who becomes a journeyman, all know, in a greater or less degree, this loosening of the wings, this bounding over the limits of maturity into the lists of philosophy. We all strive after a wider field, and rush thither like the stream which at length loses itself in the ocean.

Then for the first time does the youthful soul rightly feel her freedom, and, therefore, feels it doubly; the soul struggles for activity, she comprehends her individuality; it has been proved and not found too light; she is still in possession of the dreams of childhood, which have not yet proved delusive. Not even the joy of love, not the enthusiasm for art and science, so thrills through all the nerves as the words, "Now am I a student!"

This spring-day of life, on which the ice-covering of the school is broken, when the tree of Hope puts forth its buds and the sun of Freedom shines, falls with us, as is well known, in the month of October, just when Nature loses her foliage, when the evenings begin to grow darker, and when heavy winter-clouds draw together, as though they would say to youth,—"Your spring, the birth of the examination, is only a dream! even now does your life become earnest!" But our happy youths think not of these things, neither will we be joyous with the gay, and pay a visit to their circle. In such a one our story takes its commencement.

CHAPTER II

"At last we separate:
To Jutland one, to Fünen others go;
And still the quick thought comes,
—A day so bright, so full of fun,
Never again on us shall rise."—CARL BAGGER.

It was in October of the year 1829. Examen artium had been passed through. Several young students were assembled in the evening at the abode of one of their comrades, a young Copenhagener of eighteen, whose parents were giving him and his new friends a banquet in honor of the examination. The mother and sister had arranged everything in the nicest manner, the father had given excellent wine out of the cellar, and the student himself, here the rex convivii, had provided tobacco, genuine Oronoko-canaster. With regard to Latin, the invitation—which was, of course, composed in Latin—informed the guests that each should bring his own.

The company, consisting of one and twenty persons—and these were only the most intimate friends—was already assembled. About one third of the friends were from the provinces, the remainder out of Copenhagen.

"Old Father Homer shall stand in the middle of the table!" said one of the liveliest guests, whilst he took down from the stove a plaster bust and placed it upon the covered table.

"Yes, certainly, he will have drunk as much as the other poets!" said an older one. "Give me one of thy exercise-books, Ludwig! I will cut him out a wreath of vine-leaves, since we have no roses and since I cannot cut out any."

"I have no libation!" cried a third,—"Favete linguis." And he sprinkled a small quantity of salt, from the point of a knife, upon the bust, at the same time raising his glass to moisten it with a few drops of wine.

"Do not use my Homer as you would an ox!" cried the host. "Homer shall have the place of honor, between the bowl and the garland-cake! He is especially my poet! It was he who in Greek assisted me to laudabilis et quidem egregie. Now we will mutually drink healths! Jörgen shall be magister bibendi, and then we will sing 'Gaudeamus igitur,' and 'Integer vitae.'"

"The Sexton with the cardinal's hat shall be the precentor!" cried one of the youths from the provinces, pointing toward a rosy-cheeked companion.

"O, now I am no longer sexton!" returned the other laughing. "If thou bringest old histories up again, thou wilt receive thy old school-name, 'the Smoke-squirter.'"

"But that is a very nice little history!" said the other. "We called him 'Sexton,' from the office his father held; but that, after all, is not particularly witty. It was better with the hat, for it did, indeed, resemble a cardinal's hat. I, in the mean time, got my name in a more amusing manner."

"He lived near the school," pursued the other; "he could always slip home when we had out free quarters of an hour: and then one day he had filled his mouth with tobacco smoke, intending to blow it into our faces; but when he entered the passage with his filled cheeks the quarter of an hour was over, and we were again in class: the rector was still standing in the doorway; he could not, therefore, blow the smoke out of his mouth, and so wished to slip in as he was. 'What have you there in your mouth?' asked the rector; but Philip could answer nothing, without at the same time losing the smoke. 'Now, cannot you speak?' cried the rector, and gave him a box on the ear, so that the smoke burst through nose and mouth. This looked quite exquisite; the affair caused the rector such pleasure, that he presented the poor sinner with the nota bene."

"Integer vitae!" broke in the Precentor, and harmoniously followed the other voices. After this, a young Copenhagener exhibited his dramatic talent by mimicking most illusively the professors of the Academy, and giving their peculiarities, yet in such a good-natured manner that it must have amused even the offended parties themselves. Now followed the healths—"Vivant omnes hi et hae!"

"A health to the prettiest girl!" boldly cried one of the merriest brothers. "The prettiest girl!" repeated a pair of the younger ones, and pushed their glasses toward each other, whilst the blood rushed to their cheeks at this their boldness, for they had never thought of a beloved being, which, nevertheless, belonged to their new life. The roundelay now commenced, in which each one must give the Christian name of his lady-love, and assuredly every second youth caught a name out of the air; some, however, repeated a name with a certain palpitation of the heart. The discourse became more animated; the approaching military exercises, the handsome uniform, the reception in the students' club, and its pleasures, were all matters of the highest interest. But there was the future philologicum and philosophicum—yes, that also was discussed; there they must exhibit their knowledge of Latin.

"What do you think," said one of the party, "if once a week we alternately met at each other's rooms, and held disputations? No Danish word must be spoken. This might be an excellent scheme."

"I agree to that!" cried several.

"Regular laws must be drawn up."

"Yes, and we must have our best Latin scholar, the Jutlander, Otto Thostrup, with us! He wrote his themes in hexameters."

"He is not invited here this evening," remarked the neighbor, the young Baron Wilhelm of Funen, the only nobleman in the company.

"Otto Thostrup!" answered the host. "Yes, truly he's a clever fellow, but he seems to me so haughty. There is something about him that does not please me at all. We are still no dunces, although he did receive nine prae caeteris!"

"Yet it was very provoking," cried another, "that he received the only Non in mathematics. Otherwise he would have been called in. Now he will only have to vex himself about his many brilliant characters."

"Yes, and he is well versed in mathematics!" added Wilhelm "There was something incorrect in the writing; the inspector was to blame for that, but how I know not. Thostrup is terribly vehement, and can set all respect at defiance; he became angry, and went out. There was only a piece of unwritten paper presented from him, and this brought him a cipher, which the verbal examination could not bring higher than non. Thostrup is certainly a glorious fellow. We have made a tour together in the steamboat from Helsingöer to Copenhagen, and in the written examination we sat beside each other until the day when we had mathematics, and then I sat below him. I like him very much, his pride excepted; and of that we must break him."

"Herr Baron," said his neighbor, "I am of your opinion. Shall not we drink the Thou-brotherhood?"

"To-night we will all of us drink the Thou!" said the host; "it is nothing if comrades and good friends call each other *you*."

"Evoe Bacchus!" they joyously shouted. The glasses were filled, one arm was thrown round that of the neighbor, and the glasses were emptied, whilst several commenced singing "dulce cum sodalibus!"

"Tell me what thou art called?" demanded one of the younger guests of his new Thou-brother.

"What am I called?" replied he. "With the exception of one letter, the same as the Baron."

"The Baron!" cried a third; "yes, where is he?"

"There he stands talking at the door; take your glasses! now have all of us drank the Thou-brotherhood?"

The glasses were again raised; the young Baron laughed, clinked his glass, and shouted in the circle, "Thou, Thou!" But in his whole bearing there lay something constrained, which, however, none of the young men remarked, far less allowed themselves to imagine that his sudden retreat, during the first drinking, perhaps occurred from the sole object of avoiding it. But soon was he again one of the most extravagant; promised each youth who would study theology a living on his estate when he should once get it into his own hands; and proposed that the Latin disputations should commence with him, and on the following Friday. Otto Thostrup, however, should be of the party—if he chose, of course being understood; for he was a capital student, and his friend they had made a journey together and had been neighbors at the green table.

Among those who were the earliest to make their valete amici was the Baron. Several were not yet inclined to quit this joyous circle. The deepest silence reigned in the streets; it was the most beautiful moonlight. In most houses all had retired to rest—only here and there was a light still seen, most persons slept, even those whose sense of duty should leave banished the god of sleep: thus sat a poor hackney-coachman, aloft upon his coach-box, before the house where he awaited his party, and enjoyed, the reins wound about his hand, the much-desired rest. Wilhelm (henceforth we will only call the young Baron by his Christian name) walked alone through the street. The wine had heated his northern blood—besides which it never flowed slowly; his youthful spirits, his jovial mood, and the gayety occasioned by the merry company he had just quitted did not permit him quietly to pass by this sleeping Endymion. Suddenly it occurred to him to open the coach-door and leap in; which having done, he let the glass fall and called out with a loud voice, "Drive on!" The coachman started up out of his blessed sleep and asked, quite confused, "Where to?" Without reflecting about the matter, Wilhelm cried, "To the Ship in West Street." The coachman drove on; about half-way, Wilhelm again opened the coach-door, a bold spring helped him out, and the coach rolled on. It stopped at the public-house of the Ship. The coachman got down and opened the door; there was no one within; he thrust his head in thoroughly to convince himself; but no, the carriage was empty! "Extraordinary!" said the fellow; "can I have dreamed it? But still I heard, quite distinctly, how I was told to drive to the Ship! Lord preserve us! now they are waiting for me!" He leaped upon the box and drove rapidly back again.

In the mean time Wilhelm had reached his abode in Vineyard Street; he opened a window to enjoy the beautiful night, and gazed out upon the desolate church-yard which is shut in by shops. He had no inclination for sleep, although everything in the street, even the watchmen not excepted, appeared to rejoice the gift of God. Wilhelm thought upon the merry evening party, upon his adventure with the poor hackney-coachman, then took down his violin from the wall and began to play certain variations.

The last remaining guests from the honorable carousal, merrier than when Wilhelm left them, now came wandering up the street. One of them jodeled sweetly, and no watchman showed himself as a disturbing principle. They heard Wilhelm violin and recognized the musician.

"Play us a Française, thou up there!" cried they.

"But the watchman?" whispered one of the less courageous.

"Zounds, there he sits!" cried a third, and pointed toward a sleeping object which leaned its head upon a large wooden chest before a closed booth.

"He is happy!" said the first speaker. "If we had only the strong Icelander here, he would soon hang him up by his bandelier upon one of the iron hooks. He has done that before now; he has the strength of a bear. He seized such a lazy fellow as this right daintily by his girdle on one of the hooks at the weighing-booth. There hung the watchman and whistled to the others; the first who hastened to the spot was immediately hung up beside him, and away ran the Icelander whilst the two blew a duet."

"Here, take hold!" cried one of the merry brothers, quickly opening the chest, the lid of which was fastened by a peg. "Let us put the watchman into the chest; he sleeps indeed like a horse!" In a moment, the four had seized the sleeper, who certainly awoke during the operation, but he already lay in the chest. The lid flew down, and two or three of the friends sprang upon it whilst the peg was stuck in again. The watchman immediately seized his whistle and drew the most heart-rending tones from it. Quickly the tormenting spirits withdrew themselves; yet not so far but that they could still hear the whistle and observe what would take place.

The watchmen now came up.

"The deuce! where art thou?" cried they, and then discovered the place.

"Ah, God help me!" cried the prisoner. "Let me out, let me out! I must call!"

"Thou hast drunk more than thy thirst required, comrade!" said the others. "If thou hast fallen into the chest, remain lying there, thou swine!" And laughing they left him.

"O, the rascals!" sighed he, and worked in vain at opening the lid. Through all his powerful exertions the box fell over. The young men now stepped forth, and, as though they were highly astonished at the whole history which he related to them, they let themselves be prevailed upon to open the box, but only upon condition that he should keep street free from the interference of the other watchmen whilst they danced a Française to Wilhelm's violin.

The poor man was delivered from his captivity, and must obligingly play the sentinel whilst they arranged them for the dance. Wilhelm was called upon to play, and the dance commenced; a partner, however, was wanting. Just then a quiet citizen passed by. The gentleman who had no partner approached the citizen with comic respect, and besought him to take part in the amusement.

O. T., A Danish Romance | 13

"I never dance!" said the man, laughing, and wished to pursue his way.

"Yes," replied the cavalier, "yet you must still do me this pleasure, or else I shall have no dance." Saying this he took hold of him by the waist and the dance commenced, whether the good man would or no.

"The watchman should receive a present from every one!" said they, when the Française was at an end. "He is an excellent man who thus keeps order in the street, so that one can enjoy a little dance."

"These are honest people's children!" said the watchman to himself, whilst he with much pleasure thrust the money into his leathern purse.

All was again quiet in the street; the violin was also silent.

CHAPTER III

"Who looks into the shadowy realm of my heart?"
A. V. CHAMISSO.

In the former chapter we heard mention made of a young student, Otto Thostrup, a clever fellow, with nine prae caeteris, as his comrades said, but also of a proud spirit, of which he must be broken. Not at the disputations, which have been already mentioned, will we make his acquaintance, although there we must be filled with respect for the good Latin scholar; not in large companies, where his handsome exterior and his speaking, melancholy glance must make him interesting; as little in the pit of the Opera although his few yet striking observations there would show him to be a very intellectual young man; but we will seek him out for the first time at the house of his friend, the young Baron Wilhelm. It is the beginning of November: we find them both with their pipes in their mouths; upon the table lie Tibullus and Anacreon, which they are reading together for the approaching philologicum.

In the room stands a piano-forte, with a number of music-books; upon the walls hang the portraits of Weyse and Beethoven, for our young Baron is musical, nay a composer himself.

"See, here we have again this lovely, clinging mist!" said Wilhelm. "Out of doors one can fairly taste it; at home it would be a real plague to me, here it only Londonizes the city."

"I like it!" said Otto. "To me it is like an old acquaintance from Vestervovov. It is as though the mist brought me greetings from the sea and sand-hills."

"I should like to see the North Sea, but the devil might live there! What town lies nearest to your grandfather's estate?"

"Lernvig," answered Otto. "If any one wish to see the North Sea properly, they ought to go up as far as Thisted and Hjörring. I have travelled there, have visited the family in Börglum-Kloster; and, besides this, have made other small journeys. Never shall I forget one evening; yes, it was a storm of which people in the interior of the country can form no conception. I rode—I was then a mere boy, and a very wild lad—with one of our men. When the storm commenced we found ourselves among the sand-hills. Ah! that you should have seen! The sand forms along the strand high banks, which serve as dikes against the sea; these are overgrown with sea-grass, but, if the storm bursts a single hole, the whole is carried away. This spectacle we chanced to witness. It is a true Arabian sand-storm, and the North Sea bellowed so that it might be heard at the distance of many miles. The salt foam flew together with the sand into our faces."

"That must have been splendid!" exclaimed Wilhelm, and his eyes sparkled. "Jutland is certainly the most romantic part of Denmark. Since I read Steen-Blicher's novels I have felt a real interest for that country. It seems to me that it must greatly resemble the Lowlands of Scotland. And gypsies are also found there, are they not?"

"Vagabonds, we call them," said Otto, with an involuntary motion of the mouth. "They correspond to the name!"

"The fishermen, also, on the coast are not much better! Do they still from the pulpit pray for wrecks? Do they still slay shipwrecked mariners?"

"I have heard our preacher, who is an old man, relate how, in the first years after he had obtained his office and dignity, he was obliged to pray in the church that, if ships stranded, they might strand in his district; but this I have never heard myself. But with regard to what is related of murdering, why, the fishermen—sea-geese, as they are called—are by no means a tender-hearted people; but it is not as bad as that in our days. A peasant died in the neighborhood, of whom it was certainly related that in bad weather he had bound a lantern under his horse's belly and let it wander up and down the beach, so that the strange mariner who was sailing in those seas might imagine it some cruising ship, and thus fancy himself still a considerable way from land. By this means many a ship is said to have been destroyed. But observe, these are stories out of the district of Thisted, and of an elder age, before my power of observation had developed itself; this was that golden age when in tumble-down fishers' huts, after one of these good shipwrecks, valuable shawls, but little damaged by the sea, might be found employed as bed-hangings. Boots and shoes were smeared with the finest pomatum. If such things now reach their hands, they know better how to turn them into money. The Strand-commissioners are now on the watch; now it is said to be a real age of copper."

"Have you seen a vessel stranded?" inquired Wilhelm, with increasing interest.

"Our estate lies only half a mile from the sea. Every year about this time, when the mist spreads itself out as it does to-day and the storms begin to rage, then was it most animated. In my wild spirits, when I was a boy, and especially in the midst of our monotonous life, I truly yearned after it. Once, upon a journey to Börglum-Kloster, I experienced a storm. In the early morning; it was quite calm, but gray, and we witnessed a kind of Fata Morgana. A ship, which had not yet risen above the horizon, showed itself in the distance, but the rigging was turned upside down; the masts were below, the hull above. This is called the ship of death, and when it is seen people are sure of bad weather and shipwreck. Later, about midday, it began to blow, and in an hour's time we had a regular tempest. The sea growled quite charmingly; we travelled on between sand-hills—they resemble hills and dales in winter time, but here it is not snow which melts away; here never grows a single green blade; a black stake stands up here and there, and these are rudders from wrecks, the histories of which are unknown. In the afternoon arose a storm such as I had experienced when riding with the man between the sand-hills. We could not proceed farther, and were obliged on this account to seek shelter in one of the huts which the fishermen hail erected among the white sand-hills. There we remained, and I saw the stranding of a vessel: I shall never forget it! An American ship lay not a musket-shot from land. They cut the mast; six or seven men clung fast to it in the waters. O, how they rocked backward and forward in the dashing spray! The mast took a direction toward the shore; at length only three men were left clinging to the mast; it was dashed upon land, but the returning waves again bore it away; it had crushed the arms and legs of the clinging wretches—ground them like worms! I dreamed of this for many nights. The waves flung the hull of the vessel up high on the shore, and drove it into the sand, where it was afterward found. Later, as we retraced our steps, were the stem and sternpost gone: you saw two strong wooden walls, between which the road took its course. You even still travel through the wreck!"

"Up in your country every poetical mind must become a Byron," said Wilhelm. "On my parents' estate we have only idyls; the whole of Funen is a garden. We mutually visit each other upon our different estates, where we lead most merry lives, dance with the peasant-girls at the brewing-feast, hunt in the woods, and fish in the lakes. The only melancholy object which presents itself with us is a funeral, and the only romantic characters we possess are a little hump-backed musician, a wise woman, and an honest schoolmaster, who still firmly believes, as Jeronimus did, that the earth is flat, and that, were it to turn round, we should fall, the devil knows where!"

"I love nature in Jutland!" exclaimed Otto. "The open sea, the brown heath, and the bushy moorland. You should see the wild moor in Vendsyssel—that is an extent! Almost always wet mists float over its unapproachable interior, which is known to no one. It is not yet fifty years since it served as an abode for wolves. Often it bursts into flames, for it is impregnated with sulphuric gas,—one can see the fire for miles."

"My sister Sophie ought to hear all this!" said Wilhelm. "You would make your fortune with her! The dear girl! she has the best head at home, but she loves effect. Hoffman and Victor Hugo are her favorites. Byron rests every night under her pillow. If you related such things of the west coast of Jutland, and of heaths and moors, you might persuade her to make a journey thither. One really would not believe that we possessed in our own country such romantic situations!"

"Is she your only sister?" inquired Otto.

"No," returned Wilhelm, "I have two—the other is named Louise; she is of quite an opposite character: I do not know of which one ought to think most. Have you no brothers or sisters?" he asked of Otto.

"No!" returned the latter, with his former involuntary, half-melancholy expression. "I am an only child. In my house it is solitary and silent. My grandfather alone is left alive. He is an active, strong man, but very grave. He instructed me in mathematics, which he thoroughly understands. The preacher taught me Latin, Greek, and history: two persons, however, occupied themselves with my religious education—the preacher and my old Rosalie. She is a good soul. How often have I teased her, been petulant, and almost angry with her! She thought so much of me, she was both mother and sister to me, and instructed me in religion as well as the preacher, although she is a Catholic. Since my father's childhood she has been a sort of governante in the house. You should have seen her melancholy smile when she heard my geography lesson, and we read of her dear Switzerland, where she was born, and of the south of France, where she had travelled as a child. The west coast of Jutland may also appear very barren in comparison with these countries!"

"She might have made you a Catholic! But surely nothing of this still clings to you?"

"Rosalie was a prudent old creature; Luther himself need not have been ashamed of her doctrine. Whatever is holy to the heart of man, remains also holy in every religion!"

"But then, to erect altars to the Madonna!" exclaimed Wilhelm; "to pray to a being; whom the Bible does not make a saint!—that is rather too much. And their tricks with burning of incense and ringing of bells! Yes, indeed, it would give me no little pleasure to cut off the heads of the Pope and of the whole clerical body! To purchase indulgence!—Those must, indeed, be curious people who can place thorough faith in such things! I will never once take off my hat before the Madonna!"

"But that will I do, and in my heart bow myself before her!" answered Otto, gravely.

"Did I not think so? she has made you a Catholic!"

"No such thing! I am as good a Protestant as you yourself: but wherefore should we not respect the mother of Christ? With regard to the ceremonials of Catholicism, indulgence, and all these additions of the priesthood, I agree with you in wishing to strike off the heads of all who, in such a manner, degrade God and the human understanding. But in many respects we are unjust: we so easily forget the first and greatest commandment, 'Love thy neighbor as thyself!' We are not tolerant. Among our festivals we have still one for the Three Kings—it is yet celebrated by the common people; but what have these three kings done? They knelt before the manger in which Christ lay, and on this account we honor them. On the contrary, the mother of God has no festival-day; nay, the multitude even smile at her name! If you will only quietly listen to my simple argument, we shall soon agree. You will take off your hat and bow before the Madonna. Only two things are to be considered—either Christ was entirely human, or He was, as the Bible teaches us, a divine being. I will now admit the latter. He is God Himself, who in some inexplicable manner, is born to us of the Virgin Mary. She must therefore be the purest, the most perfect feminine being, since God found her worthy to bring into the world the Son, the only one; through this she becomes as holy as any human being can, and low we must bow ourselves before the pure, the exalted one. Take it for granted that Christ was human, like ourselves, otherwise He cannot, according to my belief, call upon us to imitate Him; neither would it be great, as God, to meet a corporeal death, from which He could remove each pain. Were He only a man, born of Mary, we must doubly admire Him; we must bow in the dust before His mighty spirit, His enlightening and consoling doctrine. But can we then forget how much the mother has must have influenced the child, how sublime and profound the soul must have been which spoke to His heart? We must reverence and honor her! Everywhere in the Scriptures where she appears we see an example of care and love; with her whole soul she adheres to her Son. Think how uneasy she became, and sought for Him in the temple—think of her gentle reproaches! The words of the Son always sounded harsh in my ears. 'Those are the powerful expressions of the East!' said my old preacher. The Saviour was severe, severe as He must be! Already there seemed to me severity in His words! She was completely the mother; she was it then, even as when she wept at Golgotha. Honor and reverence she deserves from us!"

"These she also receives!" returned Wilhelm; and striking him upon the shoulder he added, with a smile, "you are, according to the Roman Catholic manner, near exalting the mother above the Son! Old Rosalie has made a proselyte; after all, you are half a Catholic!"

"That am I not!" answered Otto, "and that will I not be!"

"See! the thunder-cloud advances!"

resounded below in the court: the sweet Neapolitan song reached the ears of the friends. They stepped into the adjoining room and opened the window. Three poor boys stood below in the wind and rain, and commenced the song. The tallest was, perhaps, fourteen or fifteen years old, his deep, rough voice seemed to have attained its strength and depth more through rain and bad weather than through age. The dirty wet clothes hung in rags about his body; the shoes upon the wet feet, and the hat held together with white threads, were articles of luxury. The other two boys had neither hat nor shoes, but their clothes were whole and clean. The youngest appeared six or seven years old; his silvery white hair formed a contrast with his brown face, his dark eyes and long brown eyelashes. His voice sounded like the voice of a little girl, as fine and soft, beside the voices of the others, as the breeze of an autumnal evening beside that of rude November weather.

"That is a handsome boy!" exclaimed the two friends at the same time.

"And a lovely melody!" added Otto.

"Yes, but they sing falsely!" answered Wilhelm: "one sings half a tone too low, the other half a tone too high!"

"Now, thank God that I cannot hear that!" said Otto. "It sounds sweetly, and the little one might become a singer. Poor child!" added he gravely: "bare feet, wet to the very skin; and then the elder one will certainly lead him to brandy drinking! Within a month, perhaps, the voice will be gone! Then is the nightingale dead!" He quickly threw down some skillings, wrapped in paper.

"Come up!" cried Wilhelm, and beckoned. The eldest of the boys flew up like an arrow; Wilhelm, however, said it was the youngest who was meant. The others remained standing before the door; the youngest stepped in.

"Whose son art thou?" asked Wilhelm. The boy was silent, and cast down his eyes in an embarrassed manner. "Now, don't be bashful! Thou art of a good family—that one can see from thy appearance! Art not thou thy mother's son? I will give thee stockings and—the deuce! here is a pair of boots which are too small for me; if thou dost not get drowned in them they shall be thy property: but now thou must sing." And he seated himself at the piano-forte and struck the keys. "Now, where art thou?" he cried, rather displeased. The little one gazed upon the ground.

"How! dost thou weep; or is it the rain which hangs in thy black eyelashes?" said Otto, and raised his head: "we only wish to do thee a kindness. There—thou hast another skilling from me."

The little one still remained somewhat laconic. All that they learned was that he was named Jonas, and that his grandmother thought so much of him.

"Here thou hast the stockings!" said Wilhelm; "and see here! a coat with a velvet collar, a much-to-be-prized keepsake! The boots! Thou canst certainly stick both legs into one boot! See! that is as good as having two pairs to change about with! Let us see!"

The boy's eyes sparkled with joy; the boots he drew on, the stockings went into his pocket, and the bundle he took under his arm.

"But thou must sing us a little song!" said Wilhelm, and the little one commenced the old song out of the "Woman-hater," "Cupid never can be trusted!"

The lively expression in the dark eyes, the boy himself in his wet, wretched clothes and big boots, with the bundle under his arm; nay, the whole had something so characteristic in it, that had it been painted, and had the painter called the picture "Cupid on his Wanderings," every one would have found the little god strikingly excellent, although he were not blind.

"Something might be made of the boy and of his voice!" said Wilhelm, when little Jonas, in a joyous mood, had left the house with the other lads.

"The poor child!" sighed Otto. "I have fairly lost my good spirits through all this. It seizes upon me so strangely when I see misery and genius mated. Once there came to our estate in Jutland a man who played the Pandean-pipes, and at the same time beat the drum and cymbals: near him stood a little girl, and struck the triangle. I was forced to weep over this spectacle; without understanding how it was, I felt the misery of the poor child. I was myself yet a mere boy."

"He looked so comic in the big boots that I became quite merry, and not grave," said Wilhelm. "Nevertheless what a pity it is that such gentle blood, which at the first glance one perceives he is, that such a pretty child should become a rude fellow, and his beautiful voice change into a howl, like that with which the other tall Laban saluted us. Who knows whether little Jonas might not become the first singer on the Danish stage? Yes, if he received education of mind and voice, who knows? I could really have, pleasure in attempting it, and help every one on in the world, before I myself am rightly in the way!"

"If he is born to a beggar's estate," said Otto, "let him as beggar live and die, and learn nothing higher. That is better, that is more to be desired!"

Wilhelm seated himself at the piano-forte, and played some of his own compositions. "That is difficult," said he; "every one cannot play that."

"The simpler the sweeter!" replied Otto.

"You must not speak about music!" returned the friend "upon that you know not how to pass judgment. Light Italian operas are not difficult to write."

In the evening the friends separated. Whilst Otto took his hat, there was a low knock at the door. Wilhelm opened it. Without stood a poor old woman, with pale sharp features; by the hand she led a little boy—it was Jonas: thus then it was a visit from him and his grandmother.

The other boys had sold the boots and shoes which had been given him. They ought to have a share, they maintained. This atrocious injustice had induced the old grandmother to go immediately with little Jonas to the two good gentlemen, and relate how little the poor lad had received of flint which they had assigned to him alone.

Wilhelm spoke of the boy's sweet voice, and thought that by might make his fortune at the theatre; but then he ought not now to be left running about with bare feet in the wind and rain.

"But by this means he brings a skilling home," said the old woman. "That's what his father and mother look to, and the skilling they can always employ. Nevertheless she had herself already thought of bringing him out at the theatre,—but that was to have been in dancing, for they got shoes and stockings to dance in, and with these they might also run home; and that would be an advantage."

"I will teach the boy music!" said Wilhelm; "he can come to me sometimes."

"And then he will, perhaps, get a little cast-off clothing, good sir," said the grandmother; "a shirt, or a waistcoat, just as it happens?"

"Become a tailor, or shoemaker," said Otto, gravely, and laid his hand upon the boy's head.

"He shall be a genius!" said Wilhelm.

CHAPTER IV

"Christmas-tide,

When in the wood the snow shines bright."

OEHLENSCHLÄGER'S Helge

We again let several weeks pass by; it was Christmas Eve, which brings us the beautiful Christmas festival. We find the two friends taking a walk.

Describe to an inhabitant of the south a country where the earth appears covered with the purest Carrara marble, where the tree twigs resemble white branches of coral sprinkled with diamonds, and above a sky as blue as that belonging to the south, and he will say that is a fairy land. Couldst thou suddenly remove him from his dark cypresses and olive-trees to the north, where the fresh snow lies upon the earth, where the white hoar-frost has powdered the trees over, and the sun shines down from the blue heaven, then would he recognize the description and call the north a fairy land.

This was the splendor which the friends admired. The large trees upon the fortification-walls appeared crystallized when seen against the blue sky. The Sound was not yet frozen over; vessels, illuminated by the red evening sun, glided past with spread sails. The Swedish coast seemed to have approached nearer; one might see individual houses in Landskrona. It was lovely, and on this account there were many promenaders upon the walls and the Langelinie.

"Sweden seems so near that one might swim over to it!" said Wilhelm.

"The distance would be too far," answered Otto; "but I should love to plunge among the deep blue waters yonder."

"How refreshing it is," said Wilhelm, "when the water plays about one's cheeks! Whilst I was at home, I always swam in the Great Belt. Yes, you are certainly half a fish when you come into the water."

"I!" repeated Otto, and was silent; but immediately added, with a kind of embarrassment which was at other times quite foreign to him, and from which one might infer how unpleasant confessing any imperfection was to him, "I do not swim."

"That must be learned in summer!" said Wilhelm.

"There is so much to learn," answered Otto; "swimming will certainly be the last thing." He now suddenly turned toward the fortress, and stood still. "Only see how melancholy and quiet!" said he, and led the conversation again to the surrounding scenery. "The sentinel before the prison paces so quietly up and down, the sun shines upon his bayonet! How this reminds me of a sweet little poem of Heine's; it is just as though he described this fortress and this soldier, but in the warmth of summer: one sees the picture livingly before one, as here; the weapon glances in the sun, and the part ends so touchingly,—'Ich wollt', er schösse mich todt!' It is here so romantically beautiful! on the right the animated promenade, and the view over the Sund; on the left, the desolate square, where the military criminals are shot, and close upon it the prison with its beam-fence. The sun scarcely shines through those windows. Yet, without doubt, the prisoner can see us walking here upon the wall."

"And envy our golden freedom!" said Wilhelm.

"Perhaps he derides it," answered Otto. "He is confined to his chamber and the small courts behind the beam-lattice; we are confined to the coast; we cannot fly forth with the ships into the mighty, glorious world. We are also fastened with a chain, only ours is somewhat longer than that of the prisoner. But we will not think of this; let us go down to where the beautiful ladies are walking."

"To see and to be seen," cried Wilhelm. "'Spectatum veniunt; veniunt spectentur ut ipsae,' as Ovid says."

The friends quitted the wall.

"There comes my scholar, little Jonas!" cried Wilhelm. "The boy was better dressed than at his last appearance; quickly he pulled his little cap off and stood still: a young girl in a wretched garb held him by the hand.

"Good day, my clever lad!" said Wilhelm, and his glance rested on the girl: she was of a singularly elegant form; had she only carried herself better she would have been a perfect beauty. It was Psyche herself who stood beside Cupid. She smiled in a friendly manner; the little lad had certainly told her who the gentlemen were; but she became crimson, and cast down her eyes when Wilhelm looked back after her: he beckoned to Jonas, who immediately came to him. The girl was his sister, he said, and was called Eva. Wilhelm nodded to her, and the friends went on.

"That was a beautiful girl!" said Wilhelm, and looked back once more. "A rosebud that one could kiss until it became a full blown rose!"

"During the experiment the rosebud might easily be broken!" answered Otto; "at least such is the case with the real flower. But do not look back again, that is a sin!"

"Sin?" repeated Wilhelm; "no, then it is a very innocent sin! Believe me, it flatters the little creature that we should admire her beauty. I can well imagine how enchanting a loving look from a rich young gentleman may be for a weak, feminine mind. The sweet words which one can say are as poison which enters the blood. I have still a clear conscience. Not ONE innocent soul have I poisoned!"

"And yet you are rich and young enough to do so," returned Otto, not without bitterness. "Our friends precede us with a good example: here come some of our own age; they are acquainted with the roses!"

"Good evening, thou good fellow!" was the greeting Wilhelm received from three or four of the young men.

"Are you on Thou-terms with all these?" inquired Otto.

"Yes," answered Wilhelm; "we became so at a carouse. There all drank the Thou-brotherhood. I could not draw myself back. At other times I do not willingly give my 'thou' to any but my nearest friends. *Thou* has something to my mind affectionate and holy. Many people fling it to the first person with whom they drink a glass. At the carouse I could not say no."

"And wherefore not?" returned Otto; "that would never have troubled me."

The friends now wandered on, arm-in-arm. Later in the evening we again meet with them together, and that at the house of a noble family, whose name and rank are to be found in the "Danish Court Calendar;" on which account it would be wanting in delicacy to mention the same, even in a story the events of which lie so near our hearts.

Large companies are most wearisome. In these there are two kinds of rank. Either you are riveted to a card-table, or placed against the wall where you must stand with your hat in your hand, or, later in the evening, with it at your feet, nay, even must stand during supper. But this house was one of the most intellectual. Thou who dost recognize the house wilt also recognize that it is not to be reckoned with those, —

> *"Where each day's gossiping stale fish*
> *Is served up daily for thy dish."*

This evening we do not become acquainted with the family, but only with their beautiful Christmas festival.

The company was assembled in a large apartment; the shaded lamp burned dimly, but this was with the intention of increasing the effect when the drawing-room doors should open and the children joyfully press in together.

Wilhelm now stepped to the piano-forte; a few chords produced stillness and attention. To the sounds of low music there stepped forth from the side-doors three maidens arrayed in white; each wore a long veil depending from the back of her head,—one blue, the other red, and the third white. Each carried in her arms an urn, and thus they represented fortune-tellers from the East. They brought good or ill luck, which each related in a little verse. People were to draw a number, and according to this would he receive his gift from the Christmas-tree. One of the maidens brought blanks—but which of them? now it was proved whether you were a child of fortune. All, even the children, drew their uncertain numbers: exception was only made with the family physician and a few elderly ladies of the family; these had a particular number stuck into their hands—their presents had been settled beforehand.

"Who brings me good luck?" inquired Otto, as the three pretty young girls approached him. The one with a white veil was Wilhelm's eldest sister, Miss Sophie, who was this winter paying a visit to the family. She resembled her brother. The white drapery about her head increased the expression of her countenance. She rested her gaze firmly upon Otto, and, perhaps, because he was the friend of her brother, she raised her finger. Did she wish to warn or to challenge him? Otto regarded it as a challenge, thrust his hand into the urn, and drew out number 33. All were now provided. The girls disappeared, and the folding-doors of the drawing-room were opened.

A dazzling light streamed toward the guests. A splendid fir-tree, covered with burning tapers, and hung over with tinsel-gold, gilt eggs and apples, almonds and grapes, dazzled the eye. On either side of the tree were grottoes of fir-trees and moss, hung with red and blue paper lamps. In each grotto was an altar; upon one stood John of Bologna's floating Mercury; upon the other, a reduced cast in plaster of Thorwaldsen's Shepherd-boy. The steps were covered with presents, to which were attached the different numbers.

"Superbe! lovely!" resounded from all sides; and the happy children shouted for joy. People arranged themselves in a half-circle, one row behind the other. One of the cousins of the family now stepped forth, a young poet, who, if we mistake not, has since then appeared among the Anonymouses in "The New Year's Gift of Danish Poets." He was appareled this evening as one of the Magi, and recited a little poem which declared that, as each one had himself drawn out of the urn of Fate, no one could be angry, let him have procured for himself honor or derision—Fate, and not Merit, being here the ruler. Two little boys, with huge butterfly wings and in flowing garments, bore the presents to the guests. A number, which had been purposely given to one of the elder ladies, was now called out, and the boys brought forward a large, heavy, brown earthen jug. To the same hung a direction the length of two sheets of paper, upon which was written, "A remedy against frost." The jug was opened, and a very nice boa taken out and presented to the lady.

"What number have you?" inquired Otto of Wilhelm's sister, who, freed from her long veil, now entered the room and took her place near him.

"Number 34," she answered. "I was to keep the number which remained over when the others had drawn."

"We are, then, neighbors in the chain of Fate," returned Otto; "I have number 33."

"Then one of us will receive something very bad!" said Sophie. "For, as much as I know, only every other number is good." At this moment their numbers were called out. The accompanying poem declared that only a poetical, noble mind deserved this gift. It consisted of an illuminated French print, the subject a simple but touching idea. You saw a frozen lake, nothing but one expanse of ice as far as the horizon. The ice was broken, and near to the opening lay a hat with a red lining, and beside it sat a dog with grave eyes, still and expectant. Around the broken opening in the ice were seen traces of the dog having scratched into the hard crust of ice. "Il attend toujours" was the simple motto.

"That is glorious!" exclaimed Otto. "An affecting thought! His master has sunk in the depth, and the faithful log yet awaits him. Had that picture only fallen to my lot!"

"It is lovely!" said Sophie, and a melancholy glance made the young girl still more beautiful.

Soon after Wilhelm's turn came.

"Open the packet, thou shalt see

The very fairest gaze on thee!"

ran the verse. He opened the packet, and found within a small mirror. "Yes, that was intended for a lady," said he; "in that case it would have spoken the truth! in my hands it makes a fool of me.

"For me nothing certainly remains but my number!" said Otto to his neighbor, as all the gifts appeared to be distributed.

"The last is number 33," said the cousin, and drew forth a roll of paper, which had been hidden among the moss. It was unrolled. It was an old pedigree of an extinct race. Quite at the bottom lay the knight with shield and armor, and out of his breast grew the many-branched tree with its shields and names. Probably it had been bought, with other rubbish, at some auction, and now at Christmas, when every hole and corner was rummaged for whatever could be converted into fun or earnest, it had been brought out for the Christmas tree. The cousin read the following verse:—

"Art thou not noble?—then it in far better;

This tree unto thy father is not debtor;

Thyself alone is thy ancestral crown.

From thee shall spring forth branches of renown,

And if thou come where blood gives honor's place,

This tree shall prove thee first of all thy race!

From this hour forth thy soul high rank hath won her,

Not will forget thy knighthood and thy honor."

"I congratulate you," said Wilhelm, laughing. "Now you will have to pay the nobility-tax!"

Several of the ladies who stood near him, smiling, also offered a kind of congratulation. Sophie alone remained silent, and examined the present of another lady—a pretty pincushion in the form of a gay butterfly.

The first row now rose to examine more nearly how beautifully the Christmas tree was adorned. Sophie drew one of the ladies away with her.

"Let us look at the beautiful statues," said she; "the Shepherd-boy and the Mercury."

"That is not proper," whispered the lady; "but look there at the splendid large raisins on the tree!"

Sophie stepped before Thorwaldsen's Shepherd-boy. The lady whispered to a friend, "It looks so odd that she should examine the figures!"

"Ah!" replied the other, "she is a lover of the fine arts, as you well know. Only think! at the last exhibition she went with her brother into the great hall where all the plaster-casts stand, and looked at them!—the Hercules, as well as the other indecent figures! they were excellent, she said. That is being so natural; otherwise she is a nice girl."

"It is a pity she is a little awry."

Sophie approached them; both ladies made room for her, and invited her most lovingly to sit clown beside them. "Thou sweet girl!" they flatteringly exclaimed.

CHAPTER V

"Hark to trumpets and beaten gongs,
Squeaking fiddles, shouts and songs.
Hurra! hurra!
The Doctor is here;
And here the hills where fun belongs."
    J. L. HEIBERG.

We will not follow the principal characters of our story step for step, but merely present the prominent moments of their lives to our readers, be these great or small; we seize on them, if they in any way contribute to make the whole picture more worthy of contemplation.

The winter was over, the birds of passage had long since returned; the woods and fields shone in the freshest green, and, what to the friends was equally interesting, they had happily passed through their examen philologicum. Wilhelm, who, immediately after its termination, had accompanied his sister home, was again returned, sang with little Jonas, reflected upon the philosophicum, and also how he would thoroughly enjoy the summer,—the summer which in the north is so beautiful, but so short. It was St. John's Day. Families had removed from Copenhagen to their pretty country-seats on the coast, where people on horseback and in carriages rushed past, and where the highway was crowded with foot-passengers. The whole road presented a picture of life upon the Paris Boulevard. The sun was burning, the dust flew up high into the air; on which account many persons preferred the pleasanter excursion with the steamboat along the coast, from whence could be seen the traffic on the high-road without enduring the annoyance of dust and heat. Boats skimmed past; brisk sailors, by the help of vigorous strokes of the oar, strove to compete with the steam-packet, the dark smoke from which, like some demon, partly rested upon the vessel, partly floated away in the air.

Various young students, among whom were also Wilhelm and Otto, landed at Charlottenlund, the most frequented place of resort near Copenhagen. Otto was here for the first time; for the first time he should see the park.

A summer's afternoon in Linken's Bad, near Dresden, bears a certain resemblance to Charlottenlund, only that the Danish wood is larger; that instead of the Elbe we have the Sound, which is here three miles broad, and where often more than a hundred vessels, bearing flags of all the European nations, glide past. A band of musicians played airs out of "Preciosa;" the white tents glanced like snow or swans through the green beech-trees. Here and there was a fire-place raised of turf, over which people boiled and cooked, so that the smoke rose up among the trees. Outside the wood, waiting in long rows, were the peasants' vehicles, called "coffee-mills," completely answering ho the couricolo of the Neapolitan and the coucou of the Parisian, equally cheap, and overladen in the same manner with passengers, therefore forming highly picturesque groups. This scene has been humorously treated in a picture by Marstrand. Between fields and meadows, the road leads pleasantly toward the park; the friends pursued the foot-path.

"Shall I brush the gentlemen?" cried five or six boys, at the same time pressing upon the friends as they approached the entrance to the park. Without waiting for an answer, the boys commenced at once brushing the dust from their clothes and boots.

"These are Kirsten Piil's pages," said Wilhelm, laughing; "they take care that people show themselves tolerably smart. But now we are brushed enough!" A six-skilling-piece rejoiced these little Savoyards.

The Champs Elysées of the Parisians on a great festival day, when the theatres are opened, the swings are flying, trumpets and drums overpowering the softer music, and when the whole mass of people, like one body, moves itself between the booths and tents, present a companion piece to the spectacle which the so-called Park-hill affords. It is Naples' "Largo dei Castello," with its dancing apes, shrieking Bajazzoes, the whole deafening jubilee which has been transported to a northern wood. Here also, in the wooden booths, large, tawdry pictures show what delicious plays you may enjoy within. The beautiful female horse-rider stands upon the wooden balcony and cracks with her whip, whilst Harlequin blows the trumpet. Fastened to a perch, large, gay parrots nod over the heads of the multitude. Here stands a miner in his black costume, and exhibits the interior of a mine. He turns his box, and during the music dolls ascend and descend. Another shows the splendid fortress of Frederiksteen: "The whole cavalry and infantry who have endured an unspeakable deal; here a man without a weapon, there a weapon without a man; here a fellow without a bayonet, here a bayonet without a fellow; and yet they are merry and contented, for they have conquered the victory." [Note: Literal translation of the real words of a showman.] Dutch wafer-cake booths, where the handsome

Dutch women, in their national costume, wait on the customers, entice old and young. Here a telescope, there a rare Danish ox, and so forth. High up, between the fresh tree boughs, the swings fly. Are those two lovers floating up there? A current of air seizes the girl's dress and shawl, the young man flings his arm round her waist; it is for safety: there is then less danger. At the foot of the hill there is cooking and roasting going on; it seems a complete gypsy-camp. Under the tree sits the old Jew—this is precisely his fiftieth jubilee; through a whole half-century has he sung here his comical Doctor's song. Now that we are reading this he is dead; that characteristic countenance is dust, those speaking eyes are closed, his song forgotten tones. Oehlenschläger, in his "St. John's Eve," has preserved his portrait for us, and it will continue to live, as Master Jakel (Punch), our Danish Thespis, will continue to live. The play and the puppets were transferred from father to son, and every quarter of an hour in the day the piece is repeated. Free nature is the place for the spectators, and after every representation the director himself goes round with the plate.

This was the first spectacle which exhibited itself to the friends. Not far off stood a juggler in peasant's clothes, somewhat advanced in years, with a common ugly countenance. His short sleeves were rolled up, and exhibited a pair of hairy, muscular arms. The crowd, withdrawing from Master Jakel when the plate commenced its wanderings, pushed Otto and Wilhelm forward toward the low fence before the juggler's table.

"Step nearer, my gracious gentlemen, my noble masters!" said the juggler, with an accentuation which betrayed his German birth. He opened the fence; both friends were fairly pushed in and took their places upon the bench, where they, at all events, found themselves out of the crowd.

"Will the noble gentleman hold this goblet?" said the juggler, and handed Otto one from his apparatus. Otto glanced at the man: he was occupied with his art; but Otto's cheek and forehead were colored with a sudden crimson, which was immediately afterward supplanted by a deathly paleness: his hand trembled, but this lasted only a moment; he gathered all his strength of mind together and appeared the same as before.

"That was a very good trick!" said Wilhelm.

"Yes, certainly!" answered Otto; but he had seen nothing whatsoever. His soul was strangely affected. The man exhibited several other tricks, and then approached with the plate. Otto laid down a mark, and then rose to depart. The juggler remarked the piece of money: a smile played about his mouth; he glanced at Otto, and a strange malicious expression lay in the spiteful look which accompanied his loudly spoken thanks: "Mr. Otto Thostrup is always so gracious and good!"

"Does he know you?" asked Wilhelm.

"He has the honor!" grinned the juggler, and proceeded.

"He has exhibited his tricks in the Jutland villages, and upon my father's estate," whispered Otto.

"Therefore an acquaintance of your childhood?" said Wilhelm.

"Of my childhood," repeated Otto, and they made themselves a way through the tumult.

They met with several young noblemen, relatives of Wilhelm, with the cousin who had written the verses for the Christmas tree; also several friends from the carouse, and the company increased. They intended, like many others, to pass the night in the wood, and at midnight drink out of Kirsten Piil's well. "Only with the increasing darkness will it become thoroughly merry here," thought they: but Otto had appointed to be in the city again toward evening. "Nothing will come out of that!" said the poet; "if you wish to escape, we shall bind you fast to one of us."

"Then I carry him away with me on my back," replied Otto; "and still run toward the city. What shall I do here at night in the wood?"

"Be merry!" answered Wilhelm. "Come, give us no follies, or I shall grow restive."

Hand-organs, drums, and trumpets, roared against each other; Bajazzo growled; a couple of hoarse girls sang and twanged upon the guitar: it was comic or affecting, just as one was disposed. The evening approached, and now the crowd became greater, the joy more noisy.

"But where is Otto?" inquired Wilhelm. Otto had vanished in the crowd. Search after him would help nothing, chance must bring them together again. Had he designedly withdrawn himself? no one knew wherefore, no one could dream what had passed within his soul. It became evening. The highway and the foot-path before the park resembled two moving gay ribbons.

In the park itself the crowd perceptibly diminished. It was now the high-road which was become the Park-hill. The carriages dashed by each other as at a race; the people shouted and sung, if not as melodiously as the barcarole of the fisher men below Lido, still with the thorough carnival joy of the south. The steamboat moved along the coasts. From the gardens surrounding the pretty country-houses arose rockets into the blue sky, the Moccoli of the north above the Carnival of the Park.

Wilhelm remained with his young friends in the wood, and there they intended, with the stroke of twelve, to drink out of Kirsten's well. Men and women, girls and boys of the lower class, and jovial young men, meet, after this manner, to enjoy St. John's Eve. Still sounded the music, the swings were in motion, lamps hung out, whilst the new moon shone through the thick tree boughs. Toward midnight the noise died away; only a blind peasant still scratched upon the three strings which were left on his violin; some servant-girls wandered, arm-in-arm, with their sweethearts, and sang. At twelve o'clock all assembled about the well, and drank the clear, ice-cold water. From no great distance resounded, through the still night, a chorus of four manly voices. It was as if the wood gods sang in praise of the nymph of the well.

Upon the hill all was now deserted and quiet. Bajazzo and il Padrone slept behind the thin linen partition, under a coverlid. The moon set, but the night was clear; no clear, frosty winter night has a snore beautiful starry heaven to exhibit. Wilhelm's party was merry, quickly flew the hours away; singing in chorus, the party wandered through the wood, and down toward the strand. The day already dawned; a red streak along the horizon announced its approach.

Nature sang to them the mythos of the creation of the world, even as she had sung it to Moses, who wrote down this voice from God, interpreted by Nature. Light banished the darkness, heaven and earth were parted; at first birds showed themselves in the clear air; later rose the beasts of the field; and, last of all, appeared man.

"The morning is fairly sultry," said Wilhelm; "the sea resembles a mirror: shall we not bathe?"

The proposal was accepted.

"There we have the Naiades already!" said one of the party, as a swarm of fishermen's wives and daughters, with naked feet, their green petticoats tucked up, and baskets upon their backs, in which they carried fish to Copenhagen, came along the road. The gay young fellows cast toward the prettiest glances as warm and glowing as that cast by the sun himself, who, at this moment, came forth and shone over the Sound, where a splendid three-masted vessel had spread all her sails to catch each breeze. The company reached the strand.

"There is some one already swimming out yonder," said Wilhelm. "He stands it bravely. That is an excellent swimmer!"

"Here lie his clothes," remarked another.

"How!" exclaimed Wilhelm: "this is Otto Thostrup's coat! But Otto cannot swim; I have never been able to persuade him to bathe. Now, we will out and make a nearer acquaintance."

"Yes, certainly it is he," said another; "he is now showing his skill."

"Then he must have been all night in the wood," exclaimed Wilhelm. "Yes, indeed, he's a fine bird. Does he fly us? He shall pay for this. Good night in the water, or in any other improper place? To quit friends without saying a word does not appertain to the customs of civilized people. Since you, therefore, show yourself such a man of nature, we will carry away your garments; it cannot annoy you in puris naturalibus to seek us out in the wood."

Otto raised his head, but was silent.

"Now, will you not come forth?" cried Wilhelm. "Only kneeling before each of us can you receive the separate articles of your dress, so that you may again appear as a civilized European." And saying this he divided the clothes among the others; each one held an article in his hand.

"Leave such jokes!" cried Otto with singular earnestness. "Lay down the clothes, and retire!"

"Aye, that we will, presently," returned Wilhelm. "You are a fine fellow! You cannot swim, you say. Now, if you should not kneel" —

"Retire!" cried Otto, "or I will swim out into the stream, and not return again!"

"That might be original enough," answered Wilhelm. "Swim forth, or come and kneel here!"

"Wilhelm!" cried Otto, with an affecting sigh, and in a moment swam forth with quick strokes.

"There he shoots away," said one of the party. "How he cuts the waves! He is a splendid swimmer!"

Smiling they gazed over the expanse; Otto swam even farther out.

"But where will he swim to?" exclaimed, somewhat gravely, one of the spectators. "He will certainly lose his strength before he returns the same distance."

They unmoored the boat. Otto swam far out at sea; with quick strokes of the oars they rowed after him.

"Where is he now?" cried Wilhelm shortly afterwards; "I see him no longer."

"Yes, there he comes up again," said another; "but his strength is leaving him."

"On! on!" cried Wilhelm; "he will be drowned if we do not come to his help. Only see—he sinks!"

Otto had lost all power; his head disappeared beneath the water. The friends had nearly reached him; Wilhelm and several of the best swimmers flung from themselves boots and coats, sprang into the sea, and dived under the water. A short and noiseless moment passed. One of the swimmers appeared above water. "He is dead!" were the first words heard. Wilhelm and the three others now appeared with Otto; the boat was near oversetting as they brought him into it. Deathly pale lay he there, a beautifully formed marble statue, the picture of a young gladiator fallen in the arena.

The friends busied themselves about him, rubbing his breast and hands, whilst two others rowel toward the land.

"He breathes!" said Wilhelm.

Otto opened his eyes; his lips moved; his gaze became firmer; a deep crimson spread itself over his breast and countenance; he raised himself and Wilhelm supported him. Suddenly a deep sigh burst from his breast; he thrust Wilhelm from him, and, like a madman, seized an article of dress to cover himself with; then, with a convulsive trembling of the lips, he said to Wilhelm, who held his hand, "I HATE YOU!"

CHAPTER VI

—"Art thou Prometheus, pierced with wounds?
The Vulture thou that tugs at his heart?"
J. CHR. V. ZEDLITZ'S Todtenkränze.

Not half an hour after this adventure a carriage rolled toward the city—a large carriage, containing three seats, but, beside the coachman, there was only one person within. This was Otto; his lips were pale; death, it is true, had touched them. Alone he dashed forward; his last words to Wilhelm had been his only ones.

"He has lost his wits," said one of the friends.

"It is a fit of madness," answered another, "such as he was seized with at the examination, when he only sent in a scrap of white paper for the mathematical examination, because he felt himself offended by the inspector."

"I could quite vex myself about my stupid joke," said Wilhelm. "I ought to have known him better; he is of a strange, unhappy character. Give me your hands! We will mention to no one what has occurred; it would only give occasion to a deal of gossip, and wound him deeply, and he is an excellent, glorious fellow."

They gave their hands upon it, and drove toward the city.

The same day, toward evening, we again seek Otto. We find him in his chamber. Silent, with crossed arms, he stands before a print, a copy of Horace Vernet's representation of Mazeppa, who, naked and bound upon a wild horse, rushes through the forest. Wolves thrust forth their heads and exhibit their sharp teeth.

"My own life!" sighed Otto. "I also am bound to this careering wild horse. And no friend, not a single one! Wilhelm, I could kill thee! I could see you all lying in your blood! O, Almighty God!" He pressed his hands before his face and threw himself into a seat; his eyes, however, again directed themselves toward the picture; it exhibited a moment similar to the condition of his own mind.

The door now opened, and Wilhelm stood before him.

"How do you find yourself, Thostrup?" he inquired. "We are still friends as before?" and he wished to give his hand. Otto drew back his. "I have done nothing which could so much offend you," said Wilhelm; "the whole was merely a joke! Give me your hand, and we will speak no more of the affair!"

"To the man whom I hate, I never reach my hand," replied Otto and his lips were white like his cheeks.

"A second time to-day you speak these words to me," said Wilhelm, and the blood rushed to his face. "We were friends, wherefore cannot we be so still? Have people slandered me to you? Have they told lies about me? Only tell me faithfully, and I shall be able to defend myself."

"You must fight with me!" said Otto; and his glance became more gloomy. Wilhelm was silent; there reigned a momentary stillness. Otto suppressed a deep sigh. At length Wilhelm broke silence, and said, with a grave and agitated voice,—"I am so thoughtless, I joke so often, and regard everything from the ridiculous side. But for all that I have both heart and feeling. You must have known how much dearer you were to me than most other people. You are so still, although you offend me. At this moment your blood is in a fever; not now, but after a few days, you yourself will best see which of us is the offended party. You demand that I fight with you; I will if your honor requires this satisfaction: but you must lay before me an acceptable reason. I will know wherefore we risk our lives. Let some days pass by; weigh all with your understanding and your heart! It will still depend upon yourself whether we remain friends as before. Farewell!" And Wilhelm went.

Each of his words had penetrated to Otto's heart. A moment he stood silent and undecided, then his limbs trembled involuntarily, tears streamed from his eyes—it was a convulsive fit of weeping; he pressed his head back. "God, how unfortunate I am!" were his only words.

So passed some minutes; he had ceased to weep, and was calm; suddenly he sprang up, shot the bolt in the door, drew down the blinds, lighted his candle, and once more looked searchingly around: the key-hole was also stopped up. He then flung his coat away from him and uncovered the upper part of his body.

CHAPTER VII

"The towers pass by, even before we perceive them."
OEHLENSCHLÄER'S Journey to Fünen.

Early the following morning, whilst Wilhelm still slept and dreamed of his beloved sisters, well-known footsteps sounded on the stairs, the door opened, and Otto stepped into the sleeping-room. Wilhelm opened his eyes. Otto was pale; a sleepless night and sorrow of heart had breathed upon his brow and eyes.

"Thostrup!" cried Wilhelm, with joyous surprise, and stretched forth his hand toward him, but it again sank; Otto seized it, and pressed it firmly in his own, adding at the same time, with gravity, — "You have humbled me! Is that sufficient satisfaction for you?"

"We are then friends!" said Wilhelm. "Friends must be very indulgent toward each other. Yesterday you were a little strange, to-morrow I may be so; that is the way in which one retaliates."

Otto pressed his hand. "We will never speak again of the occurrence of yesterday!"

"Never!" repeated Wilhelm, affected by the strange gravity of his friend.

"You are a noble, a good creature!" said Otto, and bent over him; his lips touched Wilhelm's forehead.

Wilhelm seized his hand, and gazed frankly into his eye. "You are not happy!" exclaimed he. "If I cannot assist you, I can, at least, dear Otto, honestly share the grief of a friend!"

"Even on that very point we may never speak!" replied Otto. "Farewell! I have determined on travelling home; we have only vacation for a few weeks, and I have not been in Jutland since I became a student. Even a month's sojourn there cannot throw me back; I am well prepared for the philosophicum."

"And when will you set out?" asked Wilhelm.

"To-morrow, with the steamboat. It is hot and sultry here in the city: my blood becomes heated: it will, also, soon be a year since I saw my family."

"Thostrup!" exclaimed Wilhelm, through whom a thought suddenly flashed, "I should also like to see my family; they have written to me to come. Listen: make your journey through Funen, and only remain three or four days with us. My mother's carriage shall convey you then to Middelfart. Say 'Yes,' and we will set out this evening."

"That cannot be done!" replied Otto; but half an hour later, as both sat together over the tea-table, and Wilhelm repeated his wish, Otto consented, but certainly more through a feeling of obligation than through any pleasure of his own. Toward evening, therefore, they set out in the beautiful summer night to travel through Zealand.

Smartly dressed families wandered pleasantly through the city gate toward the summer theatre and Fredericksberg. The evening sun shone upon the column of Liberty; the beautiful obelisk, around which stand Wiedewelt's statues, one of which still weeps,

> *"In white marble clothing,*
>
> *Hand upon the breast,*
>
> *Ever grief-oppressed,*
>
> *Looking down upon the gloomy sea,"*

where were closed the eyes of the artist. Was it the remembrance which here clouded Otto's glance, as his eye rested upon the statues as they drove past, or did his own soul, perhaps, mirror itself in his eyes?

"Here it is gay and animated!" said Wilhelm, wishing to commence a conversation. "Vesterbro is certainly your most brilliant suburb. It forms a city by itself,—a little state! There upon the hill lies the King's Castle, and there on the left, between the willows, the poet's dwelling, where old Rahbek lived with his Kamma!"

"Castle and poet's dwelling!" repeated Otto; "the time will be when they will inspire equal interest!"

"That old place will soon be pulled down!" said Wilhelm; "in such a beautiful situation, so near the city, a splendid villa will be raised, and nothing more remind one of Philemon and Baucis!"

"The old trees in the park will be spared!" said Otto; "in the garden the flowers will scent the air, and remind one of Kamma's flowers. Rahbek was no great poet, but he possessed a true poet's soul, labored faithfully in the great vineyard, and loved flowers as Kamma loved them."

The friends hail left Fredericksberg behind them. The white walls of the castle glanced through the green boughs; behind Söndermark, the large, wealthy village stretched itself out. The sun had set before they reached the Dam-house, where the wild swans, coming from the ocean, build in the fresh water fake. This is the last point of beauty; nothing but lonely fields, with here and there a cairn, extend to the horizon.

The clear summer's night attracted their gaze upward; the postilion blew his horn, and the carriage rolled toward the town of Roeskilde, the St. Denis of Denmark, where kings turn to dust; where Hroar's spring still flows, and its waters mingle with those of Issefjords.

They drove to a public-house to change horses. A young girl conducted the friends into the public room; she lighted the way for them. Her slender figure and her floating gait drew Wilhelm's attention toward her; his hand touched her shoulder, she sprang aside and fixed her beautiful grave eyes upon him; but their expression became milder, she smiled and colored at the same time.

"You are the sister of little Jonas!" cried Wilhelm, recognizing the young girl he had seen with him at Christmas.

"I must also thank you," said she, "for your kindness toward the poor boy!" She quickly placed the lights on the table, and left the room with a gentle glance.

"She is beautiful, very beautiful!" exclaimed Wilhelm. "That was really quite a pleasant meeting."

"Is it then you, Herr Baron, who honor me thus?" cried the host, stepping in—an elderly man with a jovial countenance. "Yes, the Baron will doubtless visit his dear relations in hunch? It is now some little time since you were there."

"This is our host!" said Wilhelm to Otto. "He and his wife were born upon my parent's estate."

"Yes," said the host, "in my youth I have shot many a snipe and wild duck with the Herr Baron's father. But Eva should spread the table; the gentlemen will certainly take supper, and a glass of good punch the Herr Baron will certainly not despise, if he is like his blessed father."

The young girl spread the cloth in an adjoining room.

"She is pretty!" Wilhelm whispered to the old man.

"And just as pious and innocent as she is pretty!" returned he; "and that is saying much, as she is a poor girl, and from Copenhagen. She is of good service to us, and my wife says Eva shall not leave us until she is well married."

Wilhelm invited the host to join them at a glass. The old man became more animated, and now confided to him, half mysteriously, what made Eva so honorable in the eyes of his wife, and what was, indeed, really very nice of her. "My old woman," said he, "was in Copenhagen, in search of a waiting-girl. Yes, there are enough to be had, and they are fine girls; but mother has her own thoughts and opinions: she has good eyes—that she has! Now, there came many, and among others Eva; but, good Lord! she was very poorly clad, and she looked feeble and weak, and what service could one get out of her! But she had a good countenance, and the poor girl wept and besought mother to take her, for she was not comfortable at home, and would not remain at Copenhagen. Now, mother knows how to make use of her words: it is unfortunate that she is not at home to-night; how pleased she would have been to see the Herr Baron! Yes, what I would say is, she so twisted her words about, that Eva confessed to her why she wished to leave home. You see the girl is petty; and the young gallant gentlemen of Copenhagen had remarked her smooth face,—and not alone the young, but the old ones also! So an old gentleman—I could easily name him, but that has nothing to do with the affair—a very distinguished man in the city, who has, besides, a wife and children, had said all sorts of things to her parents; and, as eight hundred dollars is a deal of money to poor people, one can excuse them: but Eva wept, and said she would rather spring into the castle-ditch. They represented all sorts of things to the poor girl; she heard of the service out here with us. She wept, kissed my old woman's hand, and thus came to us; and since then we have had a deal of service from Eva, and joy also!"

Some minutes after Eva stepped in, Otto's eye rested with a melancholy expression upon the beautiful form: never had he before so gazed upon a woman. Her countenance was extraordinarily fine, her nose and forehead nobly formed, the eyebrows dark, and in the dark-blue eyes lay something pensive, yet happy: one might employ the Homeric expression, "smiling through tears," to describe this look. She announced that the carriage was ready.

A keen observer would soon have remarked what a change the host's relation had worked in the two friends. Wilhelm was no longer so free toward poor Eva. Otto, on the contrary, approached her more,—and at their leave-taking they offered her a greater present than they would otherwise have given.

She stood with Otto at the door, and assisted him on with his travelling cloak.

"Preserve your heart pure!" said he, gravely; "that is more than beauty!"

The young girl blushed, and gazed at him with astonishment; in such a manner had no one of his age ever before spoken to her.

"The poor girl!" said Otto; "but I think she is come to good people."

"She has a strange glance!" said Wilhelm. "Do you know that there is really a certain affinity between you and her? It was to me quite striking."

"That is a compliment which I cannot accept," returned Otto, smiling. "Yet, perhaps, I might resemble her."

It was not yet three o'clock when the friends reached Ringsted.

"I have never before been so far in Zealand," said Otto.

"Shall I be your guide?" returned Wilhelm. "Ringsted has a street and an inn, and one is very badly served there, as you will soon both see and experience yourself. Meanwhile, one can think of Hagbarth and Signe; not far from here, at Sigersted, he hung his mantle on the oak, and Signelil's abode stood in flames. Now only remain fields and meadows, a cairn, and the old popular song. Then we rush past the friendly Soroe, that mirrors itself with the wood in the lake, which forms itself into so many bays; but we do not see much of it. We have here another romantic spot, an old castle converted into a church, high up on the hill near the lake, and close to it the dismal place of execution. We then reach Slagelse, an animated little town; with the Antvorskov convent, the poet Frankenau's grave, and a Latin school, celebrated on account of its poets. It was there Baggesen and Ingemann learned their Latin. When I once questioned the hostess regarding the lions of the town, she would only acknowledge two,—Bastholm's library, and the English fire-engine. The curtain in the theatre represents an alley with a fountain, the jets of which are painted as if spouting out of the prompter's box; or is this, perhaps, the English fire-engine? I know not. The scene-decoration for towns represents the market-place of Slagelse itself, so that the pieces thus acquire a home-feeling. This is the modern history of the little town; and, with regard to its older and romantic history, learn that the holy Anders was preacher here! Yes, indeed, that was a man! He has been also sung of by our first poets. We end with Korsöer, where Baggesen was born and Birckner lies buried. In the more modern history of this town, King Solomon and Jörgen the hatter play a considerable rôle. Besides this, I know that the town is said once to have possessed a private theatre; but this soon was done for, and the decorations were sold; a miller bought them, and patched his windmill sails with them. Upon one sail was a piece of a wood, upon another a shred of a room, or a street; and so they rushed round one after the other. Perhaps this is mere slander, for I have my information from Slagelse; and neighboring towns never speak well of each other."

In this manner Wilhelm gossiped on, and the friends travelled over the way he had described. Slagelse, and the peasant village of Landsgrav, they had already behind them, when Wilhelm ordered the coachman to diverge from the high-road toward the right.

"Where will you take us to?" asked Otto.

"I will give you a pleasure!" returned Wilhelm. "We shall reach the weariful Korsöer early enough: the steamboat leaves at ten, and it is not yet seven. You shall be surprised—I know well that you are half a Catholic; I will conduct you where you may believe yourself carried back several centuries, and may imagine yourself in a Catholic country. That is right pleasant, is it not?"

Otto smiled. The friends alighted from the coach and walked over a corn-field. They found themselves upon a hill, the whole landscape spread itself out before them—they saw the Belt, with Sprogöe and Funen. The surrounding country was certainly flat, but the variety of greens, the near meadow, the dark stretch of wood in the neighborhood of Korsöer, the bay itself, and all this seen in a warm morning light, produced effect. The friends diverged to the right; and before them, upon a hill, stood a large wooden cross, with the figure of the Crucified One. Above the cross was built a small roof to carry off the rain,—such as one may yet find in Bavaria. The figure of the Redeemer was of wood, painted with strong, tawdry colors; a withered garland of corn-flowers still hung around his bowed head.

"It is extraordinary," said Otto, "to find in our time, in the year 1830, such a Catholic symbol in Lutheran Denmark! And yet—yes, you will laugh at me, but I find it lovely: it affects me, moves me to worship."

"That tawdry, tasteless figure!" cried Wilhelm. "Only see how coarse! the hair is covered with tar to keep off the rain! The peasants here have their peculiar superstition. If they allow the cross to fall they have no luck with their lands. It was upon this hill that the holy Anders, the celebrated preacher of Slagelse, awoke. He visited the sepulchre of Christ, but through praying there too long the ship sailed without him, and he was forced to stay behind. Then came a man and took him upon his horse, and they would ride to Joppa: the holy Anders fell asleep; but when he awoke he lay here, and heard the bells ringing in Slagelse. Upon a foal, only one night old, he rode round the extensive city lands, whilst King Waldemar lay in his bath. He could hang his glove upon the beams of the sun. This hill, where he awoke, was called Rest-hill; and the cross, with the figure of the Redeemer erected upon it, which still stands here, reminds us of the legend of the holy Anders."

A little peasant girl at this moment mounted the hill, but paused when she perceived the strangers.

"Don't be afraid, my child!" said Wilhelm. "What hast thou there? a garland! shall it hang here upon the cross? Only come, we will help thee."

"It should hang over our Lord," said the little one, holding, in an embarrassed manner, the garland of pretty blue cornflowers in her hand. Otto took the garland, and hung it up in place of the faded one.

"That was our morning adventure!" said Wilhelm, and soon they were rolling in the deep sand toward Korsöer, toward the hill where the poet watched the sun and moon sink into the sea, and wished that he had wings that he might catch them.

Melancholy and silent lies the town on the flat coast, the old castle turned into a farm-house—high grass grows upon the walls. In a storm, when the wind blows against the city, the surf beats against the outermost houses. High upon the church stands a telegraph; the black wooden plates resemble mourning-flags hung above the sinking town. Here is nothing for the stranger to see, nothing except a grave—that of the thinker Birckner. The friends drove to the public-house on the strand. No human being met them in the street except a boy, who rung a hand-bell.

"That calls to church," said Wilhelm. "Because there are no bells in the tower, they have here such a wandering bell-ringer as this. Holla! there lies the inn!"

"Baron Wilhelm!" cried a strong voice, and a man in a green jacket with pockets in the breast, the mighty riding-boots splashed above the tops, and with whip in hand, approached them, pulled his horse-hair cap, and extended his hand to Wilhelm.

"The Kammerjunker from Funen!" said Wilhelm; "my mother's neighbor, one of the most industrious and rich noblemen in all Funen."

"You will come one of the first days to me!" said the Kammerjunker; "you shall try my Russian steam-bath: I have erected one upon my estate. All who visit me, ladies and gentlemen without any exception, must try it!"

"And do the cherry-trees bear well this year?" asked Wilhelm.

"No, no," answered the Kammerjunker, "they are good for nothing; but the apples are good! All the old trees in the hill-garden stand in full splendor: I've brought them into condition! Two years ago there was not, on all the trees together, a bushel of fruit. But I had all the horses which had to be bled led under the trees, and had the warm blood sprinkled upon the roots; this happened several times, and it has been a real inoculation for life."

"The wind is certainly favorable," said Otto, whom this conversation began to weary.

"No, just the contrary!" said the Kammerjunker. "The vane upon the little house yonder lies; it points always to Nyborg, always shows a good wind for us when we want to leave. In Nyborg is also a vane, which stands even as firmly as this, and prates to the folk there of good wind. I regard both vanes as a kind of guide-post, which merely says, There goes the way! No, if we had had a wind I should have gone with the boat, and not with the little splashing thing, as the seamen call the steamboat. The carriage is doubtless awaiting the young gentleman in Nyborg?" pursued he. "I will join company with you—my brown horse waits for me at Schalburg. You should see him! He has sinews like steel springs, and legs like a dancing-master! He is my own brown."

"No one knows that we are coming," answered Wilhelm. "We shall, therefore, take a carriage from Nyborg."

"We will join company," said the Kammerjunker, "and then you will pay me a visit with the young gentleman. You shall sleep in the black chamber! Yes, you will give me the pleasure?" said he to Otto. "If you are a lover of the antique, my estate will afford you pleasure; you find there moats, towers, guard-rooms, ghosts, and hobgoblins, such as belong to an old estate. The black chamber! after all, it is not quite secure there; is it, Herr Baron?"

"No, the deuce remain a night with you!" said Wilhelm; "one gets to bed late, and even then it is not permitted one to close one's eyes. You, your sister, and the Mamsell,—yes, you are a pretty clover-leaf! Yes, Thostrup, you cannot believe what pranks are hatched upon the Kammerjunker's estate! One must be prepared for it! It is said to be haunted, but if the dead will not take that trouble the living do. The Kammerjunker is in the plot with his women-folk. They sewed me lately live cockchafers into my pillow, and they crawled and scrambled about till I did not know what the deuce it could be! A live cock they had also placed under my bed, and just in the morning, when I would go to sleep, the creature began to crow!"

"The women-folk had done that," said the Kammerjunker. "Did they not the very same night fasten a door-bell to the head of my bed? I never thought of it; fat Laender slept in the same room, and had fastened along the wall a string to the bell. I awoke with the ringing. 'What the devil is that bell?' said I, and glanced about the room, for I could not conceive what it was. 'Bell?' asked Laender—'there is no bell here!' The ringing also ceased. I thought I must have dreamed, or that our merry evening must have left some buzzing in my ears. Again it began to ring. Laender looked so innocent all the time, I could not comprehend myself; I thought it must be my imagination. I became quite fainthearted, I denied my own hearing, and said, 'No, I have only dreamed!' and commenced reckoning and counting to employ my mind; but that did no good, and it nearly drove me mad! I sprang out of bed, and then I found out the trick: but how Laender grinned! he was swollen and red in the face with his mirth."

"Do you play such jokes on your estate?" inquired Otto, addressing himself to Wilhelm.

"No, not such refined ones!" returned the Kammerjunker; "perhaps a piece of wood, or a silly mask, is laid in your bed. Miss Sophie gives us other clever things for amusement—tableaux and the magic-lantern. I was once of the party. Yes, what was it I represented? Ah, I played, Heaven help me! King Cyrus: had a paper crown on my head, and Miss Sophie's cloak about me, the wrong side turned outward, for it is lined with sable. I looked like Satan!"

The steamboat passengers were summoned on board, the company went down to the vessel, and soon it was cutting through the waves of the Belt.

CHAPTER VIII

"See now, Fünen signifieth fine,
And much in that word lies;
For Fünen is the garden fine,
Where Denmark glads its eyes."

The nakedness which the last aspect of Zealand presents occasions one to be doubly struck by the affluent abundance and luxuriance with which Funen steps forth. Green woods, rich corn-fields, and, wherever the eye rests, noblemen's seats and churches. Nyborg itself appears a lively capital in comparison with the still melancholy Korsöer. One now perceives people upon the great bridge of boats, on the ramparts, and in the broad streets with their high houses; one sees soldiers, hears music, and, what is especially animating upon a journey, one comes to an excellent inn. The drive out through the arched gateway is an astonishment; it is the same length and breadth as one of the gates of Copenhagen. Villages and peasants' houses here assume a more well-to-do aspect than in Zealand, where one often on the way-side imagines one sees a manure-heap heaped upon four poles, which upon nearer examination one finds is the abode of a family. On the highroads in Funen one perceives only clean houses; the window-frames are painted; before the doors are little flower-gardens, and wherever flowers are grown, as Bulwer strikingly remarks, the peasant is in a higher state of civilization; he thinks of the beautiful. In the ditches along the highway one sees lilac with their white and lilac flowers. Nature herself has here adorned the country with a multitude of wild poppies, which for splendor of color might vie with the most admired and beautiful in a botanic garden. Especially in the neighborhood of Nyborg do they grow in exceeding abundance.

"What a dazzling color!" exclaimed Otto, as the friends rolled past these beautiful red flowers.

"That is a proud color!" said the Kammerjunker, who rode near them upon his brown steed, "a proud color! but they are manured with the blood of Andalusian horses. It was just here where the battle between these beasts took place. You know that sit the year 1808 the Spaniards lay in Funen;

the English ships were cruising about in the Belt, and Romana fled with his whole army on board, but they could net take their horses with them. These were the most splendid Andalusian creatures that eyes ever saw. The Spaniards took off their bridles, and left them here to scamper about the fields like wild horses. The horses of Nyborg chanced also to graze here, and as soon as the Andalusian steeds became aware of ours they arranged themselves in a row, and fell upon the Danish horses: that was a combat! At length they fell upon each other, and fought until they fell bleeding to earth. Whilst still a boy I saw little skull of one of these beasts. This is the last adventure left us from the visit of the Spaniards to Denmark. In the village through which we shall now pass are some outer remembrances. Remark the young lads and lasses,—they are of a darker complexion than the inhabitants of other Funen valleys; that is Spanish blood, it is said. It was in this village that the story took its rise of the preacher's servant-girl, who wept and was so inconsolable at the departure of the Spaniards. But not on account of her bridegroom did she weep,—not over her own condition. The preacher consoled her, and then she said she only wept to think that if the innocent child resembled its father it certainly would speak Spanish, and then not a soul would understand it! Yes, such histories as this have we in Funen!" said he laughingly to Otto.

With similar relations, and some agricultural observations, according as they were called forth by surrounding objects, did our excellent landed proprietor amuse our young gentlemen. They were already distant several miles from Nyborg, when he suddenly broke off in the midst of a very interesting discourse upon a characteristic of a true inhabitant of Funen, which is, that whenever he passes a field of buckwheat he moves his mouth as if chewing, and made Wilhelm observe a Viennese carriage, which approached them by a neighboring road. To judge from the coachman and the horses, it must be the family from the hall.

This was the case—they returned from paying a visit. Where the roads crossed they met each other. Otto immediately recognized Miss Sophie, and near to her sat an elderly lady, with a gentle, good-humored countenance; this was the mother. Now there was surprise and joy. Sophie blushed—this blush could not have reference to the brother; was it then the Kammerjunker? No: that appeared impossible! therefore, it must concern Otto. The mother extended her hand to him with a welcome, whilst at the same time she invited the Kammerjunker to spend the afternoon with them. There lay, in the manner with which she proposed this, so much attention and consideration, that Otto felt the man was here held in greater esteem, and was otherwise regarded than he, during their short acquaintance, had imagined possible.

Sophie added, smiling, "You must stay!" To which the Kammerjunker replied with an apology for his travelling-dress.

"We are not strangers!" said the mother; "it is only a family meal! You see the usual circle. You, Mr. Thostrup," added she, with a most obliging manner, "I know so well from Wilhelm's letters, that we are no strangers. The gentlemen are acquainted with each other!"

"I accept the invitation," said the Kammerjunker, "and I will now show you into what a gallop I can put my steed! It is Carl Rise, [Translator's Note: Name of one of the heroes in Waldemar the Conqueror, a romance by Ingemann.] as you see, young lady—you called him so yourself!"

"Yes, ride forward," said Sophie, smiling. "By that means you will oblige my sister. She might otherwise be quite frightened, did she see such a mighty caravan approach the house, did she had not properly prepared the dinner-table."

"As my gracious young lady commands!" said the rider, and sprang forward.

The country became more woody; the road passed various small lakes, almost overgrown with water-lilies and shaded by old trees; the old-fashioned, indented gable-ends of the hall now peeped forth. They drove through an avenue of wild chestnut-trees; the stone pavement here threatened to smash the carriage axles. On the right lay the forge, through the open door of which flew the sparks. A little girl, with bare feet, opened a gate, and they now found themselves in a large open space before the red-painted out-buildings. The ground was covered with straw, and all the cows of the farm were collected here for milking. Here they were obliged to drive, step by step, until by the gateway they reached the larger courtyard, which was inclosed by the barns and the principal building itself. This was surrounded by broad ditches, almost grown over with reeds. Over a solid bridge, resting upon pillars of masonry, and through a principal wing which bore the armorial bearings and initials of the old possessor, they arrived in the innermost court, which was shut in by three wings, the antique one already mentioned, and two others: the fourth side was inclosed by a low trellis-work which adjoined the garden, where the canals lost themselves in a small lake.

"That is an interesting old court!" exclaimed Otto.

"O, that is not to be compared with the Kammerjunker's!" returned Wilhelm: "you should first see his!"

"Yes, you must come over some of these days," said the Kammerjunker. "Silence, Fingal! Silence, Valdine!" cried he to the barking dogs. A couple of turkey-cocks spread their feathers out, and gobbled with all their might. Men and women servants stood at the door: that was their reception!

"Thostrup will have the red room, will he not?" said Wilhelm, and the friends ascended the stairs together.

A pale young girl, not free from freckles, but with eyes full of soul, hastened toward them; this was Wilhelm's youngest sister. She pressed her brother to her breast, and took Otto's hand with kindness. She is not beautiful! was the first impression she made upon him. His chamber was vaulted, and the walls painted in the style of Gobelin tapestry; they represented the whole of Olympus. On the left was an old fire-place, with decorations and a gilt inscription; on the right stood an antiquated canopy-bed, with red damask hangings. The view was confined to the moat and the interior court. But a few minutes and Otto and Wilhelm were summoned to table. A long gallery through two wings of the hall, on one side windows, on the other entrances to the rooms, led to the dining-room. The whole long passage was a picture-gallery. Portraits the size of life, representing noble knights and ladies shining forth in red powdered periwigs, children adorned like their elders, with tulips in their hands, and great hounds by their sides, together with some historical pieces, decorated the walls.

"Have we no garland on the table?" asked Sophie, as she entered the dining-room with the others.

"Only a weak attempt to imitate my sister!" said Louise, smiling.

"But there is not a single flower in the garland! What economy! And yet it is sweet!"

"How tasteful!" exclaimed Otto, examining the garland which Louise had laid.

All kinds of green leaves, with their innumerable shades, a few yellow linden-leaves, and some from the copper-beech, formed, through their varied forms and colors, a tasteful garland upon the white table-cloth.

"You receive a thistle and a withered leaf!" whispered Wilhelm, as Otto seated himself.

"But yet the most beautiful!" answered he. "The copper beech contrasts so sweetly with the whitish-green thistle and the yellow leaf."

"My sister Sophie," said Louise, "lays us each day a different garland;— it is such a pretty decoration! If she is not here we get none; that would have been the case to-day, but when I learned that Wilhelm was coming, and that we," she added, with a friendly glance, "should have two other guests, I in great haste, made an attempt, and"—

"And wished to show how nicely it could be made without robbing your flowers!" interrupted Sophie, laughing. "In reality, I am very cruel! I cut all the heads of her favorites off. To-morrow, as a parody upon her garland of to-day, will I make one of green cabbage and pea-shells!"

"Madeira or port wine?" asked the Kammerjunker, and led the conversation from flowers to articles of food and drink.

"One feels one's self comfortable here at the hall! Miss Louise cares for the body, and Miss Sophie for the soul!"

"And mamma bestows a good cup of coffee," said the mother; "you must also praise me a little!"

"I give music after dinner!" cried Wilhelm; "and thus the whole family will have shown their activity!"

"But no voluntaries!" said the Kammerjunker; "no voluntaries, dear friend! No, a brisk song, so that one can hear what it is! but none of your artificial things!" A right proper blow on the shoulders was intended to soften his expression.

CHAPTER IX

"She sees if the cloth is clean and white
—If the bed has pillows and sheets;
If the candle fits in the candlestick....

"Modest she is, although you know
She makes the whole of the place;
And in she slips in the evening glow,
To light the room with her merry face "—OEHLENSCHLÄGER

A quiet, busy house-fairy was Louise; the beautiful, fragrant flowers were her favorites. Good-humoredly she smiled at the raillery of her sister, quietly listened to each thoughtless jest; but if any one, in joke, touched upon what was holy to her soul, she was aroused from her calmness and attained a certain eloquence.

We will now become more nearly acquainted with the sisters, and on this account pass over to one of the following days.

An abode together of a week, at a country-seat, will often bring about a greater intimacy than if, throughout a whole winter, people had met in large companies in cities. Otto soon felt himself at home; he was treated as a near relative. Wilhelm related all he knew of the beautiful Eva, and Sophie discovered that she was a romantic character. Mamma pitied the poor child, and Louise wished she had her on the estate: an inn was, after all, no proper place for a respectable girl. They then spoke of the winter enjoyments in Copenhagen, of art, and the theatre. Louise could not speak much with them upon these subjects, although she had seen one play, "Dyveke:" the amiable nature of the actress had spoken deeply to her heart.

Several days had passed; the sky was gray; the young people assembled round the table; they were at no loss for a subject of conversation. All those who have brothers or sons who study well, have remarked how much they are especially fascinated by the lectures on natural philosophy and astronomy; the world, as it were, expands itself before the intellectual eye. We know that the friends, during the past summer, had participated in these lectures, and, like the greater number, were full of these subjects, from the contemplation of a drop of water, with its innumerable animalculae, to the distance and magnitude of stars and planets.

To most of us these are well-known doctrines; to the ladies, also, this was nothing entirely new: nevertheless, it interested them; perhaps partly owing to Otto's beautiful eloquence. The gray, rainy weather led the conversation to the physical explanation of the origin of our globe, as the friends, from Orsted's lectures, conceived it to have been.

"The Northern and Grecian myths agree also with it!" sail Otto. "We must imagine, that in infinite space there floated an eternal, unending mist, in which lay a power of attraction. The mist condensed itself now to one drop—our globe was one enormous egg-shaped drop; light and warmth operated upon this huge world egg, and hatched, not alone ONE creature, but millions. These must die and give way to new ones, but their corpses fell as dust to the centre: this grew; the water itself condensed, and soon arose a point above the expanse of ocean. The warmth of the sun developed moss and plants; fresh islands presented themselves; for centuries did a more powerful development and improvement show themselves, until the perfection was attained which we now perceive!"

"But the Bible does not teach us thus!" said Louise.

"Moses invented his account of the creation," answered Otto; "we keep to Nature, who has greater revelations than man."

"But the Bible is to you a holy book?" asked Louise, and colored.

"A venerable book!" returned Otto. "It contains the profoundest doctrines, the most interesting histories, but also much which belongs not at all to a holy book."

"How can you say such things?" exclaimed Louise.

"Do not touch upon religion in her presence," said Sophie; "she is a pious soul, and believes, without desiring to know wherefore."

"Yes," said Wilhelm, "this winter she became quite angry, and, as I believe, for the first time angry with me, because I maintained that Christ was a man."

"Wilhelm!" interrupted the young girl, "do not speak of that; I feel myself unhappy at this thought; I can and will not see the Holy brought down to my level, and to that of every-day life. It lies in my nature that I commit a sin if I think otherwise than I have learned and than my heart allows me. It is profane, and if you speak longer of religion in this strain I shall leave the room."

At this moment the mother entered. "The festival has commenced," said she; "I have been forced to give my brightest silver skilling. Does Mr. Thostrup know the old custom which is observed here in the country, when beer is brewed for the mowing-feast?"

A piercing cry, as from a horde of savages, at this moment reached the ears of the party.

The friends descended.

In the middle of the brew-house stood a tub, around which danced all the female servants of the estate, from the dairymaids down to the girl who tended the swine; their iron-bound wooden shoes dashed against the uneven flag-stones. The greater number of the dancers were without their jackets, but with their long chemise-sleeves and narrow bodices. Some screamed, others laughed, the whole was blended together in a howl, whilst they danced hand in hand around the tub in which the beer should be brewed. The brewing-maid now flung into it the silver skilling, upon which the girls, like wild Maenades, tore off each other's caps, and with bacchanalian wildness whirled round the tub. By this means should the beer become stronger, and work more intoxicatingly at the approaching mowing-feast.

Among the girls, one especially distinguished herself by her Strong frame of body, and her long black hair, which, now that her cap was torn off, hung in disorder over her red face. The dark eyebrows were grown together. All seemed to rage most violently within her, and in truth she assumed something wild, nay almost brutal. Both arms she raised high in the air, and with outstretched fingers she whirled around.

"That is disgusting!" whispered Otto: "they all look like crazy people."

Wilhelm laughed at it. The wild merriment was lost in a joyous burst of laughter. The girl with the grown-together eyebrows let fall her arms; but still there lay in her glance that wild expression, which the loose hair and uncovered shoulders made still more striking. Either one of the others had had the misfortune to scratch her lip, or else she herself had bitten it in bacchanalian wildness until it bled: she accidentally glanced toward the open door where stood the friends. Otto's countenance became clouded, as was ever the case when anything unpleasant affected him. She seemed to guess his thoughts, and laughed aloud. Otto stepped aside; it was as though he in anticipation felt the shadow which this form would one day cast across his life.

When he and Wilhelm immediately afterward returned to Sophie and Louise, he related the unpleasant impression which the girl had made upon him.

"O, that is my Meg Merrilies!" exclaimed Sophie. "Yes, spite of her youth, do you not find that she has something of Sir Walter Scott's witch about her? When she grows older, she will be excellent. She has the appearance of being thirty, whereas she is said not to be more than twenty years old: she is a true giantess."

"The poor thing!" said Louise; "every one judges from the exterior. All who are around her hate her, I believe, because her eyebrows are grown together, and that is said to be a sign that she is a nightmare:

[Note: This superstition of the people is mentioned in
Thieles's Danish traditions: "When a girl at midnight
stretches between four sticks the membrane in which the foal
lies when it is born, and then creeps naked through it, she
will bear her child without pains; but all the boys she
conceives will become were-wolves, and all the girls
nightmares. You will know them in the daytime by their
eyebrows grown together over the nose. In the night she
creeps in through the key-hole, and places herself upon the
sleeper's bosom. The same superstition is also found in
German Grimm speaks thus about it: If you say to the
nightmare, —

Old hag, come to-morrow,
And I from you will borrow,
it retreats directly, and comes the next morning in the
shape of a man to borrow something."]

they are angry with her, and how could one expect, from the class to which she belongs, that she should return scorn with kindness? She is become savage, that she may not feel their neglect. In a few days, when we have the mowing-feast, you yourself will see how every girl gets a partner; but poor Sidsel may adorn herself as much as she likes, she still stands alone. It is truly hard to be born such a being!"

"The unfortunate girl!" sighed Otto.

"O, she does not feel it!" said Wilhelm: "she cannot feel it; for that she is too rude, too much of an animal."

CHAPTER X

"Were the pease not tender, and the vegetables fresh and
sweet as sugar What was the matter with the hams, the smoked
goose-breasts, and the herrings? What with the roasted lamb,
and the refreshing red-sprinkled head-lettuce? Was not the
vinegar sharp, and the nut-oil balmy? Was not the butter as
sweet as a nut, the red radishes tender? What?"—VOSS'S
Louise.

"Mr. Thostrup shall see the Kammerjunker's old country-seat; to-morrow we must go over."

Louise could not go with them, a hundred small duties chained her to the house. The most important of them all was ironing.

"But that the house-maid can do," said Sophie. "Do come with us."

"When thou seest thy linen nice and neat in thy drawers," returned Louise, "thou wilt certainly pardon me for remaining at home."

"Yes, thou art a glorious girl!" said Sophie; "thou dost deserve to have been known by Jean Paul, and made immortal in one of his books. Thou dost deserve the good fortune of being sung of by such a poet."

"Dost thou call it good fortune," answered the sister, "when the whole world directs its attention to one person?—that must be painful! unhappy! No, it is much better not to be remarked at all. Take my greetings with you, and ask for my Claudius back; they have had it now a whole half year."

"There, they have kept half my sister's library," said Sophie, smiling to Otto. "You must know she has only two books: Mynster's Sermons, and the 'Wandsbecker Boten.'"

The carriage rolled away through the chestnut avenue. "There upon the hill, close by the wood, did I act the elf-maiden," said Sophie. "I was not yet confirmed; there were strangers staying with us at the hall, and we wandered in the beautiful moonlight through the wood. Two of my friends and I hastened toward the hill, took hold of each other's hands and danced in a ring. The day after, two persons of the congregation told the preacher about three elfin-maidens, clad in white, who had danced upon the hill in the moonlight. The elfin-maidens were we; but that our backs were hollow as baking-troughs, and that the hill glanced like silver, was their own invention."

"And in this oak," exclaimed Wilhelm, "when a boy, I killed the first bird which fell from my shot. It was a crow, and was very honorably interred."

"Yes, beneath my sister's weeping-willow," said Sophie. "We buried it in an old chapeaubras, adorned with white bows; the grave was decorated with peony-leaves and yellow lilies. Wilhelm, who was then a big boy, made an oration, and Louise strewed flowers."

"You were little fools!" said the mother. "But see, who comes here?"

"O, my little Dickie, my dwarf of Kenilworth!" exclaimed Sophie, as a little hump-backed man, with thin legs and an old face, approached. He was dressed as a peasant, and bore upon his back a little knapsack of red calfskin, the hairy side turned outward: in this he carried his violin.

"Is he called Dickie?" asked Otto.

"No, that is only a joke of Sophie's," pursued Wilhelm; "she must always make suitable people romantic. He is called commonly 'Musikanti.' The inhabitant of Funen Italianizes most names; otherwise he is called Peter Cripple."

"You will hear his tones," said Sophie. "The day after to-morrow, when we have the mowing-feast, he will he number one. He understands music with which you are scarcely acquainted; he will play you the 'Shoemaker's Dance' as well as 'Cherry-soup:' such dances as these have people here in the country."

"We are now beyond my lands, and upon our neighbor's," said the old lady. "You will see a thorough old mansion."

"Now, I should like to know how the inhabitants will please Mr. Thostrup," said Sophie. "The Kammerjunker you know; he is an excellent country gentleman. His sister, on the contrary, is a little peculiar: she belongs to that class of people who always, even wily the best intentions, say unpleasant things. She has for this quite a rare talent—you will soon experience this; but she does not intend anything so bad. She can also joke! Thank God that you will not remain there over night, otherwise you would experience what she and the Mamsell can invent!"

"Yes, the Mamsell is my friend!" said Wilhelm. "You will see her work-box with all the curiosities. That little box plays a great part: it is always taken out with her when she pays a visit—for the sake of conversation it is brought out; all is then looked through, and every article goes the round of the company. Yes, there are beautiful things to be seen: a little wheelbarrow with a pincushion, a silver fish, and the little yard-measure of silk ribbon."

"Yes, and the amber heart!" said Sophie; "the little Napoleon of cast iron, and the officer who is pasted fast to the bottom of the box: that is a good friend in Odense, she lately told to me in confidence."

"See what beautiful stone fences the Kammerjunker has made!" said the mother. "And how beautifully the cherry-trees grow! He is an industrious man!"

They approached the garden. It was laid out in the old French style, with straight walks, pyramids of box, and white painted stone figures: satyrs and goddesses peeped through the green foliage. You now caught sight of a high tower with a spire; and soon the whole of the old mansion presented itself to view. The water was conveyed away from the broad moats, where the weeping willows with bowed heads and uncovered roots stood in the warm sunshine. A number of work-people were busily employed in clearing the moats of mud, which was wheeled in barrows on both sides.

They soon reached the principal court-yard. The barns and the out-buildings lay on the opposite side. A crowd of dogs rushed forth barking toward the carriage—all possible races, from the large Danish hound, which is known to the Parisian, down to the steward's little pug-dog, which had mixed with this company. Here stood the greyhound, with his long legs, beside the turnspit. You saw all varieties, and each had its peculiar and melodious bark. A couple of peacocks, with bright outspread tails, raised at the same time a cry, which must have made an impression. The whole court-yard had a striking air of cleanliness. The grass was weeded from between the stones; all was swept and arranged in its appointed order. Before the principal flight of steps grew four large lime-trees; their tops, from youth bent together and then clipped short, formed in spring and summer two large green triumphal arches. On the right stood upon an upright beam, which was carved and formed into a pillar, a prettily painted dove-cot; and its gay inhabitants fluttered and cooed around. The peacock-pigeon emulated the peacock in spreading its tail; and the cropper-pigeon elevated itself upon its long legs, and drew itself up, as though it would welcome the strangers with the air of a grand gentleman. The reddish-brown tiles and the bright window-panes were the only things which had a modern air. The building itself, from the stone window-seats to the old-fashioned tower through which you entered, proclaimed its antiquity. In the vaulted entrance-hall stood two immense presses: the quantity of wood which formed them, and the artistical carving, testified to their great age. Above the door were fastened a couple of antlers.

The Kammerjunker's sister, Miss Jakoba, a young lady of about thirty, neither stout nor thin, but with a strange mixture of joviality and indolence, approached them. She appeared to rejoice very much in the visit.

"Well, you are come over, then!" said she to Wilhelm. "I thought you had enough to do with your examination."

Wilhelm smiled, and assured her that after so much study people required relaxation.

"Yes, you doubtless study in handsome boots!" said the young lady, and in a friendly manner turned toward Sophie. "Good heavens, miss!" she exclaimed, "how the sun has burnt your nose! That looks horrible! Don't you ever wear a veil? you, who otherwise look so well!"

Otto was a stranger to her. He escaped such unpleasant remarks. "They should spend the whole day there," insisted Miss Jakoba; but mamma spoke of being at home by noon.

"Nothing will come of that!" said Jakoba. "I have expected you; and we have cooked a dinner, and made preparations, and I will not have had all this trouble in vain. There are some especial dishes for you, and of these you shall eat." This was all said in such a good-humored tone that even a stranger could not have felt himself offended. The Kammerjunker was in the fields looking after his flax; he would soon be back. Squire Wilhelm could in the mean time conduct Mr. Thostrup about the premises: "he would otherwise have nothing to do," said she.

No one must remain in the sitting-room; it was so gloomy there! The walls were still, as in by-gone days, covered with black leather, upon which were impressed gold flowers. No, they should go to the hall—that had been modernized since the Baroness was last there. The old chimney-piece with carved ornaments was removed, and a pretty porcelain stove had taken its place. The walls were covered with new paper from Paris. You could there contemplate all the public buildings of that city,—Notre Dame, Saint Sulpice, and the Tuileries. Long red curtains, thrown over gilt rods, hung above the high windows. All this splendor was admired.

"I prefer the antique sitting-room, after all," said Sophie; "the old chimney-piece and the leather hangings. One fairly lives again in the days of chivalry!"

"Yes, you have always been a little foolish!" said Jakoba, but softened her words by a smile and a pressure of the hand. "No, the hall is more lively. Ah!" she suddenly exclaimed; "Tine has placed her work-box in the window! That is disorder!"

"O, is that the celebrated work-box, with its many fool's tricks?" inquired Wilhelm, as he laughingly took it up.

"There are neither fools nor tricks in the box," said Jakoba. "But only look in the mirror in the lid, and then you will perhaps see one of the two."

"No rude speeches, my young lady!" said Wilhelm; "I am an academical burgher!"

The Kammerjunker now entered, attired in the same riding dress in which we made his acquaintance. He had visited his hay and oats, had seen after the people who were working at the fences, and had been also in the plantation. It had been a warm forenoon.

"Now, Miss Sophie," said he, "do you see how I am clearing out the court? It costs me above five hundred dollars; and still they are the peasants of the estate who clear away the mud. But I shall get a delicate manure-heap, so fit and rich that it's quite a pleasure. But, Jakoba, where is the coffee?"

"Only let it come in through the door," said Jakoba, somewhat angrily. "You certainly ate something before you went from home. Let me attend to the affairs of the ladies, and do thou attend to the gentlemen, so that they may not stand and get weary."

The Kammerjunker conducted the friends up the winding stone stairs into the old tower.

"All solid and good!" said he. "We no longer build in this manner. The loop-holes here, close under the roof, were walled up already in my father's time. But only notice this timber!"

The whole loft appeared a gigantic skeleton composed of beams, one crossing the other. On either side of the loft was a small vaulted chamber, with a brick fire-place. Probably these chambers had been used as guard-rooms; a kind of warder's walk led from these, between the beam-palisade and the broad wall.

"Yes, here," said the Kammerjunker, "they could have had a good lookout toward the enemy. Look through my telescope. You have here the whole country from Vissenberg to Munkebobanke, the Belt, and the heights of Svendborg. Only see! The air is clear. We see both Langeland and Zealand. Here one could, in 1807, have well observed the English fleet."

The three climbed up the narrow ladder and came past the great clock, the leaden weights of which, had they fallen, would have dashed through the stone steps, and soon the gentlemen sat on the highest point. The Kammerjunker requested the telescope, placed it and exclaimed:—

"Did I not think so? If one has not them always under one's eyes they begin playing pranks! Yes, I see it very well! There, now, the fellows who are working at the fences have begun to romp with the girls! they do nothing! Yes, they don't believe that I am sitting here in the tower and looking at them!"

"Then a telescope is, after all, a dangerous weapon!" exclaimed Wilhelm. "You can look at people when they least expect it. Fortunately, our seat lies hidden behind the wood: we are, at all events, safe."

"Yes, that it is, my friend," returned the other; "the outer sides of the garden are still bare. Did I not, last autumn, see Miss Sophie quite distinctly, when she was gathering service-berries in her little basket? And then, what tricks did she not play? She certainly did not think that I sat here and watched tier pretty gambols!"

They quitted the tower, and passed through the so-called Knight's Hall, where immense beams, laid one on the other, supported the roof. At either end of the hall was a huge fireplace, with armorial bearings painted above: the hall was now used as a granary; they were obliged to step over a heap of corn before reaching the family pew in the little chapel, which was no longer used for divine service.

"This might become a pretty little room," said the Kammerjunker, "but we have enough, and therefore we let this, for curiosity's sake, remain in its old state. The moon is worth its money!" and he pointed toward the vaulted ceiling, where the moon was represented as a white disk, in which the painter, with much naïveté, had introduced a man bearing a load of coals upon his back; in faithful representation of the popular belief regarding the black spot in the moon, which supposes this to be a man whom the Lord has sent up there because he stole his neighbor's coal. "That great picture on the right, there," pursued he, "is Mrs. Ellen Marsviin; I purchased it at an auction. One of the peasants put up for it; I asked him what he would do with this big piece of furniture—he could never get it in through his door. But do you know what a speculation he had? It was not such a bad one, after all. See! the rain runs so beautifully off the painted canvas, he would have a pair of breeches made out of it, to wear in rainy weather behind the plough; they would keep the rain off! I thought, however, I ought to prevent the portrait of the highly honorable Mrs. Ellen Marsviin being so profaned. I bought it: now she hangs there, and looks tolerably well pleased. The peasant got a knight instead—perhaps one of my own ancestors, who was now cut up into breeches. See, that is what one gets by being painted!"

"But the cupboard in the pillar there?" inquired Otto.

"There, certainly, were Bibles and Prayer-books kept. Now I have in it what I call sweetmeats for the Chancery-counselor Thomsen: old knives of sacrifice, coins and rings, which I have found in the horse-pond and up yonder in the cairns: not a quarter of a yard below the turf we found one pot upon another; round each a little inclosure of stones—a flat stone as covering, and underneath stood the pot, with burnt giants' bones, and a little button or the blade of a knife. The best things are already gone away to Copenhagen, and should the Counselor come, he will, God help me! carry away the rest. That may be, then, willingly, for I cannot use the stuff, after all."

After coffee, the guests wandered through the old garden: the clearing away of the mud was more closely observed, the dairy and pig-sty visited, the new threshing-machine inspected. But now the Russian bath should be also essayed; "it was heated!" But the end of the affair was, that only the Kammerjunker himself made use of it. The dinner-table was prepared, and then he returned. "But here something is wanting!" exclaimed he; left the room, and returned immediately with two large bouquets, which he stuck into an ale-glass which he placed upon the table. "Where Miss Sophie dines, the table must be ornamented with flowers: certainly we cannot lay garlands, as you do!" He seated himself at the end of the table, and wished, as he himself said, to represent the President Lars: they had had the "Wandsbecker Boten" half a year in the house, and it would certainly please Miss Sophie if they betrayed some acquaintance with books. This Lars and the flowers, here, meant quite as much as in the south a serenade under the windows of the fair one.

When, toward evening, the carriage for their return drew up before the door, Otto still stood contemplating some old inscriptions which were built into the tower-wall.

"That you can look at another time," said Jakoba; "now you must be of use a little!" And she reached him the ladies' cloaks.

Amidst promises of a return visit and the parting yelping of the dogs the carriage rolled away.

"I have fairly fallen in love with the old place!" said Sophie.

"The Kaminerjunker gains much upon nearer acquaintance," said Otto.

They bad now reached the furthest extremity of the garden. A flower-rain showered itself over them and the carriage. The Kammerjunker, Jakoba, and the Mamsell, had taken a shorter way, and now waved an adieu to the travellers, whilst at the same time they scattered hyacinths and stocks over them. With a practiced hand Jakoba threw, as a mark of friendship, a great pink straight into Otto's face. "Farewell, farewell!" sounded from both sides, and, accompanied by the sound of the evening-bell from the near village, for it was sunset, the carriage rolled away.

CHAPTER XI

"Dance and stamp
Till the shoe-soles drop!"
—*Danish Popular Song.*

On the following day should the much-talked-of mowing-festival take place. It was the hay-harvest which occasioned all this merriment. [Author's Note: It is true that serfdom is abolished, but the peasant is still not quite free; neither can he be so. For his house and land he must pay a tribute, and this consists in labor. His own work must give way to that of his lord. His wagon, which he has had prepared to bring home his own harvest, must, if such be commanded, go to the nobleman's land, and there render service. This is, therefore, a kind of tax which he pays, and for the faithful payment of which he is rewarded by a harvest and mowing-feast; at the latter he receives a certain quantity of brandy, and as much ale as he can drink. The dance generally takes place in the middle of the court-yard, and the dancers themselves must pay their musicians.]

During three afternoons in succession, in the inner court and under free heaven, should a ball be held. Along the walls, rough planks, laid upon logs of wood, formed a row of benches. At both ends of the court lay two barrels of the newly brewed ale, which had received more malt than usual, and which, besides, through the silver skilling, and the magic dance of the maidens round the tub, had acquired extraordinary strength. A large wooden tankard, containing several measures of brandy, stood upon a table; the man who watched the bleaching-ground was placed as a kind of butler to preside at this sideboard. A bread-woman, with new white bread from Nyborg upon her barrow, wheeled into the court, and there established her stall for every one; for it was only liquors the guests received gratis.

The guests now entered the court by pairs; the men, part in jackets, part in long coats which hung down to their ankles. Out of the waistcoat-pocket protruded a little nosegay of sweet-williams and musk. The girls carried their "posies," as they called them, in their neatly folded pocket-handkerchiefs. Two musicians—one quite a young blade, in a laced coat with a stiff cravat, mid the other the well-known Peter Cripple, "Musikanti" as he was called—led the procession. They both played one and the same piece, but each according to his own manner. It was both good and old.

They now began to draw lots, who should dance before the door of the family and who before that of the steward; after which the two parties drew lots for the musicians. The girls seated themselves in a row upon the bench, from whence they were chosen. The gallantry accorded with the ball-room,—the hard stone pavement. Not even had the grass been pulled up, but that would be all right after dancing there the first day. "Nay, why art thou sitting there?" spoken with a kind of morose friendliness, was the invitation to dance; and this served for seven dances. "Only don't be melancholy!" resounded from the company, and now the greater portion moved phlegmatically along, as if in sleep or in a forced dance: the girl with her eyes staring at her own feet, her partner with his head bent toward one side, and his eyes in a direct line with the girl's head-dress. A few of the most active exhibited, it is true, a kind of animation, by stamping so lustily upon the stone pavement that the dust whirled up around them. That was a joy! a joy which had occupied them many weeks, but as yet the joy had not reached its height; "but that will soon come!" said Wilhelm, who, with his sister and Otto, had taken his place at an open window.

The old people meanwhile kept to the ale-barrels, and the brandy. The latter was offered to the girls, and they were obliged, at least, to sip. Wilhelm soon discovered the prettiest, and threw them roses. The girls immediately sprang to the spot to collect the flowers: but the cavaliers also wished to have them, and they were the stronger; they, therefore, boldly pushed the ladies aside, so that some seated themselves on the stone pavement and got no roses: that was a merry bit of fun! "Thou art a foolish thing! It fell upon thy shoulder and thou couldst not catch it!" said the first lover to his lady, and stuck the rose into his waistcoat-pocket.

All got partners—all the girls; even the children, they leaped about to their own singing out upon the bridge. Only ONE stood forlorn,—Sidsel, with the grown-together eyebrows; she smiled, laughed aloud; no one would become her partner. Peter Cripple handed his violin to one of the young men and asked him to play, for he himself wished to stretch his legs a little. The girls drew back and talked with each other; but Peter Cripple stepped quietly forward toward Sidsel, flung his arms around her, and they danced a whirling dance. Sophie laughed aloud at it, but Sidsel directed her extraordinary glance maliciously and piercingly toward her. Otto saw it, and the girl was doubly revolting and frightful in his eyes. With the increasing darkness the assembly became more animated; the two parties of dancers were resolved into one. At length, when it was grown quite dark, the ale barrels become empty, the tankard again filled and once more emptied, the company withdrew in pairs, singing. Now commenced the first joy, the powerful operation of the ale. They now wandered through the wood, accompanying each other home, as they termed it; but this was a wandering until the bright morning.

Otto and Wilhelm were gone out into the avenue, and the peasants shouted to them a grateful "Good night!" for the merry afternoon.

"Now works the witchcraft!" said Wilhelm; "the magical power of the ale! Now begins the bacchand! Give your hand to the prettiest girl, and she will immediately give you her heart!"

"Pity," answered Otto, "that the Maenades of the north possess only that which is brutal in common with those of the south!"

"See, there goes the smith's pretty daughter, to whom I threw the best rose!" cried Wilhelm. "She has got two lovers, one under either arm!"

"Yes, there she goes!" simpered a female voice close to them. It was Sidsel, who sat upon the steps of a stile almost concealed in the darkness, which the trees and the hedge increased still more.

"Has Sidsel no lover?" asked Wilhelm.

"Hi, hi, hi," simpered she; "the Herr Baron and the other gentleman seek, doubtless, for a little bride. Am I beautiful enough? At night all cats are gray!"

"Come!" whispered Otto, and drew Wilhelm away from her. "She sits like some bird of ill omen there in the hedge."

"What a difference!" exclaimed Wilhelm, as he followed; "yes, what a difference between this monster, nay, between the other girls and Eva! She was, doubtless, born in the same poverty, in similar circumstances, and yet they are like day and night. What a soul has been given to Eva! what inborn nobility! It must be, really, more than a mere freak of Nature!"

"Only do not let Nature play her freaks with you!" said Otto, smiling, and raised his hand. "You speak often of Eva."

"Here it was association of ideas," answered Wilhelm. "The contrast awoke remembrance."

Otto entered his chamber—he opened the window; it was a moonlight night. From the near wood resounded laughter and song. They came from the young men and girls, who, on their wandering, gave themselves up to merriment. Otto stood silent and full of thought in the open window. Perhaps it was the moon which lent her paleness to his countenance. On what did he reflect? Upon his departure, perhaps? Only one more day would he remain here, where he felt himself so much at home; but then the journey was toward his own house, to his grandfather, to Rosalie, and the old preacher, who all thought so much of him. Otto stood listening and silent. The wind bore the song more distinctly over from the wood.

"That is their joy, their happiness!" said he. "It might have been my joy also, my happiness!" lay in the sigh which he heaved. His lips did not move, his thoughts alone spoke their silent language. "I might have stood on a level with these; my soul might have been chained to the dust, and yet it would have been the same which I now possess, with which I long to compass all worlds! the same, endowed with this sentiment of pride, which drives me on to active exertion. My fate wavered whether I should become one such as these or whether I should rise into that circle which the world calls the higher. The mist-form did not sink down into the mire, but rose above into the high refreshing air. And am I become happy through this?" His eye stared upon the bright disk of the moon. Two large tears rolled over his pale cheeks. "Infinite Omnipotence! I acknowledge Thy existence! Thou dost direct all; upon Thee will I depend!"

A melancholy smile passed over his lips; he stepped back into the chamber, folded his hands, prayed, and felt rest and peace.

CHAPTER XII

"The travellers roll through the world of men,

Like rose leaves in a stream.

The past will ne'er come back again,

But fade into a dream." —B. S. INGEMANN.

The following day, the last before Otto's departure, whilst he and Wilhelm were walking in the garden, Sophie approached them with a garland made of oak-leaves: this was intended for Otto; they were now really to lose him.

"Sophie will scarcely be up so early to-morrow morning," said Louise; "she is, therefore, obliged to present her garland to-day. I am never missing at the breakfast-table, as you well know; and I shall then bring my bouquet."

"I shall preserve both until we meet again," returned Otto; "they are vignettes to my beautiful summer-dream. When I again sit in Copenhagen, when the rain patters and the winter approaches with cold and a joyless sky, I shall still see before me Funen with its green woods, flowers, and sunshine; it will appear to me that it must still be so there, and that the garland and bouquet are only withered because they are with me in the winter cold."

"In Copenhagen we shall meet again!" said Sophie.

"And I shall see you again with the swallows!" said Louise, "when my flowers spring up again, when we have again warm summer days! As far as I am concerned, you belong to the summer, and not to the cold, calm winter."

Early on the following morning was Sophie, after all, at the breakfast table. That was to honor Otto. Mamma showed herself as the carriage was at the door. Wilhelm would accompany him as far as Odense. It was, therefore, a double leave taking, here and there.

"We will always remain friends, faithful friends!" said Wilhelm, when they parted.

"Faithful friends!" repeated Otto, and they rolled away toward Middelfart; thus far should mamma's own carriage convey the excellent Otto. Wilhelm remained behind in Odense; his coachman drove Otto, and they discoursed upon the way. They passed Vissenberg: the high, wooded hills there have received the name of the Funen Alps. The legend relates of robbers who had here deep passages underneath the high-road, where they hung bells which rang when any one passed above. The inhabitants are still looked upon with suspicion. Vissenberg appears a kind of Itri, between Copenhagen and Hamburg. [Author's Note: "Itri," Fra Diavolo's birthplace, lies in the Neapolitan States, on the highway between Rome and Naples. The inhabitants are not, without reason, suspected of carrying on the robber's trade.] Near the church there formerly lay a stone, on which Knud, the saint, is said to have rested himself when flying from the rebellious Jutlanders. In the stone remained the impression of where he had sat; the hard stone had been softer than the hearts of the rebellious people.

This, and similar legends, the coachman knew how to relate; he was born in this neighborhood, but not in Vissenberg itself, where they make the false notes. [Author's Note: A number of years ago a band of men were seized in Vissenberg who had forged bank-notes.] Every legend gains in interest when one hears it in the place with which it is connected. Funen is especially rich in such relations.

"That cairn elevates itself at Christmas upon four red posts, and one can then see the dance and merriment of the goblins within. Through that peasant's farm there drives every night a glowing coach, drawn by four coal-black horses. Where we now see a pond overgrown with reeds and roots there once stood a church, but it sank as the godless desecrated it; at midnight we still hear their sighs, and hymns of repentance."

It is true that the narrator mixed up together certain leg-ends which related to other places in the country—that he took little springs, and mingled his own thoughts with his relations; but Otto listened to him with great interest. The discourse turned also upon the family at the hall.

"Yes, they are very much liked!" said the coachman; "the gentleman may believe we know how to value them."

"And now, which of the young ladies is the best?" asked Otto.

"Yes, every one is best served by Miss Louise," returned the fellow.

"Miss Sophie is the prettiest," said Otto.

"Yes, she is also very good,—she belongs to the learned ones! She knows German, that she does! she can act comedy very excellently! I once got permission with the rest of the people to be up-stairs in the sitting-room— we stood behind the family; she did not manage her affairs at all badly."

However much the old legends interested Otto, it seemed as though he listened with more pleasure to the simple reasonings of the coachman upon the family who were become so dear to him. Words and thoughts were busied about the objects there. Wilhelm, however, was and still remained the dearest; he recollected with what mildness Wilhelm had stretched forth his hand in reconciliation, when he himself had thrust him from him. Already the happy summer days which he had spent at the country-seat, the whole visit, appeared a beautiful but short dream.

Otto felt an inward impulse to express his gratitude; his pride even, which was a fundamental feature of his character, commanded him to do this. Wilhelm's affection, his desire for a continued friendship, Otto thought he must reward; and on this account he added the following words to the few lines which he gave the coachman before his passage over the Little Belt:—

"Wilhelm, in future we will say thou to each other; that is more confidential!" "He is the first to whom I have given my thou," said Otto, when the letter was dispatched. "This will rejoice him: now, however, I myself have for once made an advance, but he deserves it."

A few moments later it troubled him. "I am a fool like the rest!" said he, and wished he could annihilate the paper. He was summoned on board. The Little Belt is only a river between the two countries; he soon found himself upon Jutland ground; the whip cracked, the wheels turned round, like the wheels of fortune, up and down, yet ever onward.

Late in the evening he arrived at an inn. From his solitary chamber his thoughts flew in opposite directions; now toward the solitary country-seat of his grandfather, among the sand-hills; now toward the animated mansion in Funen, where the new friends resided. He had opened his box and taken out what lay quite at the top, the garland of oak-leaves and the beautiful bouquet of flowers of this morning.

Most people maintain that one dreams at night of that which one has thought much about. According to this, Otto must have thought a deal about the North Sea, for of it he dreamed the whole night,—not of the young ladies.

CHAPTER XIII

"The heat-lark warbles forth his sepulchral melodies."

S. S. BLICHER.

The peninsula of Jutland possesses nothing of the natural beauty which Zealand and Funen present—splendid beeches and odoriferous clover-fields in the neighborhood of the salt sea; it possesses at once a wild and desolate nature, in the heath-covered expanses and the far-stretching moors. East and west are different; like the green, sappy leaf, and grayish white sea-weed on the sea shore. From the Woods of Marselisborg to the woods south of Coldinger Fjord, is the land rich and blooming; it is the Danish Nature in her greatness. Here rises the Heaven Mountain, with its wilderness of coppice and heather; from here you gaze over the rich landscape, with its woods and lakes, as far down as the roaring Cattegat.

The western coast, on the contrary, lies without a tree, without bushes, with nothing but white sand-hills stretching along the roaring ocean, which scourges the melancholy coast with sand-storms and sharp winds. Between these contrasts, which the east and west coasts present, the Hesperides and Siberia, lies the vast heath which stretches itself from the Lyneborg sand to the Skagen's reef. No hedge shows here the limits of possession. Among the crossing tracks of carriage wheels must thou seek thy way. Crippled oaks, with whitish-green moss overgrown to the outermost branches, twist themselves along the ground, as if fearing storms and the sea-mist. Here, like a nomadic people, but without flocks, do the so-called Tartar bands wander up and down, with their peculiar language and peculiar ceremonies. Suddenly there shows itself in the interior of the heathy wilderness a colony—another, a strange people, German emigrants, who through industry compel the meagre country to fruitfulness.

From Veile, Otto wished to take the road through Viborg, as the most direct and the shortest to his grandfather's estate, which lay between Nisumfjord and Lemvig.

The first heath-bushes accosted him as dear friends of his childhood. The beautiful beech-woods lay behind him, the expanse of heath began; but the heath was dear to him: it was this landscape which formed the basis of many dear recollections.

The country became ever higher with brown heights, beyond which nothing was visible; houses and farms became more rare, the cherry orchards transformed themselves into cabbage-gardens. Only single spots were free from heather, and here grew grass, but short, and like moss or duckweed which grows upon ponds: here birds congregated by hundreds, and fluttered twittering into the air as the carriage drove past.

"You know where to find the green spot in the heath, and how to become happy through it," sighed Otto. "Could I only follow your example!"

At a greater distance rose bare hills, without ling or ploughed land; the prickly heath looked brown and yellow on the sharp declivities. A little boy and girl herded sheep by the way-side; the boy played the Pandean pipe, the little girl sang a psalm,—it was the best song which she knew how to sing to the traveller, in order to win a little present from him.

The day was warm and beautiful, but the evening brought the cold mist from the sea, which, however, in the interior of the country loses something of its power.

"That is a kiss of welcome from my home," said Otto; "the death-kiss of the mermaid! In Funen they call it the elf maiden."

Within the last few years a number of children have been sent from the Orphan Asylum to the heath, in order that, instead of Copenhagen rogues, they may become honest Jutland peasants. Otto had a boy of this description for his coachman. The lad was very contented, and yet Otto became low-spirited from his relation. Recollections from his own life stirred within his breast. "Return thanks to God," said he, and gave the lad a considerable present; "on the heath thou hast shelter and a home; in Copenhagen, perhaps, the sandy beach would have been thy nightly resting-place, hunger and cold the gifts which the day would bring thee."

The nearer he approached the west, the more serious became his frame of mind; it was as if the desolate scenery and cold sea-mist entered his soul. The pictures of the gay country-seat at Funen were supplanted by recollections of his home with his grandfather. He became more and more low-spirited. It was only when a single mile separated him from his home that the thought of surprising his dear friends conquered his melancholy.

He caught sight of the red roof of the house, saw the willow plantations, and heard the bark of the yard-dog. Upon the hillock before the gate stood a group of children. Otto could no longer endure the slow driving through the deep ruts. He sprang out of the carriage, and ran more than he walked.

The children on the hillock became aware of him, and all looked toward the side from whence he came.

The slow driving, and his being absorbed in melancholy fancies, had relaxed his powerful frame; but now in one moment all his elasticity returned: his cheeks glowed, and his heart beat loudly.

From the court resounded singing—it was the singing of a psalm. He stepped through the gateway. A crowd of peasants stood with bared heads: before the door stood a carriage, some peasants were just raising a coffin into it. In the doorway stood the old preacher, and spoke with a man clad in black.

"Lord Jesus! who is dead?" were Otto's first words, and his countenance became pale like that of a corpse.

"Otto!" all exclaimed.

"Otto!" exclaimed also the old preacher, astonished; then seized his hand, and said gravely, "The Lord gave, and the Lord hath taken away; blessed be the name of the Lord!"

"Let me see the face of the dead!" said Otto. Not a tear came to his eye; surprise and sorrow were too great.

"Shall I take out the screws?" inquired the man who had just screwed up the coffin.

"Let him sleep the eternal rest!" said the preacher.

Otto stared at the black coffin in which his grandfather lay. The carriage drove away with it. Otto followed after with the preacher, heard him throw earth upon it, heard words which he did not comprehend, saw the last corner of the coffin, and it was then removed from his sight. All was as a dream to him.

They returned back to the preacher's abode; a pale figure approached him: it was Rosalie—old Rosalie.

"We have here no abiding-place, we all hasten toward futurity!" said the old preacher. "Strengthen yourself now with meat and drink! The body cannot suffer like the soul. We have accompanied him to His sleeping chamber; his bed was well prepared! I have prayed the evening prayer; he sleeps in God, and will awaken to behold His glory. Amen!"

"Otto! thou dear Otto!" said Rosalie. "The bitterest day brings me this joy! How have I thought of thee! Amongst strangers shouldst thou receive the tidings of his death! with no one who could feel for thy sorrow! where thou shouldst see no eye weep for what thou hast lost! Now thou art here!

now, when I believed thee so far distant—it is a miracle! Thou couldst only have received the letter to-day which carried the intelligence of thy grandfather's death to thee!"

"I wished to surprise you," said Otto. "A melancholy surprise awaited me!"

"Sit down, my child!" said the preacher, and drew him toward the covered table. "When the tree falls which gave us shade and fruit, from which we, in our own little garden, have planted shoots and sown seeds, we may well look on with sadness and feel our loss: but we must not forget our own garden, must not forget to cherish that which we have won from the fallen tree: we must not cease to live for the living! I miss, like you, the proud tree, which rejoiced my soul and my heart, but I know that it is planted in a better garden, where Christ is the gardener."

The preacher's invitation to remain with him, during his stay, in his house, Otto declined. Already this first night he wished to establish himself in his own little chamber in the house of mourning. Rosalie also would return.

"We have a deal to say to each other," said the old preacher, and laid his hand upon Otto's shoulder. "Next summer you will hardly press my hand, it will be pressed by the turf."

"To-morrow I will come to you," said Otto, and drove back with the old Rosalie to the house.

The domestics kissed the hand and coat of the young master—he wished to prevent this; the old woman wept. Otto stepped into the room; here had stood the corpse, on account of which the furniture had been removed, and the void was all the more affecting. The long white mourning curtains fluttered in tire wind before the open window. Rosalie led him by the hand into the little sleeping-room where the grandfather had died. Here everything yet stood as formerly—the large book case, with the glass doors, behind which the intellectual treasure was preserved: Wieland and Fielding, Millot's "History of the World," and Von der Hagen's "Narrenbuch," occupied the principal place: these books had been those most read by the old gentleman. Here was also Otto's earliest intellectual food, Albertus Julius, the English "Spectator," and Evald's writings. Upon the wall hung pikes and pistols, and a large old sabre, which the grandfather had once worn. Upon the table beneath the mirror stood an hour-glass; the sand had run out. Rosalie pointed toward the bed. "There he died," said she, "between six and seven o'clock in the evening. He was only ill three days; the two last he passed in delirium: he raised himself in bed, and shook the bed posts; I was obliged to let two strong men watch beside him. 'To horse! to horse!'

said he; 'the cannons forward!' His brain dreamed of war and battles. He also spoke of your blessed father severely and bitterly! Every word was like the stab of a knife; he was as severe toward him as ever!"

"And did the people understand his words?" asked Otto with a wrinkled brow.

"No, for the uninitiated they were dark words; and even had they possessed any meaning, the men would have believed it was the sickness which spoke out of him. 'There stands the mother with the two children! The one shall fall upon the flank of the enemy and bring me honor and joy. The mother and daughter I know not!' That was all which I heard him say about you and your mother and sister. By noon on the third day the fever had spent itself; the strong, gloomy man was become as weak and gentle as a child; I sat beside his bed. 'If I had only Otto here!' said he. 'I have been severely attacked, Rosalie, but I am now much better: I will go to sleep; that strengthens one.' Smilingly he closed his eyes and lay quite still: I read my prayers, withdrew gently so as not to wake him; he lay there unchanged when I returned. I sat a little while beside his bed; his hands lay upon the coverlid; I touched them, they were ice-cold. I was frightened, touched his brow, his face—he was dead! he had died without a death-struggle!"

For a long time did they converse about the dead man; it was near midnight when Otto ascended the narrow stairs which led to the little chamber in the roof, where as child and boy he had slept. All stood here as it had done the year before, only in nicer order. Upon the wall hung the black painted target, near to the centre of which he had once shot. His skates lay upon the chest of drawers, near to the nodding plaster figure. The long journey, and the overpowering surprise which awaited him on his return, had strongly affected him: he opened the window; a large white sand-hill rose like a wall straight up before it, and deprived him of all view. How often, when a child, had the furrows made by rain in the sand, and the detached pieces, presented to him pictures,—towns, towers, and whole marching armies. Now it was only a white wall, which reminded him of a winding-sheet. A small streak of the blue sky was visible between the house and the steep slope of the hill. Never before had Otto felt, never before reflected, what it was to stand alone in the world, to be lovingly bound to no one with the band of consanguinity.

"Solitary, as in this silent night do I stand in the world! solitary in the mighty crowd of human beings! Only ONE being can I call mine! only ONE being press as kindred to my heart! And I shudder at the thought of meeting with this being—I should bless the thought that she was dead! Father! thou didst ruin one being and make three miserable. I have never loved thee;

bitterness germinated within my breast when I became acquainted with thee! Mother! thy features have died out of my recollection; I revere thee! Thou wast all love; to love didst thou offer up thy life—more than life! Pray for me with thy God! Pray for me, ye dead! if there is immortality; if the flesh is not alone born again in grass and the worm; if the soul is not lost in floods of air! We shall be unconscious of it: eternally shall we sleep! eternally!" Otto supported his forehead upon the window-frame, his arm sank languidly, "Mother! poor mother! thou didst gain by death, even if it be merely an eternal sleep,—asleep without dreams! We have only a short time to live, and yet we divide our days of life with sleep! My body yearns after this short death! I will sleep—sleep like all my beloved ones! They do not awaken!" He threw himself upon the bed. The cold air from the sea blew through the open window. The wearied body conquered; he sank into the death-like sleep, whilst his doubting soul, ever active, presented him with living dreams.

CHAPTER XIV

"Man seems to me a foolish being; he drives along over the
waves of time, endlessly thrown up and down, and descrying a
little verdant spot, formed of mud and stagnant moor and of
putrid green mouldiness, he cries out, Land! He rows
thither, ascends—and sinks and sinks—and is no more to be
seen." —The Golden Fleece of GRILLPARZER.

Old Rosalie was pouring out coffee when Otto came down the next morning. Peace and resignation to the will of God lay in her soft countenance. Otto was pale, paler than usual, but handsomer than Rosalie had seen him before: a year had rendered him older and more manly; a handsome, crisp beard curled over his chin; manly gravity lay in his eyes, in which, at his departure, she had only remarked their inborn melancholy glance. With a kind of satisfaction she looked upon this beautiful, melancholy countenance, and with cordial affection she stretched forth her hand toward him.

"Here stands thy chair, Otto; and here thy cup. I will drink to thy welcome. It seems to me long since I saw thee, and yet it is, now I have thee again, only a short time. Were that place only not empty!" and she pointed to the place at the table which the grandfather had used to occupy.

"If I had only seen him!" said Otto.

"His countenance was so gentle in death," said Rosalie. "The severity and gravity which had settled in his eyes were softened away. I was myself present when he was dressed. He had his uniform on, which he always wore upon occasions of ceremony, the sabre by his side and the great hat upon his head. I knew that this was his wish!" Quietly she made the sign of the cross.

"Are all my grandfather's papers sealed?" inquired Otto.

"The most important—those which have the greatest interest for thee," said Rosalie, "are in the hands of the preacher. Last year, the day after thy departure, he gave them to the preacher; thy father's last letter I know is amongst them."

"My father!" said Otto, and glanced toward the ground. "Yes," continued he, "there is truth in the words of Scripture,—the sins of the fathers are visited upon the children unto the third and fourth generation!"

"Otto!" said Rosalie, with a beseeching and reproachful look, "thy grandfather was a severe man. Thou last known him, hast seen his darkest moments, and yet then age and cares had softened him: his love to thee calmed every outbreak. Had he only loved thy father as he loved thee, things would, perhaps, have ended better: but we may not judge!"

"And what have I done?" said Otto. "Thou, Rosalie, knowest the history of my life. Is it not as if a curse rested upon me? I was a high-spirited boy, I often occasioned thee tears; yet didst thou always place thyself between me and punishment. It was my evil blood, the blood of my birth in which the curse lay, that drove me on!"

"But thou didst become good and full of love, as thou art now!" said Rosalie.

"Only when I became acquainted with myself and my destiny. In the thoughtlessness of childhood, unacquainted with myself and the world, did I myself have that sign of my misery, which now presses down my soul, cut into my flesh. Yes, Rosalie! I remember this very well, and have clearly preserved this, my earliest recollection before my grandfather took me, and I came here a boy. I remember the great building from whence I was brought, the number of people who there worked, sang, and laughed, and who told me extraordinary stories of how badly people were treated in the beautiful world. This was my parents' home, thought I, when I began to ponder upon parents and their connection with children. It was a large manufactory which they possessed, thought I; I remembered the number of work-people. All played and romped with me. I was wild and full of boisterous spirits a boy of only six years old, but with the perseverance and will of one of ten. Rosalie, thou sawest many proofs of the evil which lay in my blood; it bordered upon insolence. I remembered well the strong, merry Heinrich, who always sang at his loom; he showed me and the others his tattooed breast, upon which he had his whole mournful history imprinted. Upon his arm were his own and his bride's names. That pleased me; I wished to have my name also on my arm. 'It is painful!' said he; 'then thou wilt pipe, my lad!' That was spur enough to make me desire it. I allowed him to puncture my skin, to puncture an O and a T upon my shoulder, and did not cry,—no, not once whilst the powder burnt into it; but I was praised, and was proud to bear the initials—proud of them until three years ago, when I met Heinrich here. I recognized him, but he did not recognize me. I showed him my shoulder, and besought him to read the name, this O and

T: but he did not say Otto Thostrup; he named a name which destroyed the happiness of my childhood, and has made me miserable forever!"

"It was a fearful day!" said Rosalie. "Thou didst demand from me an explanation, thy grandfather gave it thee, and thou wast no longer the Otto thou hadst formerly been. Yet wherefore speak of it? Thou art good and wise, noble and innocent. Do not fill thy heart with sorrow from a time which is past, and which, for thy sake, shall be forgotten."

"But Heinrich still lives!" said Otto; "I have met with him, have spoken with him: it was as if all presence of mind forsook me."

"When and where?" asked Rosalie.

Otto related of his walk with Wilhelm in the park, and of the juggler, in whom he had recognized Heinrich. "I tore myself from my friends, I wandered the whole night alone in the wood. O Rosalie, I thought of death! I thought of death as no Christian ought to do. A beautiful morning followed, I wandered beside the sea which I love, and in which I have so often dived. Since that explanation of the initials on my shoulder was suggested, that explanation which reminded me of my unhappy birth, I have never uncovered them before any one. O, I have rubbed thorn with a stone, until they were bloody! The letters are gone, but still I imagine I can read them in the deep scar—that in it I see a Cain's mark! That morning the desire to bathe came upon me. The fresh current infused life once more into my soul. Just then Wilhelm and several acquaintance came down; they called to me and carried off my clothes; my blood boiled; all my unhappiness, which this night had stirred within my soul, again overwhelmed me: it was as though the obliterated initials on my shoulder would reveal themselves in the scar and betray the secret of my grief. Disgust of life seized upon me. I no longer knew what I shouted to them, but it seemed to me as if I must swim out into the stream and never return. I swam until it became night before my eyes. I sank, and Wilhelm rescued me! Never since then have we spoken of this hour! O Rosalie! long is it since I have been able to open my heart as before thee at this moment. What use is it to have a friend if one cannot lay before him one's whole thoughts? To no one have I been able to unfold them but to thee, who already knowest them. I suffer, as a criminal and yet am I innocent,—just as the misshapen, the deformed man, is innocent of his ugliness!"

"I do not possess thy knowledge, Otto," said Rosalie, and pressed his hand; "have never rejoiced in such a clear head as thine; but I have that which thou canst not as yet possess—experience. In trouble, as well as in joy, youth transforms the light cobweb into the cable. Self-deception has changed the blood in thy veins, the thoughts in thy soul; but do not forever cling to this one black spot! Neither wilt thou! it will spur thee on to activity, will enervate thy soul, not depress thee! The melancholy surprise of thy grandfather's death, whom thou didst believe active and well, has now made thee dejected, and thy thoughts so desponding. But there will come better days! happy days! Thou art young, and youth brings health for the soul and body!"

She led Otto into the garden, where the willow plantations protected the other trees from the sharp west wind. The gooseberry-bushes bore fruit, but it was not yet ripe: one bush Otto had planted when a cutting; it was now large. Rosalie had tied the twigs to a palisade, so that, as an espalier, it could thoroughly drink in the sun's rays. Otto regarded the fetters more than the good intention.

"Let it grow free!" said he; "if that brittle palisade should tumble down, the twigs would be broken." And he cut the bands.

"Thou art still the old Otto," said Rosalie.

They went into her little room, where the crucifix, and before it a small vase of flowers, adorned the table. Above the cross hung a garland of withered heather.

"Two years ago didst thou give me that, Otto!" said Rosalie. "There were no more flowers, there was nothing green but the heath, and thou twinedst a garland of it for me. Afterward I would not take it down from the crucifix."

They were interrupted by a visit. It was from the old preacher.

CHAPTER XV

"His coal was coarse, its fashion old;
He asked no dress of greater worth
Than that which kept from storm and cold
The Baptist when he preached on earth."

C. J. BORE.

Not alone of Otto's affairs, but also of "the city yonder," as the preacher called Copenhagen, would he speak. Only once a week came the "Viborg Collector" to hint, and the Copenhagen papers were a whole month going their round. "One would willingly advance with the time," said he. Yesterday, at the interment, he had not found it seemly to gratify his desire of hearing dear Otto talk about the city, but to-day he thought it might well be done, and therefore he would not await Otto's visit but come over to pay one himself.

"Thou hast certainly seen our good king?" was his first question. "Lord help the anointed one! he is then as vigorous and active as ever—my good King Frederik!" And now he must relate a trait which had touched his heart, and which, in his opinion, deserved a place in the annals of history. This event occurred the last time that the king was in Jutland; he had visited the interior of the country and the western coast also. When he was leaving a public-house the old hostess ran after him, and besought that the Father would, as a remembrance, write his name with chalk upon a beam. The grand gentlemen wished to deter her, but she pulled at the king's coat; and when he had learned her wish he nodded in a friendly manner, and said, "Very willingly!" and then turned back and wrote his name on the beam. Tears came into the old man's eyes; he wept, and prayed for his king. He now inquired whether the old tree was still standing in the Regent's Court, and then spoke of Nyerup and Abrahamson, whom he had known in his student days.

In fact, after all, he was himself the narrator; each of his questions related to this or that event in his own life, and he always returned to this source—his student-days. There was then another life, another activity, he maintained. His royal idea of beauty had been Queen Matilda. [Translator's

Note: The unhappy wife of Christian VII. and daughter of our George III.]
"I saw her often on horseback," said he. "It was not then the custom in our country for ladies to ride. In her country it was the fashion; here it gave rise to scandal. God gave her beauty, a king's crown, and a heart full of love; the world gave her—what it can give—a grave near to the bare heath!"

Whilst he so perpetually returned to his own recollections, his share of news was truly not new, but he was satisfied. Copenhagen appeared to him a whole world—a royal city; but Sodom and Gomorrah had more than one street there.

Otto smiled at the earnestness with which he said this.

"Yes, that I know better than thou, my young friend!" continued the old preacher. "True, the devil does not go about like a roaring lion, but there he has his greatest works! He is well-dressed, and conceals his claws and his tail! Do not rely upon thy strength! He goes about, like the cat in the fable, 'pede suspenso,' sneakingly and cautiously! It is, after all, with the devil as it is with a Jutland peasant. This fellow comes to the city, has nothing, runs about, and cleans shoes and boots for the young gentlemen, and by this means he wins a small sum of money. He knows how to spare. He can now hire the cellar of the house in which thou livest, and there commence some small trade. The trade is successful, very successful. It goes on so well that he can hire the lower story; then he gains more profit, and before thou canst look about thee he buys the whole house. See, that is the way with the Jutland peasant, and just the same with the devil. At first he gets the cellar, then the lower story, and at last the whole house!"

CHAPTER XVI

"Sure 'tis fair in foreign land,
But not so fair as home;

Let me but see thy mountains grand
Glaciers and snowy dome!

Let me but hear the sound that tells
Of climbing cattle, dressed with bells."
The Switzer's Homesickness.

Not until after breakfast did the preacher pass over to Otto's affairs. His grandfather's will made him the sole heir to the large property; a man in Copenhagen, the merchant Berger, should be his guardian, since the preacher did not wish to undertake the office. Rosalie was not forgotten: her devotion and fidelity had won for her a relative's right. Her last days should be free from care: she had truly striven to remove all care from the dead whilst yet he lived. An old age free from care awaited her; but Otto wished that she should also have a happy old age. He imparted his plan to the preacher; but the latter shook his head, thought it was not practicable, and regarded it as a mere fancy—a whim. But such it was not.

Some days passed by. One afternoon Rosalie sat upon a small wooden bench under the cherry-trees, and was making mourning for the winter.

"This is the last summer that we shall sit here," said she; "the last summer that this is our home. Now I am become equally rooted to this spot; it grieves me that I must leave it."

"Thou wast forced to leave thy dear Switzerland," said Otto; "that was still harder!"

"I was then young," answered she. "The young tree may be easily transplanted, but the old one has shot forth deeper roots. Denmark is a good land—a beautiful land!"

"But not the west coast of Jutland!" exclaimed Otto. "For thy green pasture hast thou here heath; for thy mountains, low sand-hills."

"Upon the Jura Mountains there is also heath," said Rosalie. "The heath here often reminds me of my home on the Jura. There also is it cold, and snow can fall already in August. The fir-trees then stand as if powdered over."

"I love Switzerland, which I have never seen," pursued Otto. "Thy relation has given me a conception of the picturesque magnificence of this mountain-land. I have a plan, Rosalie. I know that in the heart of a mountaineer homesickness never dies. I remember well how thy eyes sparkled when thou toldest of the walk toward Le Locle and Neufchâtel; even as a boy I felt at thy words the light mountain air. I rode with thee upon the dizzy height, where the woods lay below us like potato fields. What below arose, like the smoke from a charcoal-burner's kiln, was a cloud in the air. I saw the Alpine chain, like floating cloud mountains; below mist, above dark shapes with glancing glaciers."

"Yes, Otto," said Rosalie, and her eyes sparkled with youthful fire; "so looks the Alpine chain when one goes from Le Locle to Neulfchâtel: so did I see it when I descended the Jura for the list time. It was in August. The trees, with their autumnal foliage, stood yellow and red between the dark firs; barberries and hips grew among the tall fern. The Alps lay in such a beautiful light, their feet blue as heaven, their peaks snow-white in the clear sunshine. I was in a sorrowful mood; I was leaving my mountains! Then I wrote in my book—O, I remember it so well!—The high Alps appear to me the folded wings of the earth: how if she should raise them! how if the immense wings should unfold, with their gay images of dark woods, glaciers, and clouds! What a picture! At the Last Judgment will the earth doubtless unfold these pinions, soar up to God, and in the rays of His sunlight disappear! I also have been young, Otto," pursued she, with a melancholy smile. "Thou wouldst have felt still more deeply at the sight of this splendor of nature. The lake at the foot of the mountains was smooth as a mirror; a little boat with white sails swam, like a swan, upon its expanse. On the road along which we drove were the peasants beating down chestnuts; the grapes hung in large black bunches. How an impression such as this can root itself in the memory! It is five and thirty years since, and yet I still see that boat with the white sail, the high Alps, and the black grapes."

"Thou shalt see thy Switzerland again, Rosalie," exclaimed Otto; "again hear the bells of the cows upon the green pastures! Thou shalt go once more to the chapel in Franche Compté, shalt visit thy friends at Le Locle, see the subterranean mill, and the Doub fall."

"The mill wheel yet goes round, the water dashes down as in my youth; but the friends are gone, my relatives dispersed! I should appear a stranger there; and when one has reached my age, nature cannot satisfy—one must have people!"

"Thou knowest, Rosalie, my grandfather has settled a sum upon thee so long as thou livest. Now I have thought thou couldst spend thy latter days with thy beloved ones at home, in the glorious Switzerland. In October I take my philosophicum; the following summer I would then accompany thee. I must also see that splendid mountain-land,—know something more of the world than I have yet known. I know how thy thoughts always dwell upon Switzerland. Thither will I reconduct thee; thou wilt feel thyself less lonely there than here in Denmark."

"Thou art carried away by the thoughts of youth, as thou shouldst and must be, thou dear, sweet soul!" said Rosalie, smiling. "At my age it is not so easy."

"We will make short days' journeys," said Otto, "go with the steamboat up the Rhine—that is not fatiguing; and from Basel one is soon in Franche Compté on the Jura."

"No, upon the heath, near Vestervovov, as it is called here, will old Rosalie die; here I have felt myself at home, here I have two or three friends. The family at Lemvig have invited me, have for me a place at table, a little room, and friendly faces. Switzerland would be no longer that Switzerland which I quitted. Nature would greet me as an old acquaintance; it would be to me music, once more to hear the ringing of the cows' bells; it would affect me deeply, once again to kneel in the little chapel on the mountain: but I should soon feel myself a greater stranger there than here. Had it been fifteen years ago, my sister would still have been living, the dear, pious Adèle! She dwelt with my uncle close on the confines of Neufchâtel, as thou knowest, scarcely a quarter of a mile from Le Locle—the town, as we called it, because it was the largest place in the neighborhood. Now there are only distant relations of mine living, who have forgotten me. I am a stranger there. Denmark gave me bread, it will also give me a grave!"

"I thought of giving thee a pleasure!" said Otto.

"That thou dost by thy love to me!" returned she.

"I thought thou wouldst have shown me thy mountains, thy home, of which thou hast so often spoken!"

"That can I still do. I remember every spot, every tree—all remains so clear in my recollection. Then we ascend together the Jura higher and higher; here are no more vineyards to be found, no maize, no chestnuts only dark pines, huge cliffs, here and there a beech, as green and large as in Denmark. Now we have the wood behind us, we are many feet above the sea; thou canst perceive this by the freshness of the air. Everywhere are green meadows; uninterruptedly reaches our ear the ringing of the cow-bells. Thou as yet seest no town, and yet we are close upon Le Locle. Suddenly the road turns; in the midst of the mountain-level we perceive a small valley, and in this lies the town, with its red roofs, its churches, and large gardens. Close beneath the windows rises the mountain-side, with its grass and flowers; it looks as though the cattle must be precipitated upon the houses. We go through the long street, past the church; the inhabitants are Protestants—it is a complete town of watchmakers. My uncle and Adèle also sat the whole day, and worked at wheels and chains. That was for Monsieur Houriet, in Le Locle. His daughters I know; one is called Rosalie, like myself. Rosalie and Lydia, they will certainly have forgotten me! But it is true that we are upon our own journey! Now, thou seest, at the end of the town we do not follow the broad road—that leads to Besançon; we remain in the lesser one, here in the valley where the town lies. The beautiful valley! The green mountain-sides we keep to our right; on it are scattered houses, with large stones upon their steep wooden roofs, and with little gardens tilled with plum-trees. Steep cliff-walls shut in the valley; there stands up a crag; if thou climbest it thou canst look straight into France: one sees a plain, flat like the Danish plains. In the valley where we are, close under the rock, lies a little house; O, I see it distinctly! white-washed and with blue painted window-frames: at the gate a great chained dog. I hear him bark! We step into that quiet, friendly little house! The children are playing about on the ground. O, my little Henry-Numa-Robert! Ah, it is true that now he is older and taller than thou! We descend the steps toward the cellar. Here stand sacks and chests of flour; under the floor one hears a strange roaring; still a few steps lower, and we must light the lamp, for here it is dark. We find ourselves in a great water-mill, a subterranean mill. Deep below in the earth rushes a river—above no one dreams of it; the water dashes down several fathoms over the rushing wheel, which threatens to seize our clothes and whirl us away into the circle. The steps on which we stand are slippery: the stone walls drip with water, and only a step beyond the depth appears bottomless! O, thou wilt love this mill as I love it! Again having reached the light of day, and under free heaven, one only perceives the quiet, friendly little house. Dost thou know, Otto, often as thou hast sat quiet and dreaming, silent as a statue, have I thought of my mill, and the repose which it presented? and yet how wildly the stream roared in its bosom, how the wheels rushed round, and how gloomy it was in the depth!"

"We will leave the mill!" said Otto, and sought to lead her from her reflections back to her own relation. "We find ourselves in the wood, where the ringing of the evening-bell reaches our ear from the little chapel in Franche Compté."

"There stands my father's house!" said Rosalie. "From the corner-window one looks over the wood toward Aubernez, [Author's Note: A village in the canton Neufchâtel, lying close upon the river Doub, where it forms the boundary between Switzerland and France.] where the ridge leads over the Doub. The sun shines upon the river, which, far below, winds along, gleaming like the clearest silver."

"And the whole of France spreads itself out before us!" said Otto.

"How beautiful! O, how beautiful!" exclaimed Rosalie, and her eyes sparkled as she gazed before her; but soon her glance became sad, and she pressed Otto's hand. "No one will welcome me to my home! I know neither their joys nor their sorrows—they are not my own family! In Denmark—I am at home. When the cold sea-mist spreads itself over the heath I often fancy I am living among my mountains, where the heather grows. The mist seems to me then to be a snow-cloud which rests over the mountains, and thus, when other people are complaining of the bad weather, I am up among my mountains!"

"Thou wilt then remove to the family at Lemvig?" asked Otto.

"There I am welcome!" returned she.

CHAPTER XVII

"Look at the calming sea. The waves still tremble in the
depths, and stem to fear the gale.—Over my head is hovering
the shadowy mist.—My curls are wet with the filling dew."
—OSSIAN.

Otto had not as yet visited the sand-hills on the strand, the fishermen, or the peasants, among whom formerly he had spent all his spare time.

The beautiful summer's day drove him forth, his heart yearned to drink in the summer warmth.

Only the roads between the larger towns are here tolerable, or rather as tolerable as the country will allow. The by-ways were only to be discerned by the traces of cart-wheels, which ran on beside each other; at certain places, to prevent the wheels sinking into the deep sand, ling had been spread; where this is not the case, and the tracks cross each other, a stranger would scarcely find the way. Here the landmark places its unseen boundary between neighboring possessions.

Every farm, every cottage, every hill, was an old acquaintance to Otto. He directed his steps toward Harbooere, a parish which, one may say, consists of sand and water, but which, nevertheless, is not to be called unfruitful. A few of the inhabitants pursue agriculture, but the majority consists of fishermen, who dwell in small houses and have no land.

His first encounter upon his wandering was with one of those large covered wagons with which the so-called eelmen, between the days of St. John and St. Bartholomew, go with eels toward the small towns lying to the south and east, and then, laden with apples and garden produce, return home—articles which are rapidly consumed by the common people. The eelman stopped when he saw and recognized Otto.

"Welcome, Mr. Otto!" said he. "Yes, you are come over abut a sad affair! That Major Thostrup should have gone off so! But there was nothing else to be expected from him he was old enough."

"Death demands his right!" replied Otto, and pressed the man's hand. "Things go, doubtless, well with you, Morten Chraenseu?"

"The whole cart full of eels, and some smoked carp! It is also good to meet with you, Mr. Otto. Upon the land a preacher is very good, but not upon the sea, as they say at home. Yes, you are certainly now a preacher, or will become one?"

"No, I am not studying to become a preacher!" answered Otto.

"No! will you then become a lawyer? It strikes me you are clever enough—you have no need to study any more! You will just go and say a few words to them at home? The grandmother sits and spins yarn for eel-nets. She has now the cataract on the other eye, but her mouth is as well as ever; she does not let herself grow dumb, although she does sit in the dark. Mother provides the baits; she has also enough to do with the hooks."

"But Maria, the lively little Maria?" said Otto.

"The girl? She has gone this year with the other fishergirls to Ringkjoebing, to be hired for the hay and corn harvest; we thought we could do without her at home. But now, God willing! I must travel on." Cordially he shook Otto's hand, and pursued his slow journey.

The brothers of the eelman were active fishermen, as their father had been before them; and although they were all married they lived together. The swarm of children was not insignificant; young and old formed one family, in which the old grandmother had the first voice.

Otto approached the dwelling; before it lay a little plot of land, planted with potatoes and carrots, and also beds of onions and thyme. Two large bull-dogs, with sharp teeth and wicked eyes, rushed toward Otto. "Tyv! Grumsling!" shrieked a voice, and the dogs let fall their tails and drew back, with a low growl, toward the house. Here at the threshold sat an old woman in a red woolen jacket, with a handkerchief of the same material and same color about her neck, and upon her head a man's black felt hat. She spun. Otto immediately recognized the old blind grandmother.

"God's peace be in the house!" said he.

"That voice I have not heard for a year and a day!" replied the old woman, and raised her head, as if she would see him with her dead eyes. "Are not you Major Thostrup's Otto? You resemble him in the voice. I thought, truly, that if you came here you would pay us a visit. Ide shall leave the baits and put on the kettle, that you may have a cup of coffee. Formerly you did not use to despise our entertainment. You have not grown proud with your journey, have you? The coffee-vetch [Author's Note: Astragalus baeticus is used as a substitute for coffee, and is principally grown upon the sand-hills west of Holmsland. It is first freed from the husk, and then dried and roasted a little.] is good; it is from Holmsland, and tastes better than the merchant's beans." The dogs still growled at Otto. "Cannot you stupid beasts, who have still eyes in your heads to see with, recognize that this is the Major's Otto?" cried she wrathfully, and gave them several good blows with her hand.

Otto's arrival created a great stir in the little household that he was welcome, you might see by every countenance.

"Yes," said the grandmother, "now you are grown much wiser in the town, could, very likely, were it needful, write an almanac! You will very likely have found for yourself a little bride there, or will you fetch one out of Lemvig? for no doubt she must be from a town! Yes, I have known him ever since he was a little fellow; yonder, on the wall, he made, out of herrings' heads, the living devil, just as he lives and breathes. He thrust our sucking-pig into the eel-cart, between the casks. We sought a whole day after the sucking-pig without finding him, and he was forced to make the journey with them to Holstebro. Yes, he was a wild fellow! Later, when he was obliged to learn so much, he became sad. Yes, yes, within the last years his books have overdone him!"

"Yes, many a time has he put out to sea with my husband!" pursued one of the daughters-in-law. "One night he remained out with him. How anxious the French Mamsell at the hall was about him!"

"He was never haughtty," said the grandmother. "He nibbled his dried fish with the fresh fish, and drank a little cup of water, although he was used to better things at home. But to-day we have white bread, fresh and good; it came yesterday from Lemvig."

The brandy-glass, with its wooden, red-painted foot, was placed before Otto. Under the bed there was an anker of brandy,—"a little stock," as all stranded goods are here called.

Otto inquired after the married sons. They were with their men on the shore, ready to embark on their fishing expedition, The grandmother would accompany him thither; they were not yet departed: she should first take them provisions.

The old woman took her stick, the dog sprang forward, and now commenced their wandering among the sand-hills, where their huts or booths, built with rafters and smeared with earth, stood. Around lay the refuse of fish,—heads and entrails, thrown about. The men were just then busied in carrying the trough and fishing-tackle [Author's Note: A "Bakke" consists of three lines, each of 200 Danish ells, or about 135 yards, and of 200 fishing-hooks; the stretched "Bakke" is thus about 200 yards, with 600 hooks; these are attached to the line with strings half an ell long and as thick as fine twine. To each "Bakke" belongs a square trough, on which it is carried on board. To a larger fishing-boat are reckoned six lots of hooks; each lot has eight to nine "Bakkes."] on board.

The open sea lay before them, almost as bright as a mirror, for the wind was easterly. Near to them paused a horseman; he was partly dressed like a peasant, with riding-breeches on, which were buttoned down at the sides.

"Have you heard the news?" he cried to Otto. "I come from Ringkjoebing. At Merchant Cohen's I have read the German paper; there is a revolution in France! Charles X. is fled with the whole royal family. Yes, in Paris, there is fine work!"

"The French are a wild people!" said the grandmother. "A king and a queen they have beheaded in my time; now they will do the same with these. Will our dear Lord suffer that such things be done to His anointed?"

"There will be war again!" said one of the fishermen.

"Then more horses will go out of the country," said the stranger, pressed Otto's hand, and vanished behind the sandhills.

"Was not that the horse-dealer from Varde?" inquired Otto.

"Yes, he understands languages," said the fisherman; "and thus he is acquainted with foreign affairs sooner than we. Then they are now fighting in France! Blood flows in the streets; it will not be so in Denmark before the Turk binds his horse to the bush in the Viborg Lake. And then, according to the prophecy of the sibyl, it will be near the end of the world."

Meanwhile, everything was prepared for their embarkation. If Mr. Otto would take the further oar, and was inclined to pass the night on the sea, there was a place for him in the boat. But he had promised Rosalie to be back before evening. The grandmother now prayed, kneeling with the others, and immediately after quick strokes of the oars the flat boat rowed away from the shore. The fate of France was forgotten; their calling occupied the fishermen.

The old woman seemed to listen to the strokes of the oars; her dead eyes rested immovably on the sea. A sea-mew passed close to her in its flight. "That was a bird!" said she. "Is there no one here beside ourselves?"

"No; no one at all," answered Otto, carelessly.

"Is no one in the hut, no one behind the sand-hills?" again asked the grandmother. "It was not on account of the dried meat that I came here—it was not to wet my face on the shore; I speak with you alone, which I could not do in the house. Give me your hand! Now that the old man rests in the grave, you yourself will guide the rudder; the estate will be sold, and you will not come again to the west coast. Our Lord has made it dark before my eyes before He has closed my ears and given me leave to go. I can no longer see you, but I have you in my thought as you looked before you left our land. That you are handsomer now I can easily imagine; but gayer you are not! Talk you certainly can, and I have heard you laugh; but that was little better than the two last years you were here. Once it was different with you—no fairy could be wilder than you!"

"With years one becomes more quiet," said Otto, and gazed with astonishment at the blind woman, who did not leave go his hand. "As a boy I was far too merry—that could not continue; and that I should now be grave, I have, as you will see, sufficient reason—I have lost my last support."

"Yes, truly, truly!" repeated she slowly, and as if pondering; then shook her head. "That is not the reason. Do you not believe in the power of the devil? our Lord Christ forgive me! do not you believe in the power of wicked men? There is no greater difference between the human child and the changeling brat which the underground spirits lay in his stead in the cradle, than there is between you when you were a boy and you as you became during the last year of your stay here. 'That comes from books, from so much learning,' said I to other people. Could I only have said so to myself! But you shall become gay; the trouble of your heart shall wither like a poisonous weed. I know whence it sprung, and will, with God's help, heal it. Will you solemnly promise, that no soul in the world shall learn what we speak of in this hour?"

"What have you to say to me?" asked Otto, affected by the extraordinary earnestness of the old woman.

"The German Heinrich, the player! You remember him well? He is to blame for your grief! Yes, his name drives the blood more quickly through your pulse. I feel it, even it I cannot see youi face."

"The German Heinrich!" repeated Otto, and his hand really trembled. Had Heinrich, then, when he was here three years ago, told her and the fishermen that which no human being must know,—that which had destroyed the gayety of his youth? "What have I to do with the German Heinrich?"

"Nothing more than a pious Christian has to do with the devil!" replied she, and made the sign of the cross. "But Heinrich has whispered an evil word in your ear; he has banished your joyous humor, as one banishes a serpent."

"Has he told you this?" exclaimed Otto, and breathed more quickly. "Tell me all that he has said!"

"You will not make me suffer for it!" said she. "I am innocent, and yet I have cooperated in it: it was only a word but a very unseemly word, and for it one must account at the day of judgment!"

"I do not understand you!" said Otto, and his eyes glanced around to see whether any one heard. They were quite alone. In the far distance the boat with the fishermen showed itself like a dark speck.

"Do you remember how wild you were as a boy? How you fastened bladders to the cat's legs and tail, and flung her out of the loft-window that she might fly? I do not say this in anger, for I thought a deal of you; but when you became too insolent one might wall say, 'Can no one, then, curb this lad?' See, these words I said!—that is my whole fault, but since then have lain heavy on my heart. Three years ago came the German Heinrich, and stayed two nights in our house; God forgive it us! Tricks he could play, and he understood more than the Lord's Prayer—more than is useful to a man. With one trick you were to assist him, but when he gave you the goblet you played your own tricks, and he could make nothing succeed. You would also be clever. Then he cast an evil eye upon you, although he was still so friendly and submissive, because you were a gentleman's child. Do you remember—no, you will certainly have forgotten—how you once took the baits of the hooks off and hung my wooden shoes on instead? Then I said in anger, and the anger of man is never good, 'Can no one, then, tame this boy for me? He was making downright fun of you to your own face,' said I to the player. 'Do you not know some art by which you can tame this wild-cat?' Then he laughed maliciously, but I thought no more of the matter. The following day, however, he said, 'Now I have curbed the lad! You should only see how tame he is become; and should he ever again turn unruly, only ask him what word the German Heinrich whispered in his ear, and you shall. Then see how quiet he will become. He shall not mock this trick!' My heart was filled with horror, but I thought afterward it really meant nothing. Ei! ei! from the hour he was here you are no longer the same as formerly; that springs from the magical word he whispered in your ear. You cannot pronounce the word, he told me; but by it you have been enchanted: this, and not book-learning, has worked the change. But you shall be delivered! If you have faith, and that you must have, you shall again become gay, and I, spite of the evil words which I spoke, be able to sleep peacefully in my grave. If you will only lay this upon your heart, now that the moon is in its wane, the trouble will vanish out of your heart as the disk of the moon decreases!" And saying this she drew out of her pocket a little leather purse, opened it and took out a piece of folded paper. "In this is a bit of the wood out of which our Saviour's cross was made. This will draw forth the sorrow from your heart, and bear it, as it bore Him who took upon

Himself the sorrow of the whole world!" She kissed it with pious devotion, and then handed it to Otto.

The whole became clear to him. He recollected how in his boyish wantonness he had caused Heinrich's tricks to miscarry, which occasioned much pleasure to the spectators, but in Heinrich displeasure: they soon again became friends, and Otto recognized in him the merry weaver of the manufactory, as he called his former abode. They were alone, Otto asked whether he did not remember his name: Heinrich shook his head. Then Otto uncovered his shoulder, bade him read the branded letters, and heard the unhappy interpretation which gave the death-blow to his gayety. Heinrich must have seen what an impression his words made upon the boy: he gained through them an opportunity of avenging himself, and at the same time of bringing himself again into repute: as a sorcerer. He had tamed him, whispered he to the old woman,—he had tamed the boy with a single word. At any future wantonness of Otto's, gravity and terror would immediately return should any one ask him, What word did the German Heinrich whisper into thy ear? "Only ask him," had Heinrich said.

In a perfectly natural manner there lay, truly, enchantment in Heinrich's words, even although it were not that enchantment which the superstition of the old woman would have signified. A revelation of the connection of affairs would have removed her doubts, but here an explanation was impossible to Otto. He pressed her hand, besought her to be calm; no sorrow lay heavy on his heart, except the loss of his dear grandfather.

"Every evening have I named your name it my prayers," said the old grandmother. "Each time when the harbingers of bad weather showed themselves, and my sons were on the sea, so that we hung out flags or lighted beacons as signals, did I think of the words which had escaped my lips, and which the wicked Heinrich had caught up; I feared lest our Lord might cause my children to suffer for my injustice."

"Be calm, my dear old woman!" said Otto. "Keep for yourself the holy cross, on the virtue of which you rely; may it remove each sorrow from your own heart!"

"No, I am guilty of my own sorrow! yours has a stranger laid upon your heart! Only the sorrow of the guiltless will the cross bear."

The beautiful sentiment which, unconsciously to her, lay in these words, affected Otto. He accepted the present, preserved it, sought to calm the old woman, and once more at parting glanced toward the splendid sea expanse which formed its own boundary.

It was almost evening before he reached the house where Rosalie awaited him. His last scene with the blind fisher-woman had again thrown him into his gloomy mood. "After all, she really knows nothing!" said he to himself. "This Heinrich is my evil angel! might he only die soon!" It was in Otto's soul as if he could shoot a ball through Heinrich's heart. "Did he only lie buried under the heather, and with him my secret! I will have blood! yes, there is something devilish in man! Were Heinrich only dead! But others live who know my birth,—my sister! my poor, neglected sister, she who had the same right to intellectual development as myself! How I fear this meeting! it will be bitter! I must away. I will hence—here will my life-germ be stifled! I have indeed fortune—I will travel! This animated France will drive away these whims, and—I am away, far removed from my home. In the coming spring I shall be a stranger among strangers!" And his thoughts melted into a quiet melancholy. In this manner he reached the hall.

CHAPTER XVIII

"*L'Angleterre jalouse et la Grèce homérique,*
Toute l'Europe admire, et la jeune Amérique
Se lève et bat des mains du bord des océans.

Trois jours vous ont suffi pour briser vos entraves.
Vous êtes les aînés d'une race de braves,
Vous êtes les fits des géans!"
V. HUGO, Chants du Crépuscule.

"*Politiken, mine Herrer!"*
MORTONS' Lystspil: den Hjemkomne Nabob

"In France there is revolution!" was the first piece of information which Otto related. "Charles X. has flown with his family. This, they say, is in the German papers."

"Revolution?" repeated Rosalie, and folded her hands. "Unhappy France! Blood has flowed there, and it again flows. There I lost my father and my brother. I became a refugee—must seek for myself a new father-land." She wiped away a tear from her cheek, and sunk into deep meditation. She knew the horrors of a revolution, and only saw in this new one a repetition of those scenes of terror which she had experienced, and which had driven her out into the world, up into the north, where she struggled on, until at length she found a home with Otto's grandfather—a resting abode.

Everything great and beautiful powerfully affected Otto's soul; only in one direction had he shown no interest—in the political direction, and it was precisely politics which had most occupied the grandfather in his seclusion. But Otto's soul was too vivacious, too easily moved, too easily carried away by what lay nearest him. "One must first thoroughly enter into life, before the affairs of the world can seize upon us!" said he. "With the greater number of those who in their early youth occupy themselves with politics, it is merely affectation. It is with them like the boy who forces himself to smoke tobacco so as to appear older than he really is." Beyond his own country, France was the only land which really interested Otto. Here Napoleon had ruled, and Napoleon's name had reached his heart—he had grown up whilst this name passed from mouth to mouth; the name and the deeds of the hero sounded to him, yet a boy, like a great world adventure. How often had he heard his grandfather, shaking his head, say, "Yes, now newspaper writers have little to tell since Napoleon is quiet." And then he had related to him of the hero at Arcole and among the Pyramids, of the great campaign against Europe, of the conflagration at Moscow, and the return from Elba.

Who has not written a play in his childhood? Otto's sole subject was Napoleon; the whole history of the hero, from the snow-batteries at Brienne to the rocky island in the ocean. True, this poem was a wild shoot; but it had sprung from an enthusiastic heart. At that time he preserved it as a treasure. A little incident which is connected with it, and is characteristic of Otto's wild outbreaks of temper when a boy, we will here introduce.

A child of one of the domestics, a little merry boy with whom Otto associated a good deal, was playing with him in his garret. Otto was then writing his play. The boy bantered him, pulling the paper at the same time. Otto forbade him with the threat,—"If thou dost that again I will throw thee out of the window!" The boy again immediately pulled at the paper. In a moment Otto seized him by the waist, swung him toward the open window, and would certainly have thrown him out, had not Rosalie fortunately entered the room, and, with an exclamation of horror, seized Otto's arm, who now stood pale as death and trembling in every limb.

In this manner had Napoleon awoke Otto's interest for France. Rosalie also spoke, next to her Switzerland, with most pleasure of this country. The Revolution had livingly affected her, and therefore her discourse regarding it was living. It even seemed to the old preacher as though the Revolution were an event which he had witnessed. The Revolution and Napoleon had often fed his thoughts and his discourse toward this land. Otto had thus, without troubling himself the least about politics, grown up with a kind of interest about France. The mere intelligence of this struggle of the July days was therefore not indifferent to him. He still only knew what the horse-dealer had related; nothing of the congregation, or of Polignac's ministry: but France was to him the mighty world-crater, which glowed with its splendid eruptions, and which he admired from a distance.

The old preacher shook his head when Otto imparted this political intelligence to him. A king, so long as he lived, was in his eyes holy, let him be whatever sort of a man he might. The actions of a king, according to his opinion, resembled the words of the Bible, which man ought not to weigh; they should be taken as they were. "All authority is from God!" said he.

"The anointed one is holy; God gives to him wisdom; he is a light to whom we must all look up!"

"He is a man like ourselves!" answered Otto. "He is the first magistrate of the land, and as such we owe him the highest reverence and obedience. Birth, and not worth, gives him the high post which he fills. He ought only to will that which is good; to exercise justice. His duties are equally great with those of his subjects."

"But more difficult, my son!" said the old man. "It is nothing, as a flower, to adorn the garland; more difficult is it to be the hand which weaves the garland. The ribbon must be tight as well as gently tied; it must not cut into the stems, and yet it must not be too loose. Yes, you young men talk according to your wisdom! Yes, you are wise! quite as wise as the woman who kept a roasted chicken for supper. She placed it upon a pewter plate upon the glowing coals, and went out to attend to her affairs. When she returned the plate was melted, and the chicken lay among the ashes. 'What a wise cat I have!' said she; 'she has eaten I the plate and left the chicken!' See, you talk just so, and regard things from the same foolish point of view. Do not speak like the rest of them in the city! 'Fear God, and honor the king!' We have nothing to argue with these two; they transact their business between them! The French resemble young students; when these have made their examen artium they imagine they are equal to the whole world: they grow restive, and give student-feasts! The French must have a Napoleon, who can give their something to do! If they be left to themselves they will play mad pranks!"

"Let us first see what the papers really say," replied Otto.

The following day a large letter arrived; it was from Wilhelm:—

"My excellent Otto, We have all drunk to Otto Thostrup's health. I raised the glass, and drank the health. The friendship's dissonance YOU has dissolved itself into a harmonious THOU, and thou thyself hast given the accord. All at home speak of thee; even the Kammerjunker's Mamsell chose lately thee, and not her work-box, as a subject of conversation. The evening as thou drovest over the Jutland heaths I seated myself at the piano, and played thy whole journey to my sisters. The journey over the heath I gave them in a monotonous piece, composed of three tones, quite dissimilar to that composed by Rousseau. My sisters were near despair; but I told them it was not more uninteresting than the heath. Sometimes I made a little flight, a quaver; that was the heath-larks which flew up into the air. The introduction to the gypsy-chorus in 'Preciosa' signified the German gypsy-flock. Then came the thema out of 'Jeannot and Collin'—'O, joyous days of childhood!'—and then thou wast at home. I thundered powerfully down in the bass; that was the North Sea, the chorus in thy present grand' opéra. Thou canst well imagine that it was quite original.

"For the rest, everything at home remains in its old state. I have been in Svendborg, and have set to music that sweet poem, 'The Wishes,' by Carl Bagger. His verses seem to me a little rough; but something will certainly come out of the fellow! Thy own wishes are they which he has expressed. Besides this, the astonishing tidings out of France have given us, and all good people here, an electrical shock. Yes, thou in thy solitude hast certainly heard nothing of the brilliant July days. The Parisians have deposed Charles X. If the former Revolution was a blood-fruit, this one is a true passionflower, suddenly sprung up, exciting astonishment through its beauty, and as soon as the work is ended rolling together its leaves. My cousin Joachim, who as thou knowest is just now at Paris, has lived through these extraordinary days. The day before yesterday we received a long, interesting letter from him, which gave us—of the particulars as well as of the whole—a more complete idea than the papers can give us. People assemble in groups round the post-houses to receive the papers as they arrive. I have extracted from my cousin's letter what has struck me most, and send thee these extracts in a supplement. Thou canst thus in thy retirement still live in the world. A thousand greetings from all here. Thou hast a place in mamma's heart, but not less so in mine.

"*Thy friend and brother,*

"WILHELM.

"P. S.—It is true! My sister Sophie begs thee to bring her a stone from the North Sea. Perhaps thou wilt bring for me a bucket of water; but it must not incommode thee!"

This hearty letter transported Otto into the midst of the friendly circle in Funen. The corner of the paper where Wilhelm's name stood he pressed to his lips. His heart was full of noble friendship.

The extract which Wilhelm had made from his cousin's letter was short and descriptive. It might be compared with a beautiful poem translated into good prose.

In the theatre we interest ourselves for struggling innocence; but we are still more affected when the destiny of a whole nation is to be decided. It is on this account that "Wilhelm Tell" possesses so much interest. Not of the single individual is here the question, but of all. Here is flesh of our flesh, and bone of our bone. Greater than the play created by the poet was the effect which this description of the July days produced upon Otto. This was the reality itself in which he lived. His heart was filled with admiration for

France, who fought for Liberty the holy fight, and who, with the language of the sword, had pronounced the anathema of the age on the enemies of enlightenment and improvement.

The old preacher folded his hands as he heard it; his eyes sparkled: but soon he shook his head. "May men so judge the anointed ones of God? 'He who taketh the sword shall perish by the sword!'"

"The king is for the people," said Otto; "not the people for the king!"

"Louis XVIth's unhappy daughter!" sighed Rosalie; "for the third time is she driven from her father-land. Her parents and brothers killed! her husband dishonored! She herself has a mind and heart. 'She is the only man among the Bourbons,'" said Napoleon.

The preacher, with his old-fashioned honesty, and a royalist from his whole heart, regarded the affair with wavering opinion, and with fear for the future. Rosalie thought most of those who were made unhappy of the royal ladies and the poor children. Each followed the impulse of their own nature, and the instinctive feeling of their age; thus did Otto also, and therefore was his soul filled with enthusiasm. Enthusiasm belongs to youth. His thoughts were busied with dreams of Paris; thither flew his wishes. "Yes, I will travel!" exclaimed he; "that will give my whole character a more decided bias: I will and must," added he in thought. "My sorrow will be extinguished, the recollections of my childhood be forgotten. Abroad, no terrific figures, as here, will present themselves to me. My father is dead, foreign earth lies upon his coffin!"

"But the office—examination!" said the old preacher, "pass that first. It is always good to have this in reserve, even if thou dost make no use of it. Only make this year thy philosophicum."

"And in the spring I shall travel," said Otto.

"That depends upon thy guardian, my son!" said the preacher.

Several days passed, and Otto began to feel it solitary in his home—all moved here in such a confined circle. His mind was accustomed to a wider sphere of action. He began to grow weary, and then the hours travel with the snail's pace.

"...minutterna ligesom räcka og strärka sig.
Man känner behof at göre sa med." [Note: Sketches of Every-day Life.]

He thought of his departure.

"Thou must take the road through Lemvig," said Rosalie. "I will then visit the family there for a few days; it will make them quite happy to see thee, and I shall then be so much longer with thee. That thou wilt do, wilt thou not?"

The day was fixed when they should travel.

The evening previous, Otto paid his last visit to the preacher. They spoke together a long time about the deceased grandfather. The preacher gave up several papers to Otto; among them also his father's last letter.

In honor of Otto, a bottle of wine was placed upon the table.

"To thy health, my son!" said the preacher, raising his glass. "We shall hardly spend another evening together. Thou wilt have much to learn before thou comest as far as I. The world has more thorn-bushes than gold-mountains. The times look unsettled. France commences a new description of campaign in Europe, and certainly will draw along with it all young men: formerly it was the conquerer Napoleon who led to the field; now it is the idea of liberty! May the Lord preserve our good king, and then it will remain well with us! Thou, Otto, wilt fly out into the wide world—hadst thou only first passed thy examination for office! But when and where-ever thou mayest fly, remember on all occasions the words of Scripture.

"We all desire to rule. Phaeton wished to drive the chariot of the sun, but not understanding how to guide the reins, he set fire to the countries, precipitated himself from the chariot, and broke his neck. I have no one in the city of Copenhagen whom I can ask thee to greet for me. All the friends of my youth are scattered to the east and to the west. If any of them still be in the city, they will certainly have forgotten me. But shouldst thou ever go to the Regent's Court, and smoke with the others a pipe under the tree, think of me. I have also sat there when I was young like thee; when the French Revolution drove also the blood quicker through my veins, and thoughts of freedom caused me to carry my head more high. The dear old tree! [Author's Note: At the end of the last century it was felled, and two younger ones, which are now in full growth, planted in its stead.] Yes, but one does not perceive in it, as in me, how many years have passed since then!"

He pressed a kiss on Otto's forehead, gave him his blessing, and they parted.

Otto was in a melancholy mood; he felt that he had certainly seen the old man for the last time. When he arrived at home he found Rosalie busy hacking. The following morning, by earliest dawn, they were to travel toward Lemvig. Otto had not been there within these two last years. In old times the journey thither had always been to him a festival, now it was almost indifferent to him.

He entered his little chamber; for the last time in his life he should now sleep there. From the next morning commenced, so it seemed to him, a new chapter in his life. Byron's "Farewell" sounded in his ears like an old melody:—

"*Fare thee well, and if forever,*

Still for ever fare thee well."

At break of day the carriage rolled away with him and old Rosalie. Both were silent; the carriage moved slowly along the deep ruts. Otto looked back once more. A lark rose, singing above him.

"It will be a beautiful day!" said the coachman; his words and the song of the lark Rosalie regarded as a good omen for Otto's whole journey.

CHAPTER XIX

"Geske.—Have you put syrup in the coffee?

Henrich.—Yes, I have.

Geske.—Be so good, dear madams, be so kind as to be contented."

HOLBERG'S *Political Pewterer.*

Lemvig lies, as is well known, on an arm of the Limfjord. The legend relates, that in the Swedish war a troop of the enemy's cavalry compelled a peasant here to mount his horse and serve as a guide. Darkness came on; they found themselves already upon the high sand-banks. The peasant guided his horse toward a steep precipice; in a farm-house on the other side of the fjord they perceived a light. "That is Lemvig," said the peasant; "let us hasten!" He set spurs to his horse, the Swedes followed his example, and they were precipitated into the depth: the following morning their corpses were found. The monument of this bold Lemvig peasant consists of this legend and in the songs of the poets; and these are the monuments which endure the longest. Through this legend the bare precipice receives an intellectual beauty, which may truly compare itself with the naturally beautiful view over the city and the bay.

Rosalie and Otto drove into the town. It was two years since he had been here; everything seemed to him, during this time, to have shrunk together: wherever he looked everything was narrow and small. In his recollection, Lemvig was very much larger.

They now drew up before the merchant's house. The entrance was through the shop, which was decorated with wooden shoes, woolen gloves, and iron ware. Close within the door stood two large casks of tea. Over the counter hung an extraordinary stuffed fish, and a whole bunch of felt hats, for the use of both sexes. It was a business en gros and en détail, which the son of the house managed. The father himself was number one in Lemvig; he had ships at sea, and kept open house, as they call it, in the neighborhood.

The sitting-room door opened, and the wife herself, a stout, square woman, with an honest, contented countenance, stepped out and received the guests with kisses and embraces. Alas! her good Jutland pronunciation cannot be given in writing.

"O, how glorious that the Mamsell comes and brings Mr. Thostrup with her! How handsome he is become! and how grown! Yes, we have his mark still on the door." She drew Otto along with her. "He has shot up more than a quarter of a yard!"

He looked at the objects which surrounded him.

"Yes," said she, "that instrument we have had since you were last here; it is a present to Maren from her brother. She will now sing; you something. It is astonishing what a voice she has! Last Whitsuntide she sang in the church with the musical people; she sang louder than the organ!"

Otto approached the sofa, over which a large piece of needlework hung, in a splendid gold frame. "That is Maren's name-sampler," said the mistress of the house. "It is very pretty. See! there stand all our names! Can Mr. Thostrup guess who this is? Here are all the figures worked in open stitch. That ship, there, is the Mariane, which was called after me. There you see the Lemvig Arms—a tower which stands on the waves; and here in the corner, in regular and irregular stitches, is her name, 'Maren, October the 24th, 1828.' Yes, that is now two years since. She has now worked a cushion for the sofa, with a Turk upon it. It went the round of the city—every one wished to see it; it is astonishing how Maren can use her hands!"

Rosalie inquired after the excellent girl.

"She is preparing the table," said the lady. "Some good friends are coming to us this evening. The secretary will also come; he will then play with Maren. You will doubtless, in Copenhagen, have heard much more beautiful music; ours is quite simple, but they sing from notes: and I think, most likely the secretary will bring his musical-box with him. That is splendid! Only lately he sang a little song to the box, that was much better than to the larger instrument; for I must say he has not the strong chest which Maren has."

The whole family assembled themselves for the first time at the dinner-table. The two persons who took the lowest places at table appeared the most original; these were the shopman and the aunt. Both of them had only at dinner the honor of being with the family; they were quite shut out from the evening parties.

The shopman, who in the shop was the first person, and who could there speak a few words, sat here like a quiet, constrained creature; his hair combed toward one side, and exhibiting two red, swollen hands: no sound escaped his lips; kissing the hand of the lady of the house, at coming and going, was all he did beside eat.

The aunt, who was not alone called so by the family, but by the whole of Lemvig, was equally sparing of her words, but her face was constantly laughing. A flowered, red cotton cap fitted close to the thin face, giving something characteristic to the high cheek-bones and hanging lip. "She assisted in the household, but could take no part in genteel company," as the lady expressed herself. She could never forget how, at the Reformation Festival, when only the singers sang in the church, aunt began singing with them out of her book, so that the churchwarden was forced to beg her to be silent; but this she took very ill, and declared she had as notch right as the others to praise God, and then sang in defiance. Had she not been "aunt," and not belonged to the family to which she did, she would certainly have been turned out.

She was now the last person who entered and took her place at table. Half an hour had she been sought after before she was found. She had stood at the end of the garden, before the wooden trellis. Grass had been mown in the field behind the garden, and made into a rick; to see this she had gone to the trellis, the odor had agreeably affected her; she had pressed her face against the trellis-work, and from contemplation of it had fallen into thought, or rather out of thought. There she was found, and the dreamer was shaken into motion. She was again right lively, and laughed each time that Otto looked at her. He had his seat between Maren and the lady of the house, at the upper end of the table. Maren was a very pretty girl—little, somewhat round, white and red, and well-dressed. A vast number of bows, and a great variety of colors, were her weak side. She was reading at this time "Cabal and Love."

"Thou art reading it in German!" said the mother.

"Yes, it must be a beautiful piece. I speak German very well, but when I wish to read it I get on too slowly with it: I like to get to the end of a book!"

The husband had his place at the head of the table. A little black cap sat smoothly on his gray hair, and a pair of clever eyes sparkled in his countenance. With folded hands he prayed a silent prayer, and then bowed his head, before he allowed the dinner to be served. Rosalie sat beside him. Her neighbor on the right seemed very talkative. He was an old soldier, who in his fortieth year had gone as lieutenant with the land's troops, and had permission to wear the uniform, and therefore sat there in a kind of military coat, and with a stiff cravat. He was already deep in Polignac's ministry and the triumph of the July days; but he had the misfortune to confound Lafitte and Lafayette together. The son of the house only spoke of bull-calves. The lady at the table was a little mamsell from Holstebro, who sat beside him, dressed like a girl for Confirmation, in a black silk dress and long red shawl.

She was in grand array, for she was on a visit. This young lady understood dress-making, and could play upon the flute; which, however, she never did without a certain bashfulness: besides this, she spoke well, especially upon melancholy events. The bottle of wine only circulated at the upper end of the table; the shopman and aunt only drank ale, but it foamed gloriously: it had been made upon raisin-stalks.

"He is an excellent man, the merchant, whom you have received as guardian, Mr. Thostrup," said the master of the house. "I am in connection with him."

"But it is strange," interrupted the lady, "that only one out of his five daughters is engaged. If the young ladies in Copenhagen do not go off better than that, what shall we say here?"

"Now Mr. Thostrup can take one of them," said the husband. "There is money, and you have fortune also; if you get an office, you can live in floribus!"

Maren colored, although there was no occasion for coloring; she even cast down her eyes.

"What should Mr. Thostrup do with one of them?" pursued the wife. "He shall have a Jutland maiden! There are pretty young ladies enough here in the country-seats," added she, and laid the best piece of meat upon his plate.

"Do the royal company give pretty operas?" asked Maren, and gave another direction to the conversation.

Otto named several, among others Der Freischütz.

"That must be horrible!" said the lieutenant. "They say the wolf-glen is so natural, with a waterfall, and an owl which flutters its wings. Burgomaster Mimi has had a letter from a young lady in Aarhuus, who has been in Copenhagen, and has seen this piece. It was so horrible that she held her hand before her face, and almost fainted. They have a splendid theatre!"

"Yes, but our little theatre was very pretty!" said the lady of the house. "It was quite stupid that the dramatic company should have been unlucky. The last piece we gave is still clear in my recollection; it was the 'Sandseslöse.' I was then ill; but because I wished so much to see it, the whole company was so obliging as to act it once more, and that, too, in our sitting-room, where I lay on the sofa and could look on. That was an extraordinary mark of attention from them! Only think—the burgomaster himself acted with them!"

In honor of the strangers, coffee was taken after dinner in the garden, where, under the plum-trees, a swing was fixed. Somewhat later a sailing party was arranged. A small yacht belonging to the merchant lay, just unladen, near the bridge of boats.

Otto found Maren and the young lady from Holstebro sitting in the arbor. Somewhat startled, they concealed something at his entrance.

"The ladies have secrets! May one not be initiated?"

"No, not at all!" replied Maren.

"You have manuscript poems in the little book!" said Otto, and boldly approached. "Perhaps of your own composition?"

"O, it is only a memorandum-book," said Maren, blushing. "When I read anything pretty I copy it, for we cannot keep the books."

"Then I may see it!" said Otto. His eye fell upon the written sheet: —

"So fliessen nun zwei Wasser
Wohl zwischen mir und Dir
Das eine sind die Thränen,
Das andre ist der See!"
[Note: Des Knaben Wunderhorn.]

he read. "That is very pretty! 'Der verlorne Schwimmer,' the poem is called, is it not?"

"Yes, I have copied it out of the secretary's memorandum-book; he has so many pretty pieces."

"The secretary has many splendid things!" said Otto, smiling. "Memorandum-book, musical snuff-box" —

"And a collection of seals!" added the young lady from Holstebro.

"I must read more!" said Otto; but the ladies fled with glowing cheeks.

"Are you already at your tricks, Mr. Thostrup?" said the mother, who now entered the garden. "Yes, you do not know how Maren has thought of you—how much she has spoken of you. You never wrote to us; we never heard anything of you, except when Miss Rosalie related us something out of your letters. That was not nice of you! You and Maren were always called bride and bridegroom. You were a pair of pretty children, and your growth has not been disadvantageous to either of you."

At four o'clock the evening party assembled—a whole swarm of young ladies, a few old ones, and the secretary, who distinguished himself by a collection of seals hanging to a long watch-chain, and everlastingly knocking against his body; a white shirt-frill, stiff collar, and a cock's comb, in which each hair seemed to take an affected position. They all walked down to the bay. Otto had some business and came somewhat later. Whilst he was crossing, alone, the court-yard, he heard, proceeding from the back of the house, a fearful, wild cry, which ended in violent sobbing. Terrified, he went nearer, and perceived the aunt sitting in the middle of a large heap of turf. The priestess at Delphi could not have looked more agitated! Her close cap she had torn from her head; her long, gray hair floated over her shoulders; and with her feet she stamped upon the turf, like a willful child, until the pieces flew in various directions. When she perceived Otto she became calm in a moment, but soon she pressed her thin hands before her face and sobbed aloud. To learn from her what was the matter was not to be thought of.

"O, she is only quarrelsome!" said the girl, to whom Otto had turned for an explanation. "Aunt is angry because she was not invited to sail with the company. She always does so,—she can be quite wicked! Just lately, when she should have helped me to wring out the sheets, she always twisted them the same way that I did, so that we could never get done, and my hands hurt me very much!"

Otto walked down to the bay. The sail was unfurled, the secretary brought out his musical-box, and, accompanied by its tones, they glided in the burning sunshine over the water.

On the other side tea was to be drunk, and then Maren was to sing. Her mother asked her to sing the song with the strong tones, so that Otto might hear what a voice she had.

She sang "Dannevang." Her voice had uncommon power, but no style, no grace.

"Such a voice, I fancy, you have not heard in the theatre at Copenhagen?" said the secretary, with dogmatical gravity.

"You might wish yourself such a chest!" said the lieutenant.

The secretary should now sing; but he had a little cold, which he had always.

"You must sing to the musical-box!" said the lady, and her wish was fulfilled. If Maren had only commenced, one might have believed it a trial of skill between Boreas and Zephyr.

They now walked about, drank tea, and after this they were to return to the house, there to partake of fish and roast meat, a piece of boxed ham, and other good things.

Otto could by no means be permitted to think of leaving them the following morning; he must remain a few days, and gather strength, so that in Copenhagen he might apply himself well to work. But only one day would he enjoy all the good things which they heaped upon him. He yearned for other people, for a more intellectual circle. Two years before he had agreed splendidly with them all, had found them interesting and intellectual; now he felt that Lemvig was a little town, and that the people were good, excellent people.

The following play again brought capital cookery, good foul, and good wine—that was to honor Mr. Thostrup. His health was drunk, Maren was more confidential, the aunt had forgotten her trouble, and again sat with a laughing face beside the constrained shopman. They must, it is true, make a little haste over their dinner, for the fire-engine was to be tried; and this splendor, they maintained, Otto must see, since he so fortunately chanced to lie there.

"How can my mother think that this will give Mr. Thostrup pleasure?" said Maren. "There is nothing to see in it."

"That has given him pleasure formerly!" answered the mother. "It is, also, laughable when the boys run underneath the engine-rain, and the stream comes just in their necks."

She spoke of the former Otto and of the present one—he was become so Copenhagenish, so refined and nice, as well in the cut of his clothes as in his manners; yet she still found an opportunity of giving him a little hint to further refinement. Only think! he took the sugar for his coffee with his fingers!

"But where are the sugar-tongs, the massive silver sugar-tongs?" asked she. "Maren, dost thou allow him to take the sugar with his fingers?"

"That is more convenient!" answered Otto. "I do that always."

"Yes, but if strangers had been here," said the hostess, in a friendly but teaching tone, "we must, like that grand lady you know of, have thrown the sugar out of the window."

"In the higher circles, where people have clean fingers, they make use of them!" said Otto. "There would be no end of it if one were to take it with the sugar-tongs."

"They are of massive silver!" said the lady, and weighed them in her hand.

Toward evening Rosalie went into the garden under the plum trees.

"These, also, remind me of my mountains," said she; "this is the only fruit which will properly flourish there. Lemvig lies, like La Locle, in a valley," and she pointed, smiling, to the surrounding sand-hills. "How entirely different it is here from what it is at home on thy grandfather's estate! There I have been so accustomed to solitude, that it is almost too lively for me here. One diversion follows another."

It was precisely this which Otto did not like. These amusements of the small towns wearied him, and he could not delight himself with them, no longer mingle in this life.

He wished to set out early the following morning. It would be too exhausting to drive along the dry road in the sun's heat, they all declared; he must wait until the afternoon, then it would be cooler; it was, also, far pleasanter to travel in the night. Rosalie's prayers decided him. Thus, after dinner and coffee, the horses should be put into the carriage.

It was the last day. Maren was somewhat in a grave mood. Otto must write in her album. "He would never come to Lemvig again," said she. As children they had played with each other. Since he went to Copenhagen she had, many an evening, seated herself in the swing near the summer-house and thought of him. Who knows whether she must not have done so when she copied out of the secretary's memorandum-book, the verses,—

"So fliessen nun zwei Wasser

Wohl zwischen mir and Dir?"

The sea certainly flows between Aarhuus and Copenhagen.

"Maren will perhaps go over for the winter," said the mother; "but we dare not speak too much about it, for it is not yet quite settled. It will really make her gayer! lately she has been very much inclined to melancholy, although God knows that we have denied her no pleasure!"

There now arrived a quantity of letters from different acquaintance, and from their acquaintance: if Mr. Thostrup would have the goodness to take care of this to Viborg, these to Aarhuus, and the others as far as Copenhagen. It was a complete freight, such as one gets in little towns, just as though no post went through the country.

The carriage stopped before the door.

Rosalie melted into tears. "Write to me!" said she. "Thee I shall never see again! Greet my Switzerland when thou comest there!"

The others were merry. The lady sang, —

"*O could I, like a cloud, but fly!*"

The young lady from Holstebro bowed herself before him with an Album-leaf its her hand, upon which she must beg Mr. Thostrup to write her something. Maren gave him her hand, blushed and drew back: but as the carriage rolled away she waved her while handkerchief through the open window: "Farewell! Farewell!"

CHAPTER XX

"Stop! cried Patroclus, with mighty, thundering voice."
—*WILSTER'S Iliad.*

The parting with Rosalie, the hospitality of the family, and their sincere sympathy, touched Otto; he thought upon the last days, upon his whole sojourn in his home. The death of his grandfather made this an important era in his life. The quiet evening and the solitary road inclined him still more to meditation.

How cheering and interesting had been a visit to Lemvig in former times! Then it furnished matter for conversation with Rosalie for many weeks; it now lay before him a subject of indifference. The people were certainly the same, therefore the change must have taken place in himself. He thought of Copenhagen, which stood so high, and of the people there.

"After all, the difference is not so great!" said he. "In Copenhagen the social foci are more numerous, the interests more varied; each day brings a fresh topic of conversation, and one can choose one's society. The multitude, on the contrary, has something citizenish; it obtrudes itself even from beneath the ball-dress which shows itself at court; it is seen in the rich saloon of the wholesale merchant, as well as in the house of the brandy distiller, whose possessions give to him and his two brewers the right of election. It is the same food which is presented to us; in the small towns one has it on earthenware, in Copenhagen on china. If one had only the courage, in the so-called higher classes, to break through the gloss which life in a greater circle, which participation in the customs of the world, has called forth, one should soon find in many a lady of rank, in many a nobleman who sits not alone in the theatre, on the first bench, merely that empty common earthenware; and that, as with the merchant's wife in Lemvig, a déjeuner or a soirée, like some public event, will occupy the mind before and after its occurrence. A court-ball, at which either the son or daughter has figured, resembles the most brilliant success in an examination for office. We laugh at the authorities of Lemvig, and yet with us the crowd runs after nothing but authorities and newspapers. This is a certain state of innocence. How many a poor officer or student must play the subordinate part of the shopman at the table of the rich, and gratefully kiss the hand of the lady of the house because she has the right of demanding gratitude? And in the theatre, with the multitude, what does not 'an astonishing chest' do? A strength of voice which can penetrate right through the leather of the mind gains stormy applause, whilst taste and execution can only be appreciated by the few. The actor can be certain of applause if he only thunder forth his parting reply. The comedian is sure of a shout of bravo if he puts forth an insipidity, and rubs his legs together as if replying with spirit and humor. The massive plate in the house gives many a lady the boldness to teach that in which she herself might perhaps have been instructed. Many a lady, like the Mamsell from Holstebro, dresses always in silk and a long shawl, and if one asks after her profession one finds it consists at most in dress-making; perhaps she does not even possess the little accompanying talent of playing the flute. How many people do not copy, like Maren, out of other people's memorandum-books, and do not excel musical-boxes! still one hears a deal of musical snuff-box music, and is waited upon by voices which are equally as insignificant as the secretary's."

These were pretty much Otto's reflections, and certainly it was a good feeling which lay at the bottom of them. Let us remember in our judgment that he was so young, and that he had only known Copenhagen *one* year; otherwise he would most certainly have thought *quite differently.*

Night spread itself over the heath, the heavens were clear. Slowly the carriage wound along through the deep sand. The monotonous sound, the unchanging motion, all rendered Otto sleepy. A falling star shot like a fire column across the sky—this woke him for a moment; he soon again bowed his head and slept, fast and deep. It was an hour past midnight, when he was awoke by a loud cry. He started up—the fire burnt before them; and between it and the horse stood two figures, who had taken hold of the leather reins. Close beside them was a cart, under which was placed a sort of bed, on which slept a woman and some children.

"Will you drive into the soup-kettle?" asked a rough voice, whilst another scolded in a gibberish which was unintelligible to Otto.

It had happened to the coachman as to him, only that the coachman had fallen asleep somewhat later; the horses had lost their track, and uncertain, as they had long been, they were now traversing the impassable heath. A troop of the so-called Scavengers, who wander through these districts a nomadic race, had here taken up their quarters for the night, had made a fire and hung the kettle over it, to cook some pieces of a lamb they had stolen on their journey.

"They were about half a mile from the highway," said an elderly woman who was laying some bushes of heath under the kettle.

"Half a mile?" replied a voice from the other side of the cart, and Otto remarked a man who, wrapped in a large gray riding-cloak, had stretched himself out among the heather. "It is not a quarter of a mile to the highway if people know how to direct their course properly!"

The pronunciation of the man was somewhat foreign, but pure, and free from the gibberish which the others employed in their speech. The voice seemed familiar to Otto, his ear weighed each syllable, and his blood ran quicker through his veins: "It is the German Heinrich, the evil angel of my life!" he felt, and wrapt himself closer in his mantle, so that his countenance was concealed.

A half-grown lad came forward and offered himself as a guide.

"But the lad must have two marks!" said the woman.

Otto nodded assent, and glanced once more toward the man in whom he believed he recognized the German Heinrich; the man had again carelessly stretched himself among the heath, and did not seem inclined to enter into farther discourse.

The woman desired the payment in advance, and received it. The boy led the horses toward one side; at the moment the fire flare up between the turf-sods, a great dog, with a loose cord about his neck, sprang forward and ran barking after the carriage, which now travelled on over the heath in the gloomy night.

CHAPTER XXI

*"Poetry does not always express sorrow; the rainbow can also
arch across a cloudless blue firmament." — JEAN PAUL.*

We again find ourselves in Copenhagen, where we meet with Otto, and
may every day expect Wilhelm, Miss Sophie, and the excellent mamma;
they would only stay a few weeks. To learn tidings of their arrival, Otto
determined to pay a visit where they were expected; we know the house,
we were present at the Christmas festival: it was here that Otto received his
noble pedigree.

We will now become somewhat better acquainted with the family.
The husband had a good head, as people sat, had an excellent wine-cellar,
and was, as one of the friends maintained, a good l'hombre player. But
the soul of the house, the animating genius, which drew into this circle
all that possessed life and youth, was the wife. Beautiful one could by no
means call her, but, enchanted by her natural loveliness, her mind, and
her unaffectedness, you forgot this in a few moments. A rare facility in
appreciating the comic of every-day life, and a good-humored originality
in its representation, always afforded her rich material for conversation. It
was as if Nature, in a moment of thoughtlessness, had formed an insipid
countenance, but immediately afterward strove to make good her fault by
breathing into it a soul, which, even through pale blue eyes, pale cheeks,
and ordinary features, could make her beauty felt.

When Otto entered the room he heard music. He listened: it must be
either Weyse or Gerson.

"It is the Professor Weyse," said the servant, and Otto opened the door
softly, without knocking.

The astral-lamp burnt upon the table; upon the sofa sat two young
ladies. The mistress of the house nodded Otto a friendly welcome, but then
smiling laid her finger on her lips, as a sign of silence, and pointed to a
chair, on which he seated himself, and listened to the soft tones, which, like
spirits, floated from the piano at which the musician sat. It was as if the
slumbering thoughts and feelings of the soul, which in every breast find
a response, even among the most opposite nations, had found a voice and

language. The fantasies died away in a soft, spiritual piano. Thus lightly has Raphael breathed the Madonna di Foligno upon the clouds; she rests there as a soap-bubble rests upon velvet. That dying away of the tomes resembled the thoughts of the lover when his eye closes, and the living dream of his heart imperceptibly merges and vanishes in sleep. Reality is over.

Here also the tones ceased.

> *"Der Bettelvogt von Ninive*
> *Zog hinab zum Genfersee,*
> *Hm, hm!"*
> *[Author's Note: An old popular German song.]*

commenced the musician once more, with an originality and spirit which influenced the whole company. Far too soon did he again break off, after he had enchanted all ears by his own treasures, as well as by the curiosities of the people's life in the world of sound. Only when he was gone did admiration find words; the fantasies still echoed in every heart.

"His name deserves to be known throughout Europe!" said the gracious lady; "how few people in the world know Weyse and Kuhlau!"

"That is the misfortune of a musician being born in a small country," said Otto. "His works become only manuscript for friends; his auditory extends only from Skagen to Kiel: there the door is closed."

"One must console one's self that everything great and good becomes at length known," said the cousin of the family, who is known to us by his verses for the Christmas-tree. "The nations will become acquainted with everything splendid in the kingdom of mind, let it bloom in a small or in a large country. Certainly during this time the artist may have died, but then he must receive compensation in another world."

"I truly believe," returned the gracious lady, "that he would wish a little in advance here below, where it is so ordered that the immortal must bow himself before the mortal."

"Certainly," replied Otto; "the great men of the age are like mountains; they it is which cause the land to be seen from afar, and give it importance, but in themselves they are bare and cold; their heights are never properly known."

"Very beautiful," said the lady; "you speak like a Jean Paul."

At this moment the door opened, and all were surprised by the entrance of Miss Sophie, Wilhelm, and the dear mamma. They were not expected before the following evening. They had travelled the whole day through Zealand.

"We should have been here to dinner," said Sophie, "but my brother could not get his business finished in Roeskelde; then he had forgotten to order horses, and other little misadventures occurred: six whole hours we remained there. Mamma contracted quite a passion there—she fell fairly in love with a young girl, the pretty Eva."

"Yes, she is a nice creature!" said the old lady. "Had I not reason, Mr. Thostrup? You and my Wilhelm had already made her interesting to me. She has something so noble, so refined, which one so rarely meets with in the lower class; she deserves to come among educated people."

"Otto, what shall our hearts say," exclaimed Wilhelm, "when my good mother is thus affected?"

They assembled round the tea-table. Wilhelm addressed Otto with the confidential "thou" which Otto himself had requested.

"We will drink together in tea and renew our brotherhood."

Otto smiled, but with such a strangely melancholy air, and spoke not a word.

"He's thinking about the old grandfather," thought Wilhelm, and laid his hand upon his friend's shoulder. "The Kammerjunker and his ladies greet thee!" said he. "I believe the Mamsell would willingly lay thee in her own work-box, were that to be done."

Otto remained quiet, but in his soul there was a strange commotion. It would be a difficult thing to explain this motive, which belonged to his peculiarity of mind; it entered among the mysteries of the soul. The multitude call it in individuals singularity, the psychologist finds a deeper meaning in it, which the understanding is unable to fathom. We have examples of men, whose strength of mind and body were well known, feeling faint at the scent of a rose; others have been thrown into a convulsive state by touching gray paper. This cannot be explained; it is one of the riddles of Nature. A similar relaxing sensation Otto experienced when he, for the first time, heard himself addressed as "thou" by Wilhelm. It seemed to him as though the spiritual band which encircled them loosened itself, and Wilhelm became a stranger. It was impossible for Otto to return the "thou," yet, at the same time, he felt the injustice of his behavior and the singularity, and wished to struggle against it; he mastered himself, attained a kind of eloquence, but no "thou" would pass his lips.

"To thy health, Otto," said Wilhelm, and pushed his cup against Otto's.

"Health!" said Otto, with a smile.

"It is true," began the cousin, "I promised you the other day to bring my advertisements with me; the first volume is closed." And he drew from his pocket a book in which a collection of the most original Address-Gazette advertisements, such as one sees daily, was pasted.

"I have one for you," said the lady; "I found it a little time since. 'A woman wishes for a little child to bottle.' Is not that capital?"

"Here is also a good one," said Wilhelm, who had turned over the leaves of the book: "'A boy of the Mosaic belief may be apprenticed to a cabinet-maker, but he need not apply unless he will eat everything that happens to be in the house.' That is truly a hard condition for the poor lad."

"Almost every day," said the cousin, "one may read, 'For the play of to-day or to-morrow is a good place to be had in the third story in the Christenbernikov Street.' The place is a considerable distance from the theatre."

"Theatre!" exclaimed the master of the house, who now entered to take his place at the tea-table, "one can soon hear who has that word in his mouth; now is he again at the theatre! The man can speak of nothing else. There ought, ready, to be a fine imposed, which he should pay each time he pronounces the word theatre. I would only make it a fine of two skillings, and yet I dare promise that before a month was over he would be found to pay in fines his whole pocket-money, and his coat and boots besides. It is a real mania with the man! I know no one among my young friends," added he, with an ironical smile at Wilhelm, — "no, not one, who has such a hobby-horse as our good cousin."

"Here thou art unjust to him!" interrupted his wife; "do not place a fine upon him, else I will place thee in a vaudeville! Thy life is in politics; our cousin's in theatrical life; Wilhelm's in thorough-bass; and Mr. Thostrup's in learned subjects. Each of you is thus a little nail in the different world-wheels; whoever despises others shows that he considers his wheel the first, or imagines that the world is a wheelbarrow, which goes upon one wheel! No, it is a more complicated machine."

Later in the evening, when the company broke up, Otto and Wilhelm went together.

"I do not think," said Wilhelm, "that thou hast yet said thou to me. Is it not agreeable to thee?"

"It was my own wish, my own request," replied Otto. "I have not remarked what expressions I have employed." He remained silent. Wilhelm himself seemed occupied with unusual thoughts, when he suddenly exclaimed: "Life is, after all, a gift of blessings! One should never make one's self sorrows which do not really exist! 'Carpe diem,' said old Horace."

"That will we!" replied Otto; "but now we must first think of our examination."

They pressed each other's hands and parted.

"But I have heard no thou!" said Wilhelm to himself "He is an oddity, and yet I love him! In this consists, perhaps, my own originality."

He entered his room, where the hostess had been cleaning, and had arranged the books and papers in the nicest order. Wilhelm truly called it disorder; the papers in confusion and the books in a row. The lamp even had a new place; and this was called order!

Smiling, he seated himself at the piano; it was so long since they had said "Good day" to each other! He ran over the keys several times, then lost himself in fantasies. "That is lovely!" he exclaimed. "But it is not my property! What does it belong to? It melts into my own feelings!" He played it again. It was a thema out of "Tancredi," therefore from Rossini, even the very composer whom our musical friends most looked down upon; how could he then guess who had created those tones which now spoke to his heart? His whole being he felt penetrated by a happiness, a love of life, the cause of which he knew not. He thought of Otto with a warmth which the latter's strange behavior did not deserve. All beloved beings floated so sweetly before his mind. This was one of those moments which all good people know; one feels one's self a member of the great chain of love which binds creation together.

So long as the rose-bud remains folded together it seems to be without fragrance; yet only one morning is required, and the fine breath streams from the crimson mouth. It is only one moment; it is the commencement of a new existence, which already has lain long concealed in the bud: but one does not see the magic wand which works the change. This spiritual contrast, perhaps, took place in the past hour; perhaps the last evening rays which fell upon the leaves concealed this power! The roses of the garden must open; those of the heart follow the same laws. Was this love? Love is, as poets say, a pain; it resembles the disease of the mussel, through which pearls are formed. But Wilhelm was not sick; he felt himself particularly full of strength and enjoyment of life. The poet's simile of the mussel and the pearl sounds well, but it is false. Most poets are not very learned in natural history; and, therefore, they are guilty of many errors with regard to it. The pearl is formed on the mussel not through disease; when an enemy attacks her she sends forth drops in her defense, and these change into pearls. It is thus strength, and not weakness, which creates the beautiful. It would be unjust to call love a pain, a sickness; it is an energy of life which God has planted in the human breast; it fills our whole being like the fragrance which fills each leaf of the rose, and then reveals itself among the struggles of life as a pearl of worth.

These were Wilhelm's thoughts; and yet it was not perfectly clear to him that he loved with his whole soul, as one can only love once.

The following forenoon he paid a visit to Professor Weyse.

"You are going to Roeskelde, are you not?" asked Wilhelm. "I have heard you so often play the organ here in Our Lady's church, I should very much like to hear you there, in the cathedral. If I were to make the journey, would you then play a voluntary for me?"

"You will not come!" said the musician.

"I shall come!" answered Wilhelm, and kept his word. Two days after this conversation he rolled through the streets of Roeskelde.

"I am come for a wager! I shall hear Weyse play the organ!" said he to the host, although there was no need for an apology.

Bulwer in his romance, "The Pilgrims of the Rhine," has with endless grace and tenderness called forth a fairy world. The little spirits float there as the breath of air floats around the material reality; one is forced to believe in their existence. With a genius powerful as that which inspired Bulwer, glorious as that which infused into Shakespeare the fragrance we find breathed over the "Midsummer-night's Dream," did Weyse's tones fill Wilhelm; the deep melodies of the organ in the old cathedral had indeed attracted him to the quiet little town! The powerful tones of the heart summoned him! Through them even every day things assumed a coloring, an expression of beauty, such as Byron shows us in words, Thorwaldsen in the hard stone, Correggio in colors.

We have by Goethe a glorious poem, "Love a Landscape-painter." The poet sits upon a peak and gazes before him into the mist, which, like canvas spread upon the easel, conceals all heights and expanses; then comes the God of Love and teaches him how to paint a picture on the mist. The little one now sketches with his rosy fingers a picture such as only Nature and Goethe give us. Were the poet here, we could offer him no rock on which he might seat himself, but something, through legends and songs, equally beautiful. He would then sing,—I seated myself upon the mossy stone above the cairn; the mist resembled outstretched canvas. The God of Love commenced on this his sketch. High up he painted a glorious still, whose rays were dazzling! The edges of the clouds he made as of gold, and let the rays penetrate through them; then painted he the fine light boughs of fresh, fragrant trees; brought forth one hill after the other. Behind these, half-concealed, lay a little town, above which rose a mighty church; two tall towers with high spires rose into the air; and below the church, far out, where woods formed the horizon, drew he a bay so naturally! it seemed to play with the sunbeams as if the waves splashed up against the coast. Now appeared flowers; to the fields and meadows he gave the coloring of velvet and precious stones; and on the other side of the bay the dark woods melted away into a bluish mist. "I can paint!" said the little one; "but the most difficult still remains to do." And he drew with his delicate finger, just where the rays of the sun fell most glowingly, a maiden so gentle, so sweet, with dark blue eyes and cheeks as blooming as the rosy fingers which formed the picture. And see! a breeze arose; the leaves of the trees quivered; the expanse of water ruffled itself; the dress of the maiden was gently stirred; the maiden herself approached: the picture itself was a reality! And thus did the old royal city present itself before Wilhelm's eyes, the towers of the cathedral, she tay, the far woods, and—Eva!

The first love of a pure heart is holy! This holiness may be indicated, but not described! We return to Otto.

CHAPTER XXII

"A man only gains importance by a poet's fancy, when his
genius vividly represents to our imagination a clearer, but
not an ennobled image of men and objects which have an
existence; then alone he understands how to idealize." —H.
HERTZ.

We pass on several weeks. It was toward the end of September, the examen philosophicum was near. Preparations for this had been Otto's excuse for not yet having visited the family circle of his guardian, the merchant Berger. This was, however, brought about by Otto's finding one day, when he went to speak with his guardian, the mistress of the house in the same room. We know that there are five daughters in the house, and that only one is engaged, yet they are all well-educated girls—domestic girls, as their mother assured her friend upon more than one occasion.

"So, then, I have at length the honor of making your acquaintance," said Mrs. Berger, "this visit, truly, is not intended either for me or the children, but still you must now drink a cup of coffee with us. Within it certainly looks rather disorderly; the girls are making cloaks for the winter. We will not put ourselves out of the way for you: you shall be regarded as a member of the family: but then you must come to us in a friendly way. Every Thursday our son-in-law dines with us, will you then be contented with our dinner? Now you shall become acquainted with my daughters."

"And I must to my office," said the husband; "therefore let us consider Thursday as an appointment. We dine at three o'clock, and after coffee Laide gives us music."

The lady now conducted Otto into the sitting-room, where he found the four daughters in full activity with a workwoman. The fifth daughter, Julle, was, as they had told him, gone to the shops for patterns: yesterday she had run all over the town, but the patterns she received were not good.

The lady told him the name of each daughter; their characteristics he naturally learnt later.

All the five sisters had the idea that they were so extremely different, and yet they resembled each other to a hair. Adelaide, or Laide, as she was also called, was certainly the prettiest; that she well knew also, therefore she would have a fur cape, and no cloak; her figure should be seen. Christiane was what one might call a practical girl; she knew how to make use of everything. Alvilde had always a little attack of the tooth-ache; Julle went shopping, and Miss Grethe was the bride. She was also musical, and was considered witty. Thus she said one evening when the house-door was closed, and groaned dreadfully on its hinges, "See now, we have port wine after dinner." [Translator's Note: A pun which it is impossible to translate. The Danish word Portviin according to sound, may mean either port wine or the creaking of a door.] The brother, the only son of the house, with whom we shall become better acquainted, had written down this conceit; "but that was only to be rude toward her," said Miss Grethe. "Such good ideas as this I have every hour of the day!"

We ought really to accuse these excellent girls of nothing foolish; they were very good and wise. The lover, Mr. Svane, was also a zealous wit; he was so lively, they said. Every one with whom he became a little familiar he called immediately Mr. Petersen, and that was so droll!

"Now the father has invited Mr. Thostrup to come on Thursday!" said the lady. "I also think, if we were to squeeze ourselves a little together, he might find a place with us in the box; the room is, truly, very confined."

Otto besought them not to incommode themselves.

"O, it is a large box!" said the lady, but she did not say how many of them were already in it. Only eleven ladies went from the family itself. They were obliged to go to the theatre in three parties, so that people might not think; if they all went together, there was a mob. One evening, when the box had been occupied by eighteen persons, beside several twelve-year old children, who had sat in people's laps, or stood before them, and the whole party had returned home in one procession, and were standing before the house door to go in, people streamed together, imagining there was some alarm, or that some one had fallen into convulsions. "What is the matter?" they asked, and Miss Grethe immediately replied, "It is a select company!" [Translator's Note: A select or shut-out company. We regret that this pun, like the foregoing one, is untransferable into English.] Since that evening they returned home in separate divisions.

"It is really a good box!" said Alvilde; "if we had only other neighbors! The doors are opening and shutting eternally, and make a draught which is not bearable for the teeth. And then they speak so loud! the other night I did not hear a single word of the pretty song about Denmark."

"But did you lose much through that?" asked Otto, smiling, and soon they found themselves very much at variance, just as if they had been old acquaintances. "I do not think much of these patriotic scraps, where the poet, in his weakness, supports himself by this beautiful sentiment of patriotism in the people. You will certainly grant that here the multitude always applauds when it only hears the word 'Father-land,' or the name of 'Christian IV.' The poet must give something more; this is a left-handed kind of patriotism. One would really believe that Denmark were the only country in the world!"

"Fie, Mr. Thostrup!" said the lady: "do you not then love your father-land?"

"I believe I love it properly!" returned he: "and because it really possesses so much that is excellent do I desire that only what is genuine should be esteemed, only what is genuine be prized."

"I agree in the main with Mr. Thostrup," said Miss Grethe, who was busied in unpicking and turning her cloak, in order, as she herself said, to spoil it on the other side. "I think he is right! If a poem is well spoken on the stage, it has always a kind of effect. It is just the same as with stuffs—they may be of a middling quality and may have an unfavorable pattern, but if they are worn by a pretty figure they look well after all!"

"I am often vexed with the public!" said Otto. "It applauds at improper places, and sometimes exhibits an extraordinary innocence."

"Those are 'the lords of the kingdom of mind,'" said Miss Grethe, smiling.

> [Note: "We are the lords of the kingdom of mind!
> We are the stem which can never decay!"
> —Students' Song, by CHRISTIAN WINTHER.]

"No, the *neighbors*!" replied Otto quickly.

At this moment Miss Julle entered. She had been wandering from shop to shop, she said, until she could bear it no longer! She had had the stuffs down from all the shelves, and at length had succeeded so far as to become possessed of eight small pieces—beautiful patterns, she maintained. And now she knew very well where the different stuffs were to be had, how wide they were, and how much the yard. "And whom did I meet?" said she; "only think! down the middle of East Street came the actor—you know well! Our little passion! He is really charming off the stage."

"Did you meet him?" said Laide. "That girl is always lucky!"

"Mr. Thostrup," said the mother, presenting him, for the young lady seemed to forget him entirely, so much was she occupied with this encounter and her patterns.

Julle bowed, and said she had seen him before: he had heard Mynster, and had stood near the chair where she sat; he was dressed in an olive-green coat.

"Then you are acquainted with each other!" said the lady. "She is the most pious of all the children. When the others rave about Spindler and Johanne Schoppenhauer, she raves about the clergyman who confirmed her. You know my son? He became a student a year before you. He sees you in the club sometimes."

"There you will have seen him more amiable than you will find him at home," said Adelaide. "Heaven knows he is not gallant toward his sisters!"

"Sweet Laide, how can you say so!" cried the mother. "You are always so unjust toward Hans Peter! When you become better acquainted with him, Mr. Thostrup, you will like him; he is a really serious young man, of uncorrupted manners. Do you remember, Laide, how he hissed that evening in the theatre when they gave that immoral piece? And how angry he is with that 'Red Riding Hood?' O, the good youth! Besides, in our family, you will soon meet with an old acquaintance—in a fortnight a lady out of Jutland will come here. She remains the winter here. Do you not guess who it is? A little lady from Lemvig!"

"Maren!" exclaimed Otto.

"Yes, truly!" said the lady. "She is said to have such a beautiful voice!"

"Yes, in Lemvig," remarked Adelaide. "And what a horrible name she has! We must christen her again, when she comes. She must be called Mara, or Massa."

"We could call her Massa Carara!" said Grethe.

"No; she shall be called Maja, as in the 'Every-day Tales,'" said Christiane.

"I am of Jane's opinion!" said the mother. "We will christen her again, and call her Maja."

CHAPTER XXIII

Men are not always what they seem. —*LESSING.*

Our tale is no creation of fancy; it is the reality in which we live; bone of our bone, and flesh of our flesh. Our own time and the men of our own age we shall see. But not alone will we occupy ourselves with every-day life, with the moss on the surface; the whole tree, from the roots to the fragrant leaves, will we observe. The heavy earth shall press the roots, the moss and bark of every-day life adhere to the stern, the strong boughs with flowers and leaves spread themselves out, whilst the sun of poetry shall shine among them, and show the colors, odor, and singing-birds. But the tree of reality cannot shoot up so soon as that of fancy, like the enchantment in Tieck's "Elves." We must seek our type in nature. Often may there be an appearance of cessation; but that is not the case. It is even so with our story; whilst our characters, by mutual discourse, make themselves worthy of contemplation, there arises, as with the individual branches of the tree, an unseen connection. The branch which shoots high up in the air, as though it would separate itself from the mother-stem, only presses forward to form the crown, to lend uniformity to the whole tree. The lines which diverge from the general centre are precisely those which produce the harmony.

We shall, therefore, soon see, though these scenes out of every-day life are no digression from the principal events, nothing episodical which one may pass over. In order still sooner to arrive at a clear perception of this assertion, we will yet tarry a few moments in the house of Mr. Berger, the merchant; but in the mean time we have advanced three weeks. Wilhelm and Otto had happily passed their examen philosophicum. The latter had paid several visits, and was already regarded as an old friend of the family. The lover already addressed him with his droll "Good day, Mr. Petersen;" and Grethe was witty about his melancholy glance, which he was not always able to conquer. She called it "making faces," and besought him to appear so on the day of her funeral.

The object of the five sisters' first Platonic love had been their brother. They had overwhelmed him with caresses and tenderness, had admired and worshipped him. "The dear little man!" they called him; they had no other. But Hans Peter was so impolite and teasing toward the dear sisters, that they were found to resign him so soon as one of them had a lover. Upon this lover they all clung. Each one seemed to have a piece of him. He was Grethe's bridegroom, would be their brother-in-law. They might address him with the confidential thou, and even give him a little kiss.

Otto's appearance in the family caused these rays to change their direction. Otto was handsome, and possessed of fortune; either of which often suffices to bow a female heart. Beauty bribes the thoughtless; riches, the prudent.

Maren, or as she was here called, Maja, had arrived. The young ladies had already pulled off some of her bows, arranged her hair differently, and made one of her silk handkerchiefs into an apron; but, spite of all this finesse, she still remained the lady from Lemvig. They could remove no bows from her pronunciation. She had been the first at home; here she could not take that rank. This evening she was to see in the theatre, for the first time, the ballet of the "Somnambule."

"It is French!" said Hans Peter; "and frivolous, like everything that we have from them."

"Yes, the scene in the second act, where she steps out of the window," said the merchant; "that is very instructive for youth!"

"But the last act is sweet!" cried the lady. "The second act is certainly, as Hans Peter very justly observed, somewhat French. Good heavens! he gets quite red, the sweet lad!" She extended her hand to him, and nodded, smiling, whereupon Hans Peter spoke very prettily about the immorality on the stage. The father also made some striking observation.

"Yes," said the lady, "were all husbands like thee, and all young men like Hans Peter, they would speak in another tone on the stage, and dress in another manner. In dancing it is abominable; the dresses are so short and indecent, just as though they had nothing on! Yet, after all, we must say that the 'Somnambule' is beautiful. And, really, it is quite innocent!"

They now entered still deeper into the moral: the conversation lasted till coffee came.

Maren's heart beat even quicker, partly in expectation of the play, through hearing of the corruptions of this Copenhagen Sodom. She heard Otto defend this French piece; heard him speak of affectation. Was he then corrupted? How gladly would she have heard him discourse upon propriety, as Hans Peter had done. "Poor Otto!" thought she; "this is having no relations, but being forced to struggle on in the world alone."

The merchant now rose. He could not go to the theatre. First, he had business to attend to; and then he must go to his club, where he had yesterday changed his hat.

"Nay, then, it has happened to thee as to Hans Peter!" said the lady. "Yesterday, in the lecture-room, he also got a strange hat. But, there, thou hast his hat!" she suddenly exclaimed, as her eye fell upon the hat which her husband held in his hand. "That is Hans Peter's hat! Now, we shall certainly find that he has thine! You have exchanged them here at home. You do not know each other's hats, and therefore you fancy this occurred from home."

One of the sisters now brought the hat which Hans Peter had got in mistake. Yes, it was certainly the father's. Thus an exchange in the house, a little intermezzo, which naturally, from its insignificance, was momentarily forgotten by all except the parties concerned, for to them it was an important moment in their lives; and to us also, as we shall see, an event of importance, which has occasioned us to linger thus long in this circle. In an adjoining room will we, unseen spirits, watch the father and son. They are alone; the family is already in the theatre. We may, indeed, watch them—they are true moralists. It is only a moral drawn from a hat.

But the father's eyes rolled, his cheeks glowed, his words were sword-strokes, and must make an impression on any disposition as gentle as his son's; but the son stood quiet, with a firm look and with a smile on his lips, such as the moral bestows. "You were in the adjoining room!" said he. "Where it is proper for you to be there may I also come."

"Boy!" cried the father, and named the place, but we know it not; neither know we its inhabitants. Victor Hugo includes them in his "Children's Prayer," in his beautiful poem, "La Prière pour Tous." The child prays for all, even "for those who sell the sweet name of love."

[Note: "Prie!... Pour les femmes échevelées Qui vendent
le doux nom d'amour!"]

"Let us be silent with each other!" said the son. "I am acquainted with many histories. I know another of the pretty Eva!" —

"Eva!" repeated the father.

We will hear no more! It is not proper to listen. We see the father and son extend their hands. It appeared a scene of reconciliation. They parted: the father goes to his business, and Hans Peter to the theatre, to anger himself over the immorality in the second act of the "Somnambule."

CHAPTER XXIV

"L'amour est pour les coeurs,
Ce que l'aurore est pour les fleurs,
Et le printemps pour la nature." —VIGUE.

"Love is a childish disease and like the small-pox. Some
die, some become deformed, others are more or less scarred,
while upon others the disease does not leave any visible
trace." —The Alchemist, by C. HAUCH.

"Be candid, Otto!" said Wilhelm, as he one day visited his friend. "You cannot make up your mind to say thou to me; therefore let it be. We are, after all, good friends. It is only a form; although you must grant that in this respect you are really a great fool."

Otto now explained what an extraordinary aversion he had felt, what a painful feeling had seized upon him, and made it impossible to him.

"There you were playing the martyr!" said Wilhelm, laughing. "Could you not immediately tell me how you were constituted? So are most men. When they have no trouble, they generally hatch one themselves; they will rather stand in the cold shadow than in the warm sunshine, and yet the choice stands open to us. Dear friend, reflect; now we are both of us on the stream: we shall soon be put into the great business-bottles, where we shall, like little devils, stretch and strain ourselves without ever getting out, until life withdraws from us!" He laid his arm confidentially upon Otto's shoulder. "Often have I wished to speak with you upon one point! Yes, I do not desire that you should confess every word, every thought to me. I already know that I shall be able to prove to you that the thing lies in a region where it cannot have the power which you ascribe to it. In the cold zones a venomous bite does not operate as dangerously as in warmer ones; a sorrow in childhood cannot overpower us as it does in riper age. Whatever misfortune may have happened to you when a child, if in your wildness— you yourself say that you were wild—whatsoever you may have then done, it cannot, it ought not to influence your whole life: your understanding could tell you this better than I. At our age we find ourselves in the land of joy, or we never enter it!"

"You are a happy man!" exclaimed Otto, and gazed sorrowfully before him. "Your childhood afforded you only joy and hope! Only think of the solitude in which mine was passed. Among the sand-hills of the west coast my days glided away: my grandfather was gloomy and passionate; our old preacher lived only in a past time which I knew not, and Rosalie regarded the world through the spectacles of sorrow. Such an environment might well cast a shadow upon my life-joy. Even in dress, one is strangely remarkable when one comes from afar province to the capital; first this receives another cut, and one gradually becomes like those around one. The same thing happens in a spiritual relation, but one's being and ideas one does not change so quickly as one's clothes. I have only been a short time among strangers, and who knows?" added he, with a melancholy smile, "perhaps I shall come into equilibrium when some really great misfortune happens to me and very much overpowers me, and then I may show the same carelessness, the same phlegm as the multitude."

"A really great misfortune!" repeated Wilhelm. "You do, indeed, say something. That would be a very original means of cure, but you are an original being. Perhaps lay this means you might really be healed. 'Make no cable out of cobweb!' said a celebrated poet whose name does not occur to me at this moment. But the thought is good, you should have it embroidered upon your waistcoat, so that you might have it before your eyes when you droop your head. Do not look so grave; we are friends, are we not? Among all my young acquaintance you are the dearest to me, although there are moments when I know not how it stands with us. I could confide every secret to you, but I am not sure that you would be equally open with me. Do not be angry, my dear friend! There are secrets of so delicate a nature, that one may not confide them even to the dearest friend. So long as we preserve *our* secret it is our prisoner; it is quite the contrary, however, so soon as we have let it escape us. And yet, Otto, you are so dear to me, that I believe in you as in my own heart. This, even now, bears a secret which penetrates me with joy and love of life! I must speak cut. But you must enter into my joy, partake in it, or say nothing about it; you have then heard nothing—nothing! Otto, I love! therefore am I happy, therefore is there sunshine in my heart, life joy in my veins! I love Eva, the beautiful lovely Eva!"

Otto pressed his hand, but preserved silence.

"No, not so!" cried Wilhelm. "Only speak a word! Do you I'm in a conception of the world which has opened before me?"

"Eva is beautiful! very beautiful!" said Otto, slowly. "She is innocent and good. What can one wish for more? I can imagine how she fills your whole heart! But will she do so always? She will not always remain young, always lovely! Has she, then, mind sufficient to be everything to you? Will this momentary happiness which you prepare for her and yourself be great enough to outweigh—I will not say the sorrow, but the discontent which this union will bring forth in your family? For God's sake, think of everything!"

"My dear fellow!" said Wilhelm, "your old preacher now really speaks out of you! But enough: I can bear the confession. I answer, 'Yes, yes!' with all my heart, 'yes!' Wherefore will you now bring me out of my sunshine into shade? Wherefore, in my joy over the beauty of the rose should I be reminded that the perfume and color will vanish, that the leaves will fall? It is the course of life! but must one, therefore, think of the grave, of the finale, when the act begins?"

"Love is a kind of monomania," said Otto; "it may be combated: it depends merely upon our own will."

"Ah, you know this not at all!" said Wilhelm. "But it will come in due time, and then you will be far more violent than others! Who knows? perhaps this is the sorrow of which you spoke, the misfortune which should bring your whole being into equipoise! That was also a kind of search after the sorrowful. I will sincerely wish that your heart may be filled with love as mine is; then will the influence of the sand-hills vanish, and you will speak with me as you ought to do, and as my confidence deserves!"

"That will I!" replied Otto. "You make the poor girl miserable! Now you love Eva, but then you will no longer be able. The distance between you and her is too great, and I cannot conceive how the beauty of her countenance can thus fill your whole being. A waiting-girl! yes, I repeat the name which offends your ear: a waiting-girl! Everywhere will it be repeated. And you? No one can respect nobility less than I do—that nobility which is only conferred by birth; it is nothing, and a time will come when this will not be prized at all, when the nobility of the soul will be the only nobility. I openly say this to you, who are a nobleman yourself. The more development of mind, the more ancestors! But Eva has nothing, can have nothing, except a pretty face, and this is what has enchained you; you are become the servant of a servant, and that is degrading yourself and your nobility of mind!"

"Mr. Thostrup!" exclaimed Wilhelm, "you wound me! This is truly not the first time, but now I am weary of it. I have shown too much good nature, and that is the most unfortunate failing a man can be cursed with!"

He seated himself at the piano, and hammered away.

Otto was silent a moment, his checks glowed, but he was soon again calm, and in a joking tone said: "Do not expend your anger upon that poor instrument because we disagree in our views. You are playing only dissonances, which offend my ear more than your anger!"

"Dissonances!" repeated Wilhelm. "Cannot you hear that they are harmonies? There are many things for which you have a bad ear!"

Otto knew how to lead his anger to different points regarding which they had formerly been at variance, but he spoke with such mildness that Wilhelm's anger rather abated than increased.

They were again friends, but regarding Eva not one word more was said.

"I should not be an honest and true friend to him, were I to let him be swallowed up by this whirlpool!" said Otto to himself, when he was alone. "At present he is innocent and good but at his age, with his gay disposition!—I must warn Eva! soon! soon! The snow which has once been trodden is no longer pure! Wilhelm will scarcely forgive me! But I must!"

On the morrow it was impossible for him to travel to Roeskelde, but the following day he really would and must hasten thither.

Still, in the early morning hour, Eva occupied his thoughts; she busied Wilhelm's also, but in a different way: but they agreed in the purity of their intentions. There was still a third, whose blood was put in motion at the mention of her name, who said: "The pretty Eva is a servant there! One must speak with her. The family can make an excursion there!"

"You sweet children!" said the merchant's wife, "the autumn is charming, far pleasanter than the whole summer! The father, should the weather remain good, will make an excursion with us to Lethraborg the day after to-morrow. We will then walk in the beautiful valley of the Hertha, and pass the night at Roeskelde. Those will be two delightful days! What an excellent father you have! But shall we not invite Mr. Thostrup to go with us? We are so many ladies, and it looks well to have a few young gentlemen with us. Grethe, thou must write an invitation; thou canst write thy father's name underneath."

CHAPTER XXV

"These poetical letters are so similar to those of Baggesen, that we could be almost tempted to consider the news of his death as false, although so well affirmed that we must acknowledge it." —Monthly Journal of Literature.

"She is as slender as the poplar-willow, as fleet as the hastening waters. A Mayflower odorous and sweet." —H. P. HOLST.

"Ah, where is the rose?" —Lulu, by GUNTELBURG.

The evening before Otto was to travel with the merchant's family to Roeskelde he called upon the family where Miss Sophie was staying. Her dear mamma had left three days before. Wilhelm had wished to accompany him to Roeskelde, but the mother did not desire it.

"We have had a pleasure to-day," said Sophie, "a pleasure from which we shall long have enjoyment. Have you seen the new book, the 'Letters of a Wandering Ghost?' It is Baggesen himself in his most perfect beauty, a music which I never believed could have been given in words. This is a poet! He has made July days in the poetry of Denmark. Natural thoughts are so strikingly, and yet so simply expressed; one has the idea that one could write such verses one's self, they fall so lightly."

"They are like prose," said the lady, "and yet the most beautifully perfect verse I know. You must read the book, Mr. Thostrup!"

"Perhaps you will read to us this evening?" said Sophie. "I should very much like to hear it again."

"In a second reading one shall enter better into the individual beauties," said the lady of the house.

"I will remain and listen," said the host.

"This must be a masterpiece!" exclaimed Otto," —a true masterpiece, since all are so delighted with it."

"It is Baggesen himself; and truly as he must sing in that world where everything mortal is ennobled."

"'Meadows all fragrance, the strongholds of pleasure,

Heaven blue streamlets,

That speed through the green woods in musical measure,'" began Otto, and the spiritual battle-piece with beauty and tone developed itself more and more; they found themselves in the midst of the winter camp of the Muses, where the poet with

...*"lyre on his shoulder and sword at....*

Hastened to fight with the foes of the Muses." Otto's gloomy look won during the perusal a more animated expression. "Excellent!" exclaimed he; "this is what I myself have thought and felt, but, alas! have been unable to express."

"I am a strange girl," said Sophie; "whenever I read a new poet of distinguished talent, I consider that he is the greatest. It was so with Byron and Victor Hugo. 'Cain' overwhelmed me, 'Notre Dame' carried me away with it. Once I could imagine no greater poet than Walter Scott, and yet I forget him over Oehlenschläger; yes, I remember a time when Heiberg's vaudevilles took almost the first place among my chosen favorites. Thus I know myself and my changeable disposition, and yet I firmly believe that I shall make an exception with this work. Other poets showed me the objects of the outer world, this one shows me my own mind: my own thoughts, my own being he presents before me, and therefore I shall always take the same interest in the Ghost's Letters."

"They are true food for the mind," said Otto; "they are as words in season; there must be movement in the lake, otherwise it will become a bog."

"The author is severe toward those whom he has introduced," said the lady; "but he carries, so to say, a sweet knife. A wound from a sharp sword-blade is not so painful as that from a rusty, notched knife."

"But who may the author be?" said Sophie.

"May we never learn!" replied Otto. "Uncertainty gives the book something piquant. In such a small country as ours it is good for the author to be unknown. Here we almost tread upon each other, and look into each other's garments. Here the personal conditions of the author have much to do with success; and then there are the newspapers, where either friend or enemy has an assistant, whereas the being anonymous gives it the patent of nobility. It is well never to know an author. What does his person matter to us, if his book is only good?

"'Crush and confound the rabble dissolute That desecrate thy poet's grave?'" read Otto, and the musical poem was at an end. All were enchanted with it. Otto alone made some small objections: "The Muses ought not to come with 'trumpets and drums,' and so many expressions similar to 'give a blow on the chaps,' etc., ought not to appear."

"But if the poet will attack what is coarse," said Sophie, "he must call things by their proper names. He presents us with a specimen of the prosaic filth, but in a soap-bubble. We may see it, but not seize upon it. I consider that you are wrong!"

"The conception of idea and form," said Otto, "does not seem to be sufficiently presented to one; both dissolve into one. Even prose is a form."

"But the form itself is the most important," said the lady of the house; "with poetry as with sculpture, it is the form which gives the meaning."

"No, pardon me!" said Otto; "poetry is like the tree which God allows to grow. The inward power expresses itself in the form; both are equally important, but I consider the internal as the most holy. This is here the poet's thought. The opinion which he expresses affects us as much as the beautiful dress in which he has presented it."

Now commenced a contest upon form and material, such as was afterward maintained throughout the whole of Copenhagen.

"I shall always admire the 'Letters of a Wandering Ghost,'" said Sophie,—"always rave about these poems. To-night I shall dream of nothing but this work of art."

How little men can do that which they desire, did this very moment teach.

When we regard the fixed star through a telescope and lose ourselves in contemplation, a little hair can conceal the mighty body, a grain of dust lead us from these sublime thoughts. A letter came for Miss Sophie; a traveller brought it from her mother: she was already in Funen, and announced her safe arrival.

"And the news?" said the hostess.

"Mamma has hired a new maid, or, rather, she has taken to be with her an amiable young girl—the pretty Eva in Roeskelde. Mr. Thostrup and Wilhelm related to us this summer several things about her which make her interesting. We saw her on our journey hither, when mamma was prepossessed by her well-bred appearance. Upon her return, the young girl has quite won her heart. It really were a pity if such a pretty, respectable girl remained in a public-house. She is very pretty; is she not, Mr. Thostrup?"

"Very pretty!" answered Otto, becoming crimson, for Sophie said this with an emphasis which was not without meaning.

The following day, at an early hour, Otto found himself at the merchant's.

Spite of the changeable weather of our climate, all the ladies were in their best dresses. Three persons must sit upon each seat. Hans Peter and the lover had their place beside the coachman. It was a long time before the cold meat, the provision for several days, was packed up, and the whole company were seated. At length, when they had got out of the city, Christiane recollected that they had forgotten the umbrellas, and that, after all, it would be good to have them. The coachman must go back for them, and meantime the carriage drew up before the Column of Liberty. The poor sentinel must now become an object of Miss Grethe's interest. Several times the soldier glanced down upon his regimentals. He was a Krähwinkler, who had an eye to his own advantage. A man who rode past upon a load of straw occupied a high position. That was very interesting.

Otto endeavored to give the conversation another direction. "Have not you seen the new poem which has just appeared, the 'Letters of a Wandering Ghost?'" asked he, and sketched out their beauty and tendency.

"Doubtless, very heavy blows are dealt!" said Mr. Berger, "the man must be witty—Baggesen to the very letter."

"The 'Copenhagen Post' is called the pump!" said Hans Peter.

"That is superb!" cried Grethe. "Who does it attack besides?"

"Folks in Soroe, and this 'Holy Andersen,' as they call him."

"Does he get something?" said Laide. "That I will grant him for his milk and water. He was so impolite toward the ladies!"

"I like them to quarrel in this way!" said the merchant's lady. "Heiberg will doubtless get his share also, and then he will reply in something merry."

"Yes," said Mr. Berger, "he always knows how to twist things in such a manner that one must laugh, and then it is all one to us whether he is right or not."

"This book is entirely for Heiberg," said Otto. "The author is anonymous, and a clever man."

"Good Heavens! you are not the author, Mr. Thostrup?" cried Julle, and looked at him with a penetrating gaze. "You can manage such things so secretly! You think so highly of Heiberg: I remember well all the beautiful things you said of his 'Walter the Potter' and his 'Psyche.'"

Otto assured her that he could not confess to this honor.

They reached Roeskelde in the forenoon, but Eva did not receive them. The excursion to Lethraborg was arranged; toward evening they should again return to the inn, and then Eva would certainly appear.

The company walked in the garden at Lethraborg: the prospect from the terrace was beautiful; they looked through the windows of the castle, and at length came to the conclusion that it would be best to go in.

"There are such beautiful paintings, people say!" remarked the lover.

"We must see them," cried all the ladies.

"Do you often visit the picture-gallery of the Christiansborg?" inquired Otto.

"I cannot say that we do!" returned Mrs. Berger. "You well know that what is near one seldom sees, unless one makes a downright earnest attempt, and that we have not yet done. Besides, not many people go up: that wandering about the great halls is so wearying."

"There are splendid pieces by Ruysdal!" said Otto.

"Salvator Rosa's glorious 'Jonas' is well worth looking at!"

"Yes, we really must go at once, whilst our little Maja is here. It does not cost more than the Exhibition, and we were there three times last year. The view from the castle windows toward the canal, as well as toward the ramparts, is so beautiful, they say."

The company now viewed the interior of Lethraborg, and then wandered through the garden and in the wood. The trees had their autumnal coloring, but the whole presented a variety of tints far richer than one finds in summer. The dark fir-trees, the yellow beeches and oaks, whose outermost branches had sent forth light green shoots, presented a most picturesque effect, and formed a splendid foreground to the view over old Leire, the royal city, now a small village, and across the bay to the splendid cathedral.

"That resembles a scene in a theatre!" cried Mrs. Berger, and immediately the company were deep in dramatic affairs.

"Such a decoration they should have in the royal theatre!" said Hans Peter.

"Yes, they should have many such!" said Grethe. "They should have some other pieces than those they have. I know not how it is with our poets; they have no inventive power. Relate the droll idea which thou hadst the other day for a new piece!" said she to her lover, and stroked his cheeks.

"O," said he, and affected a kind of indifference, "that was only an idea such as one has very often. But it might become a very nice piece. When the curtain is drawn up, one should see close upon the lamps the gable-ends of two houses. The steep roofs must go down to the stage, so that it is only half a yard wide, and this is to represent a watercourse between the two houses. In each garret a poor but interesting family should dwell, and these should step forth into the watercourse, and there the whole piece should be played."

"But what should then happen?" asked Otto.

"Yes," said the lover, "I have not thought about that; but see, there is the idea! I am no poet, and have too much to do at the counting-house, otherwise one might write a little piece."

"Heavens! Heiberg ought to have the idea!" said Grethe.

"No, then it would be a vaudeville," said the lover, "and I cannot bear them."

"O, it might be made charming!" cried Grethe. "I see the whole piece! how they clamber about the roofs! The idea is original, thou sweet friend!"

By evening the family were again in Roeskelde.

The merchant sought for Eva. Otto inquired after her, so did Hans Peter also, and all three received the same answer.

"She is no longer here."

CHAPTER XXVI

*"I wish I was air, that I could beat my wings, could chase
the clouds, and try to fly over the mountain summits: that
would be life."* —F. RÜCKERT.

The first evening after Otto's return to Copenhagen he spent with
Sophie, and the conversation turned upon his little journey. "The pretty Eva
has vanished!" said he.

"You had rejoiced in the prospect of this meeting, had you not?" asked
Sophie.

"No, not in the least!" answered Otto.

"And you wish to make me believe that? She is really pretty, and has
something so unspeakably refined, that a young gentleman might well be
attracted by her. With my brother it is not all quite right in this respect; but,
candidly speaking, I am in great fear on your account, Mr. Thostrup. Still
waters—you know the proverb? I might have spared you the trouble. The
letter which I received a few evenings ago informed me of her departure.
Mamma has taken her with her. It seemed to her a sin to leave that sweet,
innocent girl in a public-house. The host and hostess were born upon our
estate, and look very much up to my mother; and as Eva will certainly gain
by the change, the whole affair was soon settled. It is well that she is come
under mamma's oversight."

"The girl is almost indifferent to me!" said Otto.

"Almost!" repeated Sophie. "But this almost, how many degrees of
warmth does it contain? 'O Vérité! Où sont les autels et tes prêtres?'" added
she, and smiling raised her finger.

"Time will show how much you are in error!" answered Otto with
much calmness.

The lady of the house now entered, she had made various calls; everywhere the Ghost's Letters were the subject of conversation, and now the conversation took the same direction.

It was often renewed. Otto was a very frequent guest at the house. The ladies sat at their embroidery frames and embroidered splendid pieces of work, and Otto must again read the "Letters of the Wandering Ghost;" after this they began "Calderon," in whom Sophie found something resembling the anonymous author. The world of poetry afforded subjects for discourse, and every-day life intermingled its light, gay scenes; if Wilhelm joined them, he must give them music, and all remarked that his fantasies were become far richer, far softer. He had gained his touch from Weyse, said they. No one thought how much one may learn from one's own heart. With this exception he was the same joyous youth as ever. No one thought of him and Eva together. Since that evening when the friends had almost quarreled, he had never mentioned her name; but Otto had remarked how when any female figure met them, Wilhelm's eyes flashed, and how, in society, he singled out the most beautiful. Otto said jokingly to him, that he was getting oriental thoughts. Oehlenschläger's "Helge," and Goethe's Italian sonnets were now Wilhelm's favorite reading. The voluptuous spirit of these poems agreed with the dreams which his warm feelings engendered. It was Eva's beauty—her beauty alone which had awoke this feeling in him; the modesty and poverty of the poor girl had captivated him still more, and caused him to forget rank and condition. At the moment when he would approach her, she was gone. The poison was now in his blood. If is gay and happy spirit did not meanwhile let him sink into melancholy and meditation; his feeling for beauty was excited, as he himself expressed it. In thought he pressed beauty to his heart, but only in thought—but even this is sin, says the Gospel.

Otto, on the contrary, moved in the lists of philosophy and poetry. Here his soul conceived beauty—inspired, he expressed it; and Sophie's eyes flashed, and rested with pleasure on him. This flattered him and increased his inspirations. For many years no winter had been to him so pleasant, had passed away so rich in change as this; he caught at the fluttering joy and yet there were moments when the though pressed upon him—"Life is hastening away, and I do not enjoy it." In the midst of his greatest happiness he experienced a strange yearning after the changing life of travel. Paris glanced before his eyes like a star of fortune.

"Out into the bustling world!" said he so often to Wilhelm, that the same thought was excited in him. "In the spring we will travel!" Now were plans formed; circumstances were favorable. Thus in the coming spring, in April, the still happier days should begin.

"We will fly to Paris!" said Wilhelm; "to joy and pleasure!"

Joy and pleasure were to be found at home, and were found: we will introduce the evening which brought them; perhaps we shall also find something more than joy and pleasure.

CHAPTER XXVII

"A midsummer day's entertainment — but how? In February?
Yea,

some here and behold it!" — DR. BALFUNGO.

With us the students form no Burschenschafts, have no colors. The professors do not alone in the chair come into connection with them; the only difference is that which exists between young and old scholars. Thus they come in contact with each other, thus they participate in their mutual pleasures. We will spend an evening of this kind in the Students' Club, and then see for ourselves whether Miss Sophie were right when she wished she were a man, merely that she might be a student and member of this club. We choose one evening in particular, not only that we may seek a brilliant moment, but because this evening can afford us more than a description.

An excursion to the park had often been discussed in the club. They wished to hire the Caledonia steam-packet. But during the summer months the number of members is less; the majority are gone to the provinces to visit their relations. Winter, on the contrary, assembles them all. This time, also, is the best for great undertakings. The long talked of excursion to the park was therefore fixed for Carnival Monday, the 14th of February, 1831. Thus ran the invitations to the professors and older members. "It will be too cold for me," replied one. "Must one take a carriage for one's self?" asked mother. No, the park was removed to Copenhagen. In the Students' Club itself, in the Boldhuus Street, No. 225, was the park-hill with its green trees, its swings, and amusements. See, only the scholars of the Black School could have such ideas!

The evening of the 114th of February drew near. The guests assembled in the rooms on the first floor. Meanwhile all was arranged in the second story. Those who represented jugglers were in their places. A thundering cracker was the steamboat signal, and now people hastened to the park, rushing up-stairs, where two large rooms had, with great taste and humor, been converted into the park-hill. Large fir-trees concealed the walls — you found yourself in a complete wood. The doors which connected the two rooms were decorated with sheets, so that it looked as if you were going through a tent. Hand-organs played, drums and trumpets roared, and from tents and stages the hawkers shouted one against the other. It was a noise such as is heard in the real park when the hubbub has reached its height. The most brilliant requisites of the real park were found here, and they were not imitated; they were the things themselves. Master Jakel's own puppets had been hired; a student, distinguished by his complete imitation of the first actors, represented them by the puppets. The fortress of Frederiksteen was the same which we have already seen in the park. "The whole cavalry and infantry,—here a fellow without a bayonet, there a bayonet without a fellow!" The old Jew sat under his tree where he announced his fiftieth park jubilee: here a student ate flax, there another exhibited a bear; Polignac stood as a wax figure outside a cabinet. The Magdalene convent exhibited its little boxes, the drum-major beat most lustily, and from a near booth came the real odor of warm wafer-cakes. The spring even, which presented itself in the outer room, was full of significance. Certainly it was only represented by a tea-urn concealed between moss and stones, but the water was real water, brought from the well in Christiansborg. Astounding and full of effect was the multitude of sweet young girls who showed themselves. Many of the youngest students who had feminine features were dressed as ladies; some of them might even be called pretty. Who that then saw the fair one with the tambourine can have forgotten her? The company crowded round the ladies. The professors paid court to them with all propriety, and, what was best of all, some ladies who were less successful became jealous of the others. Otto was much excited; the noise, the bustle, the variety of people, were almost strikingly given. Then came the master of the fire-engines, with his wife and little granddaughter; then three pretty peasant girls; then the whole Botanical Society, with their real professor at their head. Otto seated himself in a swing; an itinerant flute-player and a drummer deafened him with dissonances. A young lady, one of the beauties, in a white dress, and with a thin handkerchief over her shoulders, approached and threw herself into his arms. It was Wilhelm! but Otto found his likeness to Sophie stronger than he had ever before noticed it to be; and therefore the blood rushed to his cheeks when the fair one threw her arms around him, and laid her cheek upon his: he perceived more of Sophie than of Wilhelm in this form. Certainly Wilhelm's features were coarser—his whole figure larger than Sophie's; but still Otto fancied he saw Sophie, and therefore these marked gestures, this reeling about with the other students, offended his eyes. When Wilhelm seated himself on his knee, and pressed his cheek to his, Otto felt his heart beat as in fever; it sent a stream of fire through his blood: he thrust him away, but the fair one continued to overwhelm him with caresses.

There now commenced, in a so-called Krähwinkel theatre, the comedy, in which were given the then popular witticisms of Kellerman.

The lady clung fast to Otto, and flew dancing with him through the crowd. The heat, the noise, and, above all, the exaggerated lacing, affected Wilhelm; he felt unwell. Otto led him to a bench and would have unfastened his dress, but all the young ladies, true to their part, sprang forward, pushed Otto aside, surrounded their sick companion and concealed her, whilst they tore up the dress behind so that she might have air: but, God forbid! no gentleman might see it.

Toward evening a song was commenced, a shot was heard, and the last verse announced:—

"The gun has been fired, the vessel must fly

To the town from the green wood shady.

Come, friends, now we to the table will hie,

A gentleman and a fair lady."

And now all rushed with the speed of a steamboat downstairs, and soon sat in gay rows around the covered tables.

Wilhelm was Otto's lady—the Baron was called the Baroness; the glasses resounded, and the song commenced:—

"These will drink our good king's health,

Will drink it here, his loyal students."

And that patriotic song:—

"I know a land up in the North

Where it is good to be."

It concluded with—

"An hurrah

For the king and the rescript!"

In joy one must embrace everything joyful, and that they did. Here was the joy of youth in youthful hearts.

"No condition's like the student's;

He has chosen the better way!"

so ran the concluding verse of the following song, which ended with the toast,—

"For her of whom the heart dreams ever,

But whom the lips must never name!"

It was then that Wilhelm seemed to glow with inward fire; he struck his glass so violently against Otto's that it broke, and the wine was spilt.

"A health to the ladies!" cried one of the signors.

"A health to the ladies!" resounded from the different rooms, which were all converted into the banquet-hall.

The ladies rose, stood upon their chairs, some even upon the table, bowed, and returned thanks for the toast.

"No, no," whispered Otto to Wilhelm, at the same time pulling him down. "In this dress you resemble your sister so much, that it is quite horrible to me to see you act a part so opposed to her character!"

"And your eyes," Said Wilhelm, smiling, "resemble two eyes which have touched my heart. A health to first love!" cried he, and struck his glass against Otto's so that the half of his wine was again lost.

The champagne foamed, and amidst noise and laughter, as during the

carnival joy, a new song refreshed the image of the nark which they had

just left:— "Here if green trees were not growing

Fresh as on yon little hill,

Heard we not the fountains flowing,

We in sooth should see them still!

Tents were filled below, above,

Filled with everything but love!

Here went gratis brushing-boys— Graduated have they all!

Here stood, who would think it, sir?

A student as a trumpeter!"

"A health to the one whose eyes mine resemble!" whispered Otto, carried along with the merriment.

"That health we have already drunk!" answered Wilhelm, "but we cannot do a good thing too often."

"Then you still think of Eva?"

"She was beautiful! sweet! who knows what might have happened had she remained here? Her fate has fallen into mamma's hands, and she and the other exalted Nemesis must now conduct the affair: I wash my hands of it."

"Are you recovered?" asked Otto. "But when you see Eva again in the summer?"

"I hope that I shall not fall sick," replied Wilhelm; "I have a strong constitution. But we must now hasten up to the dance."

All rushed from the tables, and up-stairs, where the park was arranged. There was now only the green wood to be seen. Theatres and booths had been removed. Gay paper-lamps hung among the branches, a large orchestra played, and a half-bacchanalian wood-ball commenced. Wilhelm was Otto's partner, but after the first dance the lady sought out for herself a more lively cavalier.

Otto drew back toward the wall where the windows were concealed by the boughs of Fir-tree. His eye followed Wilhelm, whose great resemblance to Sophie made him melancholy; his hand accidentally glided through the branches and touched the window-seat; there lay a little bird—it was dead!

To increase the illusion they had bought a number of birds, which should fly about during the park-scene, but the poor little creatures had died from fright at the wild uproar. In the windows and corners they lay dead. It was one of these birds that Otto found.

"It is dead!" said he to Wilhelm, who approached him.

"Now, that is capital!" returned the friend; "here you have something over which you may be sentimental!"

Otto would not reply.

"Shall we dance a Scotch waltz?" asked Wilhelm laughing, and the wine and his youthful blood glowed in his cheeks.

"I wish you would put on your own dress!" said Otto. "You resemble, as I said before, your sister" —

"And I am my sister," interrupted Wilhelm, in his wantonness. "And as a reward for your charming readings aloud, for your excellent conversation, and the whole of your piquant amiability, you shall now be paid with a little kiss!" He pressed his lips to Otto's forehead; Otto thrust him back and left the company.

Several hours passed before he could sleep; at length he was forced to laugh over his anger: what mattered it if Wilhelm resembled his sister?

The following morning Otto paid her a visit. All listened with lively interest to his description of the merry St. John's day in February. He also related how much Wilhelm had resembled his sister, and how unpleasant this had been to him; and they laughed. During the relation, however, Otto could not forbear drawing a comparison. How great a difference did he now find! Sophie's beauty was of quite another kind! Never before had he regarded her in this light. Of the kisses which Wilhelm had given him, of course, they did not speak; but Otto thought of them, thought of them quite differently to what he had done before, and—the ways of Cupid are strange! We will now see how affairs stand after advancing fourteen days.

CHAPTER XXVIII

"Huzza for Copenhagen and for Paris! may they both flourish!"
The Danes in Paris by HEIBERG.

Wilhelm's cousin, Joachim, had arrived from Paris. We remember the young officer, out of whose letters Wilhelm had sent Otto a description of the struggle of the July days. As an inspired hero of liberty had he returned; struggling Poland had excited his lively interest, and he would willingly have combated in Warsaw's ranks. His mind and his eloquence made him doubly interesting. The combat of the July days, of which he had been an eye-witness, he described to them. Joachim was handsome; he had an elegant countenance with sharp features, and was certainly rather pale—one might perhaps have called him worn with dissipation, had it not been for the brightness of his eyes, which increased in conversation. The fine dark eyebrow, and even the little mustache, gave the countenance all expression which reminded one of fine English steel-engravings. His figure was small, almost slender, but the proportions were beautiful. The animation of the Frenchman expressed itself in every motion, but at the same time there was in him a certain determination which seemed to say: "I am aware of my own intellectual superiority!"

He interested every one: Otto also listened with pleasure when Cousin Joachim related his experiences, but when all eyes were turned toward the narrator, Otto fixed his suddenly upon Sophie, and found that she could moderate his attentions. Joachim addressed his discourse to all, but at the points of interest his glance rested alone on the pretty cousin! "She interests him!" said Otto to himself. "And Cousin Joachim?" Yes, he relates well; but had we only traveled we should not be inferior to him!"

"Charles X. was a Jesuit!" said Joachim; "he strove after an unrestrained despotism, and laid violent hands on the Charter. The expedition against Algiers was only a glittering fire-work arranged to flatter the national pride—all glitter and falseness! Like Peirronnet, through an embrace he would annihilate the Charter."

The conversation now turned from the Jesuits to the Charter and Polignac. The minute particulars, which only an eyewitness can relate, brought the struggle livingly before their eyes. They saw the last night, the extraordinary activity in the squares where the balls were showered, and in the streets where the barricades were erected. Overturned wagons and carts, barrels and stones, were heaped upon each other—even the hundred year-old trees of the Boulevards were cut down to form barricades: the struggle began, Frenchman fought against Frenchman—for liberty and country they sacrificed their life.

[Note:

"*Ceux qui pieusement sont morts pour la patrie*

Ont droit qu'à leur cerceuil la foule vienne et prie:

Entre le plus beaux noms, leur nom est le plus beau.

Toute gloire, près d'eux, passe et tombe éphèmere

Et, comme ferait une mère,

La voix d'un peuple entier les berce en leur tombeau!"

—*VICTOR HUGO.*]

And he described the victory and Louis Philippe, whom he admired and loved.

"That was a world event," said the man of business. "It electrified both king and people. They still feel the movement. Last year was an extraordinary year!"

"For the Copenhageners also," said Otto, "there were three colors. These things occupied the multitude with equal interest: the July Revolution, the 'Letters of a Wandering Ghost,' and Kellermann's 'Berlin Wit.'"

"Now you are bitter, Mr. Thostrup," said the lady of the house. "The really educated did not occupy themselves with these Berlin 'Eckensteher' which the multitude have rendered national!"

"But they hit the right mark!" said Otto; "they met with a reception from the citizens and people in office."

"That I can easily believe," remarked Joachim; "that is like the people here!"

"That is like the people abroad!" said the hostess. "In Paris they pass over still more easily from a revolution, in which they themselves have taken part, to a review by Jules Janin, or to a new step of Taglioni's, and from that to 'une histoire scandaleuse!'"

"No, my gracious lady, of the last no one takes any notice—it belongs to the order of the day!"

"That I can easily believe!" said Miss Sophie.

The man of business now inquired after the Chamber. The cousin's answer was quite satisfactory. The lady of the house wished to hear of the flower-markets, and of the sweet little inclosed gardens in the Places. Sophie wished to hear of Victor Hugo. She received a description of him, of his abode in the Place Royale, and of the whole Europe littéraire beside. Cousin Joachim was extremely interesting.

Otto did not pay another visit for two days.

"Where have you been for so long?" asked Sophie, when he came again.

"With my books!" replied he: there lay a gloomy expression in his eyes.

"O, you should have come half an hour earlier—our cousin was here! He was describing to me the Jardin des Plantes in Paris. O, quite excellently!"

"He is an interesting young man!" said Otto.

"The glorious garden!" pursued Sophie, without remarking the emphasis with which Otto had replied. "Do you not remember, Mr. Thostrup, how Barthélemi has spoken of it? 'Où tout homme, qui rêve à son pays absent, Retrouve ses parfums et son air caressant.' In it there is a whole avenue with cages, in which are wild beasts,—lions and tigers! In small court-yards, elephants and buffaloes wander about at liberty! Giraffes nibble the branches of high trees! In the middle of the garden are the courts for bears, only there is a sort of well in which the bears walk about; it is surrounded by no palisades, and you stand upon the precipitous edge! There our cousin stood!"

"But he did not precipitate himself down!" said Otto, with indifference.

"What is the matter?" asked Sophie. "Are you in your elegiac mood? You look as I imagine Victor Hugo when he has not made up his mind about the management of his tragic catastrophe!"

"That is my innate singularity!" replied Otto. "I should have pleasure in springing down among the bears of which you relate!"

"And in dying?" asked Sophie. "No, you must live. 'C'est le bonheur de vivre Qui fait la gloire de mourir.'"

"You speak a deal of French to-day," said Otto, with a friendliness of manner intended to soften the bitterness of the tone. "Perhaps your conversation with the lieutenant was in that language?"

"French interests me the most!" replied she. "I will ask our cousin to speak it often with me. His accent is excellent, and he is himself a very interesting man!"

"No doubt of it!" answered Otto.

"You will remain and dine with us?" said the lady of the house, who now entered.

Otto did not feel well.

"These are only whims," said Sophie.

The ladies made merry, and Otto remained. Cousin Joachim came and was interesting—very interesting, said all. He related of Paris, spoke also of Copenhagen, and drew comparisons. The quietness of home had made an especial impression on him.

"People here," said he, "go about as if they bore some heavy grief, or some joy, which they might not express. If one goes into a coffee-house, it is just as if one entered a house of mourning. Each one seats himself, a newspaper in his hand, in a corner. That strikes one when one comes from Paris! One naturally has the thought,—Can these few degrees further north bring so much cold into the blood? There is the same quiet in our theatre. Now I love this active life. The only boldness the public permits itself is hissing a poor author; but a wretched singer, who has neither tone nor manner, a miserable actress, will be endured, nay, applauded by good friends—an act of compassion. She is so fearful! she is so good! In Paris people hiss. The decoration master, the manager, every one there receives his share of applause or blame. Even the directors are there hissed, if they manage badly."

"You are preaching a complete revolution in our theatrical kingdom!" said the lady of the house. "The Copenhageners cannot ever become Parisians, and neither should they."

"The theatre is here, as well as there, the most powerful organ of the people's life. It has the greatest influence, and ours stands high, very high, when one reflects in what different directions it must extend its influence. Our only theatre must accommodate itself, and represent, at the same time, the Theatre Français, the grand Opera, the Vaudeville, and Saint-Martin; it must comprehend all kinds of theatrical entertainments. The same actors who to-day appear in tragedy, must to-morrow show themselves in a comedy or vaudeville. We have actors who might compare themselves with the best in Paris—only *one* is above all ours, but, also, above all whom I have seen in Europe, and this one is Mademoiselle Mars. You will, doubtless, consider the reason extraordinary which gives this one, in my opinion, the first place. This is her age, which she so completely compels you to forget. She is still pretty; round, without being called fat. It is not through rouge, false hair, or false teeth, that she procures herself youth; it lies in her soul, and from thence it flows into every limb—every motion becomes charming! She fills you with astonishment! her eyes are full of expression, and her voice is the most sonorous which I know! It is indeed music! How can one think of age when one is affected by an immortal soul? I rave about Léontine Fay, but the old Mars has my heart. There is also a third who stands high with the Parisians—Jenny Vertprè, at the Gymnase Dramatique, but she would be soon eclipsed were the Parisians to see our Demoiselle Pätges. She possesses talent which will shine in every scene. Vertprè has her loveliness, her whims, but not her Proteus-genius, her nobility. I saw Vertprè in 'La Reine de Seize Ans,'—a piece which we have not yet; but she was only a saucy soubrette in royal splendor—a Pernille of Holberg's, as represented by a Parisian. We have Madame Wexschall, and we have Frydendal! Were Denmark only a larger country, these names would sound throughout Europe!"

He now described the decorations in the "Sylphide," in "Natalia," and in various other ballets, the whole splendor, the whole magnificence.

"But our orchestra is excellent!" said Miss Sophie.

"It certainly contains several distinguished men," answered Joachim; "but must one speak of the whole? Yes, you know I am not musical, and cannot therefore express myself in an artistical manner about music, but certain it is that something lay in my ear, in my feeling, which, in Paris, whispered to me, 'That is excellent!' Here, on the contrary, it cries, 'With moderation! with moderation!' The voice is the first; she is the lady; the instruments, on the contrary, are the cavaliers who shall conduct the former before the public. Gently they should take her by the hand; she must stand quite foremost; but here the instruments thrust her aside, and it is to me as if each instrument would have the first place, and constantly shouted, 'Here am I! here am I!'"

"That sounds very well!" said Sophie; "but one may not believe you! You have fallen in love with foreign countries, and, therefore, at home everything must be slighted."

"By no means! The Danish ladies, for instance, appear the prettiest, the most modest whom I have known."

"Appear?" repeated Otto.

"Joachim possesses eloquence," said the lady of the house.

"That has developed itself abroad!" answered he: "here at home there are only two ways in which it can publicly develop itself—in the pulpit, and at a meeting in the shooting-house. Yet it is true that now we are going to have a Diet and a more political life. I feel already, in anticipation, the effect; we shall only live for this life, the newspapers will become merely political, the poets sing politics the painters choose scenes from political life. 'C'est un

Uebergang!' as Madame La Flèche says. [Author's Note: Holberg's Jean de France.] Copenhagen is too small to be a great, and too great to be a small city. See, there lies the fault!"

Otto felt an irresistible desire to contradict him in most things which he said about home. But the cousin parried every bold blow with a joke.

"Copenhagen must be the Paris of the North," said he, "and that it certainly would become in fifty, or twice that number of years. The situation was far more beautiful than that of the city of the Seine. The marble church must be elevated, and become a Pantheon, adorned with the works of Thorwaldsen and other artists; Christiansborg, a Louvre, whose gallery you visit; Öster Street and Pedermadsen's passage, arcades such as are in Paris, covered with glass roofs and flagged, shops on both sides, and in the evening, when thousands of gas-lamps burnt, here should be the promenade; the esplanades would be the Champs Elysées, with swings and slides, music, and mâts de cocagne. [Author's Note: High smooth poles, to the top of which victuals, clothes, or money are attached. People of the lower classes then try to climb up and seize the prizes. The best things are placed at the very top of the pole.] On the Peblinger Lake, as on the Seine, there should be festive water excursions made. Voilà!" exclaimed he, "that would be splendid!"

"That might be divine!" said Sophie.

Animation and thought lay in the cousin's countenance; his fine features became striking from their expression. Thus did his image stamp itself in Otto's soul, thus did it place itself beside Sophie's image as she stood there, with her large brown eyes, round which played thought and smiles, whilst they rested on the cousin. The beautifully formed white hand, with its taper fingers, played with the curls which fell over her cheeks. Otto would not think of it.

CHAPTER XXIX

"And if I have wept alone, it is my own sorrow." —GOETHE

Latterly Otto had been but seldom at Mr. Berger's. He had no interest about the merchant's home. The family showed him every politeness and mark of confidence; but his visits became every week more rare. Business matters, however, led him one day there.

Chance or fate, as we call it, if the shadow of a consequence shows itself, caused Maren to pass through the anteroom when Otto was about taking his departure. She was the only one of the ladies at home. In three weeks she would return to Lemvig. She said that she could not boast of having enjoyed Mr. Thostrup's society too often.

"Your old friends interest you no longer!" added she, somewhat gravely. With this exception she had amused herself very well in the city, had seen everything but the stuffed birds, and these she should see to-morrow. She had been seven times in the theatre, and had seen the "Somnambule" twice. However, she had not seen "Der Frieschütz," and she had an especial desire to see this on account of the wolf-glen. At Aarhuus there was a place in the wood, said she, called the wolf-glen; this she knew, and now wished to see whether it resembled the one on the stage.

"May I then greet Rosalie from you?" she asked at length.

"You will still remain three weeks here," said Otto: "it is too soon to speak of leave-taking."

"But you scarcely ever come here," returned she. "You have better places to go to! The Baron's sister certainly sees you oftener; she is said to be a pretty and very clever girl: perhaps one may soon offer one's congratulations?"

Otto became crimson.

"In spring you will travel abroad," pursued she; "we shall not then see you in Jutland: yes, perhaps you will never go there again! That will make old Rosalie sad: she thinks so incredibly much of you. In all the letters which I have received here there were greetings to Mr. Thostrup. Yes, I have quite a multitude of them for you; but you do not come to receive them, and I dare not pay a visit to such a young gentleman. For the sake of old friendship let me, at least, be the first who can relate at home of the betrothal!"

"How can you have got such a thought?" replied Otto. "I go to so many houses where there are young ladies; if my heart had anything to do with it, I should have a bad prospect. I have great esteem for Miss Sophie; I speak with her as with you, that is all. I perceive that the air of Copenhagen has affected you; here in the city they are always betrothing people. This comes from the ladies in the house here. How could you believe such stories?"

Maren also joked about it, but after they had parted she seated herself in a corner, drew her little apron over her head and wept; perhaps because she should soon leave the lively city, where she had been seven times to the theatre, and yet had not seen the wolf-glen.

"Betrothed!" repeated Otto to himself, and thought of Sophie, of the cousin, and of his own childhood, which hung like a storm-cloud in his heaven. Many thoughts passed through his mind: he recollected the Christmas Eve on which he had seen Sophie for the first time, when she, as one of the Fates, gave him the number. He had 33, she 34; they were united by the numbers following each other. He received the pedigree, and was raised to her nobility. The whole joke had for him a signification. He read the verse again which had accompanied it. The conclusion sounded again and again in his ears: — "From this hour forth thy soul high rank hath won her, Nor will forget thy knighthood and thy honor!"

"O Sophie!" he exclaimed aloud, and the fire which had long smouldered in his blood now burst forth in flames. "Sophie! thee must I press to my heart!" He lost himself in dreams. Dark shapes disturbed them. "Can she then be happy? Can I? The picture which she received where the covering of ice was broken and the faithful dog watched in vain, is also significant. That is the fulfillment of hopes. I sink, and shall never return!"

The image of the cousin mingled in his dreams. That refined countenance with the little mustache looked forth saucily and loquaciously; and Sophie's eyes he saw rest upon the cousin, whilst her white hand played with the brown curls which fell over her cheek.

"O Sophie!" sighed Otto, and fell asleep.

CHAPTER XXX

...″We live through others,
We think we are others; we seem
Others to be... And so think others of us. ″
SCHEFER.

When the buds burst forth we will burst forth also! had Otto and
Wilhelm often said. Their plan was, in the spring to travel immediately
to Paris, but on their way to visit the Rhine, and to sail from Cologne to
Strasburg.

"Yes, one must see the Rhine first!" said Cousin Joachim; "when one
has seen Switzerland and Italy, it does not strike one nearly as much. That
must be your first sight; but you should not see it in spring, but toward
autumn. When the vines have their full variety of tint, and the heavy grapes
hang from the stems, see, it is then the old ruins stand forth. These are the
gardens of the Rhine! Another advantage which you have in going there in
autumn is that you then enter Paris in winter, and that one must do; then
one does not come post festum; then is the heyday of gayety—the theatre,
the soirées, and everything which can interest the beau monde."

Although Otto did not generally consider the cousin's words of much
weight, he this time entered wonderfully into his views. "It would certainly
be the most prudent to commence their journey toward autumn," he
thought: "there could be no harm in preparing themselves a little more for
it!"

"That is always good!" said Joachim; "but, what is far more advantageous
abroad than all the preparations you can make at home, is said in a few
words—give up all intercourse with your own country-people! Nowadays
every one travels! Paris is not now further from us than Hamburg was some
thirty years ago. When I was in Paris I found there sixteen or seventeen of
my countrymen. O, how they kept together! Eleven of them dwelt in the
same hôtel: they drank coffee together, walked out together, went to the
restaurateur's together, and took together half a bench in the theatre. That is
the most foolish thing a person can do! I consider travelling useful for every
one, from the prince to the travelling journeyman. But we allow too many
people to travel! We are not rich, therefore restrictions should be made. The

creative artist, the poet, the engineer, and the physician must travel; but God knows why theologians should go forth. They can become mad enough at home! They come into Catholic countries, and then there is an end of them! Wherefore should book-worms go forth? They shut themselves up in the diligence and in their chambers, rummage a little in the libraries, but not so much as a pinch of snuff do they do us any good when they return! Those who cost the most generally are of the least use, and bring the country the least honor! I, thank God! paid for my journey myself, and am therefore free to speak my opinion!"

We will now hear what Miss Sophie said, and therefore advance a few days.

"We keep you then with us till August!" said she, once when she was alone with Otto. "That is wise! You can spend some time with us in Funen, and gather strength for your journey. Yes, the journey will do you good!"

"I hope so!" answered Otto. "I am perhaps able to become as interesting as your cousin, as amiable!"

"That would be requiring too much from you!" said Sophie, bantering him. "You will never have his humor, his facility in catching up character. You will only preach against the depravity of the Parisians; you will only be able to appreciate the melancholy grandeur of Switzerland and the solitude of the Hungarian forests."

"You would make a misanthrope of me, which I by no means am."

"But you have an innate talent for this character!" answered Sophie. "Something will certainly be polished away by this journey, and it is on account of this change that I rejoice."

"Must one, then, have a light, fickle mood to please you?" asked Otto.

"Yes, certainly!" answered Sophie, ironically.

"Then it is true what your cousin told me!" said Otto. "If one will be fortunate with the ladies, one must at least be somewhat frivolous, fond of pleasure, and fickle,—that makes one interesting. Yes, he has made himself acquainted with the world, he has experience in everything!"

"Yes, perfectly!" said Sophie, and laughed aloud.

Otto was silent, with contracted brow.

"I wish you sunshine!" said Sophie, and smiling raised her finger. Otto remained unchanged—he wrinkled his brow.

"You must change very much!" said she, half gravely; and danced out of the room.

Three weeks passed by, rich in great events in the kingdom of the heart; it was still a diplomatic secret: the eyes betrayed it by their pantomimic language, the mouth alone was silent, and it is after all the deciding power.

Otto visited the merchant's family. Maren had departed just the day before. In vain had she awaited his visit throughout the three weeks.

"You quite forget your true friends!" said the ladies. "Believe us, Maja was a little angry with you, and yet we have messages. Now she is sailing over the salt sea."

This was not precisely the case; she was already on land, and just at this moment was driving over the brown heath, thinking of Copenhagen and the pleasures there, and of the sorrow also—it is so sad to be forgotten by a friend of childhood! Otto was so handsome, so clever—she did not dream at all how handsome and clever she herself would appear at home. Beauty and cleverness they had discovered in her before she left; now she had been in the capital, and that gives relief.

The little birds fluttered round the carriage; perhaps they sang to her what should happen in two years: "Thou wilt be a bride, the secretary's lovely little bride; thou shalt have both him and the musical-box! Thou wilt be the grandest lady in the town, and yet the most excellent mother. Thy first daughter shall be called Maja—that is a pretty name, and reminds thee of past days!"

CHAPTER XXXI

*"The monastery is still called 'Andersskov' (the wood of
Anders) in memory of its being the habitation of the pious
Anders.*

*"The hill on which he awoke, comforted by sleep, is still
called 'Hvile höi' (the hill of rest). A cross having a
Latin inscription, half-effaced, marks the spot."—J. L.
HEIBERG.*

It was spring, fresh, life-bearing spring! Only one day and one night,
and the birds of passage were back again; the woods made themselves
once more young with green, odorous leaves; the Sound had its swimming
Venice of richly laden vessels; only one day and one night, and Sophie was
removed from Otto—they were divided by the salt sea; but it was spring
in his heart; from it flew his thoughts, like birds of passage, to the island of
Funen, and there sang of summer. Hope gave him more "gold and green
woods" than the ships bear through the Sound, more than Zealand's bays
can show. Sophie at parting pressed his hand. In her eyes lay what his heart
might hope and dream.

He forgot that hope and dreams were the opposites of reality.

Cousin Joachim had gone to Stockholm, and would not return either
in the spring or summer to Funen. On the contrary, Otto intended to spend
a few weeks at the country-seat; not before August would he and Wilhelm
travel. There would at least be one happy moment, and many perhaps almost
as happy. In his room stood a rose-bush, the first buds formed themselves,
and opened their red lips—as pure and tender as these leaves was Sophie's
cheek: he bent over the flower, smiled and read there sweet thoughts which
were related to his love. A rose-bud is a sweet mystery.

"The myriad leaves enmaze
Small labyrinthine ways
Where spicy odor flows,
Thou lovelv bud o' the rose!"

The day came on which Otto, after he had comfortably terminated his visits of leave-taking, at midday, in the company of three young students travelled away through Zealand. They had taken a carriage together as far as Slagelse, where, like Abraham's and Lot's shepherds, they should separate to the right and left. Otto remained alone, in order to travel post that night to Nyborg. It was only four o'clock in the afternoon, Otto had no acquaintance here, therefore it was but to take a walk.

"There still exist remains of the old Antvorskov convent, [Author's Note: The convent was founded by Waldemar I., 1177.] do there not?" asked he.

"Yes, but very little!" answered the host. "The convent became a castle, the castle a private house, and now within the last few years, on account of the stones, it has been still more pulled down. You will find nothing old remaining, except here and there in the garden a piece of a red wall standing out. But the situation is beautiful! If you will only take the road toward the large village called Landsgrav, you are on the way to Korsöer, and close to the cross of the holy Anders. It is a right pleasant excursion!"

"Convent ruins and the holy cross!" said Otto; "that sounds quite romantic!" And he commenced his wanderings.

A few scholars from the Latin school, with their books held together by a strait, and then a square built lancer, who greeted in military style an elderly-young lady, who was seated behind a barricade of geraniums and wall flowers, were the only individuals he met with on his way. Yet Otto remarked that the windows were opened as he passed; people wanted to see who the stranger might be who was going up the street.

A long avenue led from the town to the castle. On either side the way lay detached houses, with little gardens. Otto soon reached the remains of old Antvorskov. The way was red from the stones which were flung about, and were now ground to dust. Huge pieces of wall, where the mortar and stone were united in one piece, lay almost concealed among the high nettles. Rather more distant stood a solitary house of two stories. It was narrow, and whitewashed. A thick pilaster, such as one sees in churches, supported the strong wall. This was half of the last wing of the castle,—a mingling of the ancient and incident, of ruin and dwelling-house.

Otto went into the garden, which was laid out upon the hill itself, and its terraces. Here were only young trees; but the walks were everywhere overgrown. The view stretched itself far over the plain, toward the Belt and Funen. He descended from the terrace down to the lowest wall. In this there yet remained a piece of an old tombstone, of the age of the convent, on which you perceived the trace of a female form; and near to this the figure of a skeleton, round which was twined a snake. Otto stood sunk in contemplation, when an old man, with two water-buckets suspended from a yoke on his shoulders, approached a near well.

The old man was very ready to commence a conversation. He told of excavations, and of an underground passage which had not been discovered, but which, according to his opinion, was certainly in existence. So far they had only found a few walled-round spaces, which had most probably been prisons. In one of these was an iron chain fastened into the wall. But with regard to the underground passage, they had only not yet discovered the right place, for it must exist. It led from here, deep under the lake and forest, toward Soröe. There were large iron gates below. At Christmas one could hear how they were swung to and fro. "Whoever should have that which is concealed there," said the old man, "would be a made man, and need not neither slip nor slide."

Otto looked at the solitary wing which rose up over the terrace. How splendid it had been here in former times!

Close to the large wood, several miles in extent, which stretches itself on the other side of Soröe, down to the shore of the King's Brook, lay the rich convent where Hans Tausen spoke what the Spirit inspired him with. Times changed; the convent vanished;

> "Halls of state
>
> Tower upon that spot elate;
>
> Where the narrow cell once stood;"
>
> [Author's Note: Anders-skov, by Oehlenschläger.]

where the monks sang psalms, knights and ladies danced to the sound of beating drums: but these tone's ceased; the blooming cheeks became dust. It was again quiet. Many a pleasant time did Holberg ride over from Soröe, through the green wood, to visit the steward of Antvorskov. Otto recollected what one of his daughters, when an old woman, had related to a friend of his. She was a child, and lay in the cradle, when old Holberg came riding there, with a little wheaten loaf and a small pot of preserve in his pocket—his usual provision on such little excursions. The steward's young wife sat at her spinning-wheel. Holberg paced up and down the room with the husband; they were discussing politics. This interested the wife, and she joined in the conversation. Holberg turned round to her,—"I fancy the distaff speaks!" said he. This the wife could never forget. [Translator's Note: Rokkehoved, distaff, means also dunce in Danish.]

Otto smiled at this recollection of the witty but ungallant poet, quitted the garden, and went through a winding hollow way, where the luxuriant briers hung in rich masses over the stone fence. Slagelse, with its high hills in the background, looked picturesque. He soon reached Landsgrav. The sun went down as he walked over the field where the wooden cross stands, with its figure of the Redeemer, in memory of the holy Anders. Near it he perceived a man, who appeared to kneel. One hand held fast by the cross; in the other was a sharp knife, with which he was probably cutting out his name. He did not observe Otto. Near the man lay a box covered with green oil-cloth; and in the grass lay a knapsack, a pair of boots, and a knotty stick. It must be a wandering journeyman, or else a pedlar.

Otto was about to return, when the stranger rose and perceived him. Otto stood as if nailed to the earth. It was the German Heinrich whom he saw before him.

"Is not that Mr. Thostrup?" said the man and that horrible grinning smile played around his mouth. "No, that I did not expect!"

"Does it go well with you, Heinrich?" asked Otto.

"There's room for things to mend!" replied Heinrich "It goes better with you! Good Lord, that you should become such a grand gentleman! Who would have thought it, when you rode on my knee, and I pricked you in the arm? Things go on strangely in this world! Have you heard of your sister? She was not so much spoiled as you! But she was a beautiful child!"

"I have neither seen her nor my parents!" replied he, with a trembling which he strove to conquer. "Do you know where she is?"

"I am always travelling!" said Heinrich; "but thus much I know, that she is still in Funen. Yes, she must take one of us, an unpretending husband! You can choose a genteel young lady for yourself. That's the way when people are lucky. You will become a landed proprietor. Old Heinrich will then no doubt obtain permission to exhibit his tricks on your estate? But none of its will speak of former times!—of the red house on the Odense water!" This last he whispered quite low. "I shall receive a few shillings from you?" he asked.

"You shall have more!" said Otto, and gave to him. "But I wish us to remain strangers to each other, as we are!"

"Yes, certainly, certainly!" said Heinrich, and nodded affirmatively with his head, whilst his eyes rested on the gift Otto had presented him with. "Then you are no longer angry with my joke in Jutland?" asked he with a simpering smile, and kissed Otto's hand. "I should not have known you then. Had you not shown me your shoulder, on which I saw the letters O and T which I myself had etched, it would never have occurred to me that we knew each other! But a light suddenly flashed across me. I should have said Otto Thostrup; but I said 'Odense Tugt-huus.' [Note: Odense house of correction.] That was not handsome of me, seeing you are such a good gentleman!"

"Yes, now adieu!" said Otto, and extended to him unwillingly his hand.

"There, our Saviour looks down upon us!" said the German Heinrich, and fixed his eyes upon the figure on the cross. "As certainly as He lives may you rely upon the silence of my mouth. He is my Redeemer, who hangs there on the cross, just as he is etched upon my skin, and as he stands along the high-roads in my father-land. Here is the only place in the whole country where the sign of the cross stands under the free heaven; here I worship: for you must know, Mr. Thostrup, I am not of your faith, but of the faith of the Virgin Mary. Here I have cut into the wood the holy sign, such as is placed over every door in my father-land,—an I, an H, and this S. In this is contained my own name; for H stands for Heinrich; I, for I myself; and S means Sinner; that is, I, Heinrich, Sinner. Now I have completed my worship, and you have given me a handsome skilling, I shall now go to my bed at the public-house; and if the girl is pretty, and lets one flatter her, I am still young enough, and shall fancy that I am Mr. Thostrup, and have won that most glorious, elegant young lady! Hurrah! it is a player's life which we lead!"

Otto left him, but heard how Heinrich sang:

> "Tri, ri, ro,
> The summer comes once mo!
> To beer, boys! to beer
> The winter lies in bands, O!
> And he who won't come here,
> We'll trounce him with our wands, O!
> Yo, yo, yo,
> The summer comes once mo!"

As, suddenly on a clear sunny day, a cloud can appear, extinguish the warm sunshine, conceal the green coast, and change everything into gray mist forms, so was it now with Otto, who had but just before felt himself so happy and full of youthful joy.

"You can sleep quietly!" said the host, when Otto returned to Slagelse; "you shall be wakened early enough to leave with the mail."

But his rest was like a delirium.

The post-horn sounded in the empty street; they rolled away—it was at daybreak.

"Is that a gallows?" inquired one of the travellers, and pointed toward the hill, where at this distance the cross looked like a stake.

"That is the cross of the holy Anders!" replied Otto; and livingly stood before him the recollections of the evening before.

"Does that really exist?" said the stranger. "I have read of it in the 'Letters of a Wandering Ghost.'"

This was a beautiful morning, the sun shone warmly, the sea was smooth as a mirror, and so much the faster did the steamboat glide away. The vessel with the mail, which had set sail two hours earlier, still lay not far from land. The sails hung down loosely; not a breeze stirred them.

The steamboat glided close past her; the passengers in the mail-vessel, the greater portion coachmen, travelling journeymen, and peasants, stood on the deck to see it. They waved greetings. One of the foremost leaned on his knotty stick, pulled off his hat, and shouted, "Good morning, my noble gentlefolk!" It was the German Heinrich; he then was going to Funen. Otto's heart beat faster, he gazed down among the rushing waves which foamed round the paddle, where the sunbeams painted a glorious rainbow.

"That is lovely!" said one of the strangers, close to him.

"Very lovely!" returned Otto, and stilled the sigh which would burst forth from his breast.

Scarcely two hours were fled—the cables were flung upon the Nyborg bridge of boats, and the steamboat made fast to the island of Funen.

CHAPTER XXXII

"It is so sweet when friendly hands bid you a hearty
welcome, so dear to behold well-known features, wherever you
turn your eyes. Everything seems so home-like and quiet
about you and in your own breast." HENRIETTE HAUCK.

Otto immediately hired a carriage, and reached the hall just about dinner-time. In the interior court-yard stood two calashes and an Holstein carriage; two strange coachmen, with lace round their hats, stood in animated discourse when Otto drove in through the gate. The postilion blew his horn.

"Be quiet there!" cried Otto.

"There are strangers at the hall!" said the postilion; "I will only let them know that another is coming."

Otto gazed at the garden, glanced up toward the windows, where mine of the ladies showed themselves only out of a side building a female head was stretched out, whose hair was put back underneath a cap. Otto recognized the grown-together eyebrows. "Is she the first person I am to see here?" sighed he; and the carriage rolled into the inner court. The dogs barked, the turkey-cocks gobbled, but not Wilhelm showed himself. The Kammerjunker came—the excellent neighbor! and immediately afterward Sophie; both exclaimed with smiles, "Welcome!"

"See, here we have our man!" said the Kammerjunker; "we can make use of him in the play!"

"It is glorious you are come!" cried Sophie. "We shall immediately put you under arrest." She extended her hand to him—he pressed it to his lips. "We will have tableaux vivants this evening!" said she: "the pastor has never seen any. We have no service from Wilhelm; he is in Svendborg, and will not return for two days. You must be the officer; the Kammerjunker will represent the Somnambulist, who comes with her light through the window. Will you?"

"Everything you desire!" said Otto.

"Do not speak of it!" returned Sophie, and laid her finger on her lips. The mother descended the steps.

"Dear Thostrup!" said she, and pressed, with warm cordiality, both his hands. "I have really quite yearned after you. Now Wilhelm is away, you must for two whole days put up with us alone."

Otto went through the long passage where hung the old portraits; it was as if these also wished welcome. It only seemed a night full of many dreams which had passed since he was here; a year in the lapse of time is also not so long as a winter's night in the life of man.

Here it was so agreeable, so home-like; no one could have seen by the trees that since then they had stood stripped of leaves and covered with snow; luxuriantly green they waved themselves in the sun's warmth, just as when Otto last gazed out of this window.

He had the red room as before. The dinner-bell rang.

Louise met him in the passage.

"Thostrup!" exclaimed she, with delight, and seized his hand. "Now, it is almost a year and a day since I saw you!"

"Yes much has happened in this year!" said the Kammerjunker. "Come soon to me, and you shall see what I have had made for pastime—a bowling-green! Miss Sophie has tried her skill upon it."

The Kammerjunker took the mother to dinner. Otto approached Sophie.

"Will you not take the Kammerjunker's sister?" whispered she.

Mechanically, Otto made his bow before Miss Jakoba.

"Take one of the young ladies!" said she; "you would rather do that?"

Otto bowed, cast a glance toward Sophie; she had the old pastor. Otto smiled, and conducted Jakoba to table.

The Mamsell, renowned through her work-box, sat on his left hand. He observed the company who, beside those we have already mentioned, consisted of several ladies and gentlemen whom he did not know. One chair was empty, but it was soon occupied; a young girl, quiet in her attire, and dressed like Louise, entered.

"Why do you come so late?" asked Sophie, smiling.

"That is only known to Eva and me!" said Louise, and smiled at the young girl.

Eva seated herself. It was, perhaps, the complete resemblance of their dress which induced Otto to observe both her and Louise so closely, and even against his own will to draw comparisons. Both wore a simple dark brown dress, a small sea-green handkerchief round the neck. Louise seemed to him enchanting—pretty one could not call her: Eva, on the contrary, was ideal; there lay something in her appearance which made him think of the pale pink hyacinth. Every human being has his invisible angel, says the mythos; both are different and yet resemble each other. Eva was the angel; Louise, on the contrary, the human being in all its purity. Otto's eyes encountered those of Sophie—they were both directed to the same point. "What power! what beauty!" thought he. Her mind is far above that of Louise, and in beauty she is a gorgeous flower, and not, like Eva, a fine, delicate hyacinth. He drew eloquence from these eyes, and became interesting like the cousin, although he had not been in Paris.

The Kammerjunker spoke of sucking-pigs, but that also was interesting; perhaps be drew his inspiration out of the same source as Otto. He spoke of the power of green buckwheat, and how the swine which eat it become mad. From this doubtless originated the legend of the devil entering into the swine. It is only coal-black pigs which can digest green buckwheat; if they have a single white speck upon them, they become ill at eating. "This is extraordinary," exclaimed he.

In his enthusiasm his discourse became almost a cry, which caused Miss Jakoba to say that one might almost think that he himself had eaten green buckwheat.

Otto meantime cut out of the green melon-peel a man, and made him ride on the edge of his glass; that withdrew Sophie's attention from the Kammerjunker. The whole company found that this little cut-out figure was very pretty; and the Mamsell begged that she might have it—it should lie in her work-box.

Toward evening all were in preparation for the approaching tableaux.

Eva must represent Hero. With a torch in her hand she must kneel on a table, which was to be draped so as to represent a balcony. The poor girl felt quite unhappy at having to appear in this manner. Sophie laughed at her fear, and assured her that she would be admired, and that therefore she must and should.

"Give way to my sister," said Louise, in a beseeching voice; and Eva was ready, let down her long brown hair, and allowed Sophie to arrange the drapery.

Otto must put on an officer's uniform. He presented himself to the sisters.

"That gold is not sewn fast on the collar," said Sophie, and undertook to rectify it. He could easily keep the uniform on whilst she did this, said she. Her soft hand touched Otto's cheek, it was like an electric shock to him; his blood burned; how much he longed to press the hand to his lips!

They all burst out laughing when the Kammerjunker appeared in a white petticoat which only reached a little below the knee, and in a large white lady's dressing-jacket. Miss Sophie must arrange his hair. She did it charmingly; her hand stroked the hair away from his brow, and glided over his cheeks: he kissed it; she struck him in the face, and begged him not to forget himself! "We are ladies," said he, and rose in his full splendor. They all laughed except Otto; he could not—he felt a desire to beat him. The spectators arranged themselves in a dark room, the folding doors were opened.

Eva as Hero, in a white linen robe, her hair hanging down on her shoulders, and a torch in her hand, gazed out over the sea. No painter could have imagined anything more beautiful; the large dark-blue eyes expressed tenderness and melancholy; it was Eva's natural glance, but here you saw her quiet. The fine black eyebrows increased the expression, the whole figure was as if breathed into the picture.

Now followed a new picture—Faust and Margaret in the arbor; behind stood Mephistophiles, with his devilish smile. The Kammerjunker's Mamsell was Margaret. When the doors were opened she sent forth aloud cry, and ran away; she would not stay, she was so afraid. The group was disarranged, people laughed and found it amusing, but the Kammerjunker scolded aloud, and swore that she should come in again; at that the laughter of the spectators increased, and was not lessened when the Kammerjunker, forgetting his costume as the Somnambule, half stepped into the frame in which the pictures were represented, and seated the Mamsell on the bench. This group was only seen for one moment: the doors were again closed; the spectators applauded, but a whistle was heard. Laughter, and the hum of conversation, resounded through the room; and it was impossible to obtain perfect quiet, although a new picture already shone in the frame. It was Sophie as Correggio's "Magdalene": her rich hair fell in waves over her shoulders and round arms; before her lay the skull and the holy book.

Otto's blood flowed faster; never had he seen Sophie more beautiful. The audience, however, could not entirely forget the comic scene which they had just witnessed; there was heard a faint suppressed laughter.

This at length was able to take its free course when the following picture presented itself, where the Kammerjunker, as the Somnambule, his hand half-concealing the extinguished light, showed himself at the open window.

A most stormy burst of applause was awarded to the actors.

"Miss Sophie has arranged the whole!" cried the Kammerjunker, and now her name sounded from the lips of all the audience.

Not before two days did Wilhelm return. He and Otto slept in the same apartment. Otto told of the tableaux, and said how lovely Eva had been as Hero.

"That I can well believe," replied Wilhelm, but did not enter further into the subject; he laughed about the Kammerjunker and the disarranged group.

Otto again named Eva, but Wilhelm lightly passed over this subject in his replies. Otto could not fathom their connection.

"Shall we not go to sleep?" said Wilhelm; they wished each other good-night, and it was quiet.

The old man Sleep, as Tieck has described him, with the box out of which he brings his dream-puppets, now commenced his nightly dramatic adventures, which lasted until the sun shone in through the window.

CHAPTER XXXIII

"He draws nearer and nearer to her.

'O, give my hope an answer by this pink-flower.'

She sighs: 'O, I will—no—I will not.'"

The Dancer, by PALUDAN-MÜLLER

"I shall get to know!" thought Otto. "This violent love cannot be evaporated." He paid attention to every little occurrence. Eva was the same quiet, modest creature as formerly—a house-fairy who exercised a friendly influence over all. Wilhelm spoke with her, but not with passion, neither with affected indifference. However, we cannot entirely rely upon Otto's power of observation: his glance was directed too often toward a dearer object—his attention was really directed to Sophie.

They walked in the garden.

"Once as you certainly know," said Otto, "your brother had a fancy for the pretty Eva. Is it not, therefore, somewhat dangerous her living here? Has your mother been prudent?"

"For Wilhelm I am quite unconcerned!" answered Sophie. "Only take care of yourself! Eva is very amiable, and has very much changed for the better since she came here. My sister Louise quite raves about her, and my mother regards her almost as an adopted daughter. You have certainly remarked that she is not kept in the background. Yet she is weak; she resembles the tender mountain-flowers which grow in ice and snow, but which bow their heads in the soft mountain air, when it is warmed by the sun. It really seems to me that she is become weaker since she has enjoyed our care and happy days. When I saw her at Roeskelde she was far more blooming."

"Perhaps she thinks of your brother—thinks of him with quiet sorrow?"

"That I do not think is the case," replied Sophie; "otherwise Louise would have heard something of it. She possesses Eva's entire confidence. You may make yourself easy, if you are jealous!"

"What make you conjecture this? My thoughts are directed above, and not beneath me!" said he, with a kind of pride, "I feel that I could never fall in love with Eva. Feel love toward her? no! Even when I think of it, I feel almost as though I had some prejudice against her. But you joke; you will rally me, as you have so often done. We shall soon part! Only two months longer shall I remain in Denmark! Two long years abroad! How much may occur in that time! Will you think of me—really think of me, Miss Sophie?" He bent, and kissed her hand.

Sophie became crimson. Both were silent.

"Are you here!" said the mother, who came out of a side walk.

Otto stooped lower, and broke one of the beautiful stocks which hung over the border.

"Are you taking Louise's favorite flowers?" said she, smiling. "This bed is declared to be inviolable."

"I was so unfortunate as to break it!" said Otto, confused.

"He wished to gather the dark-red pink for my table-garland!" said Sophie. "If he took it, my conscience would be clear!"

And they all three walked along speaking of cherries, gooseberries, of the linen on the bleaching-ground, and of the warm summer's day.

In the evening Eva and the two sisters sat at their work, Otto and Wilhelm had taken their seats beside them. They spoke of Copenhagen.

Sophie knew how to introduce a number of little anecdotes, which she had gathered among the young ladies there. Otto entered into her ideas, and knew cleverly how to support what she said. What in reality interested young ladies was discussed.

"When a girl is confirmed, all manner of fancies awake!" said Otto. "She experiences a kind of inclination for the heart of man; but this may not be acknowledged, except for two friends to the clergyman and the physician. For these she has quite a passion, especially for the former; she stands in a kind of spiritual rapport with him. His physical amiability melts into the spiritual. Thus her first love one may designate clergyman-love."

"That is well said!" exclaimed Sophie.

"He preaches himself so deeply into her heart!" pursued Otto. "She melts into tears, kisses his hand, and goes to church; but not for the sake of God, but on account of the sweet clergyman!"

"O, I know that so well!" said Sophie, and laughed.

"Fie! you do not mean so!" said Louise; "and I do not know how you can say such a thing Mr. Thostrup! That is frightful! You do not in the least know a young girl's soul! do not know the pure feeling with which she inclines herself to the man who has laid open before her the holy things of religion! Do not make sport of the innocent, the pure, which is so far removed from every earthly impression!"

"I assure you," said Otto, smiling, "were I a poet, I would make the clergyman-love ridiculous in a hundred witty epigrams; and were I a teacher, I would protest against it from the chair."

"That would be scattering poison into a well!" said Louise. "You, as a man, do not know the pure, the holy sentiment which exists in a young girl's bosom. Eva, thou art certainly of my opinion?"

"Neither is this Mr. Thostrup's opinion?" answered she, and looked at him with a mild gravity.

Wilhelm laughed aloud.

CHAPTER XXXIV

"Alas, I am no sturdy oak!
Alas, I'm but the flower
That wakes the kiss of May!
And when has fled its little hour,
Will voice of Death obey." —RUCKERT.

The following afternoon came visitors—two young ladies from Nyborg, friends of Sophie and Louise. Before dinner they would take a walk through the wood to an inclosure where the flax was in bloom. Otto was to accompany them.

"I am also of the party!" said the Kammerjunker, who just galloped into the court-yard as the ladies, with Otto, were about setting out on their excursion. Thus the whole company consisted of five ladies and two gentlemen.

"The cows are not in the field over which we must go, are they?" asked Eva.

"No, my good girl!" returned Sophie; "you may be quite easy! Besides, we have two gentlemen with us."

"Yes; but they would not be able to protect us from the unruly bullocks!" said Louise. "But we have nothing to fear. Where we are going the cows do not go until after they are milked. I am no heroine! Besides, it is not long since one bullock nearly gored the cowherd to death. He also gored Sidsel a great hole in her arm just lately: you remember the girl with her eyebrows grown together?"

"There is also in the wood a wild sow, with eleven sucking pigs!" said Sophie, in ironical gravity; "it would not be agree able to meet with her!"

"She is almost as dangerous as the bullocks!" said the Kammerjunker, and laughed at Eva.

The conversation took another turn.

"Shall we not visit Peter Cripple?" asked Sophie. "The gentlemen can then see the smith's pretty daughter; she is really too beautiful to be his wife!"

"Is Peter Cripple married?" inquired Otto.

"No, the wedding will be held on Sunday!" replied the Kammerjunker; "but the bride is already in the house. The bans were published last Sunday, and they immediately commenced housekeeping together. This often takes place even earlier, when a man cannot do without a wife. She has taken him on account of his full money-bags!"

"Yes, with the peasant it is seldom love which brings about the affair!" said Louise. "Last year there was quite a young girl who married a man who might have been her grandfather. She took him only, she said, because he had such a good set of earthenware."

"These were very brittle things to marry upon!" remarked Otto.

Meantime they were nearly come to the edge of the wood. Here stood a little house; hops hung luxuriantly over the hedge, the cat stood with bent back upon the crumbling edge of the well.

Sophie, at the head of the whole company, stepped into the room, where Peter Cripple sat on the table sewing; but, light and active as an elf, he sprang down from the table to kiss her hand. The smith's pretty daughter was stirring something in an iron pot in the hearth. St. John's wort, stuck between the beams and the ceiling, shot forth in luxuriant growth, prophesying long life to the inhabitants of the house. On the sooty ceiling glittered herrings' souls, as a certain portion of the herring's entrails is called, and which Peter Cripple, following the popular belief, had flung up to the ceiling, convinced that so long as they hung there he should be freed from the ague.

Otto took no part in the conversation, but turned over a quantity of songs which he found; they were stitched together in a piece of blue tobacco-paper. The principal contents were, "New, Melancholy Songs," "Of the Horrible Murder," "The Audacious Criminal," "The Devil in Salmon Lane," "Boat's Fall," and such things; which have now supplanted, among the peasants, the better old popular songs.

With Louise, Eva, and one of the ladies from Nyborg, Otto slowly preceded the others, who had still some pleasantries to say before leaving Peter Cripple and his bride.

"Shall we not go over the inclosure to the cairn?" said Louise. "It is clear to-day; we shall see Zealand. The others will follow us; here, from the foot-path, they will immediately discover us."

Otto opened the gate and they went through the inclosure. They had already advanced a considerable way, when the Kammerjunker and his ladies reached the foot-path from which they could see the others.

"They are going to the cairn," said he.

"Then they will have a little fright!" said Sophie. "Down in the corner of the inclosure lie the young cattle. They may easily mistake them for cows, and the wild bullocks!"

"Had we not better call them back?" asked the other lady.

"But we must frighten them a little," said Sophie. "Shout to them that there are the cows!"

"Yes, that I can do with a clear conscience!" said the Kammerjunker; and he shouted as loud as he could, "There are the cows! Turn back! turn back!"

Eva heard it the first. "O God!" said she, "hear what they are calling to us!"

Otto glanced around, but saw no cows.

"They are standing still!" said Sophie; "call once again!"

The Kammerjunker shouted as before, and Sophie imitated the lowing of the cows. At this noise the young cattle arose.

Louise now became aware of them. "O heavens!" exclaimed she; "there, down in the corner of the inclosure, are all the cows!"

"Let us run!" cried Eva, and took to flight.

"For God's sake, do not run!" cried Otto; "walk slowly and quietly, otherwise they may come!"

"Come away, away!" resounded from the wood.

"O Lord!" shrieked Eva, when she saw the creatures raise their tails in the air as soon as they perceived the fugitives.

"Now they are coming!" cried the lady who accompanied them, and sent forth a loud scream.

Eva fled first, as if borne by the wind; the lady followed her, and Louise ran on after them.

Otto now really saw all the cattle, which, upon the ladies flight, had instinctively followed, chasing over the field after them in the same direction.

Nothing now remained for him but, like the others, to reach the gate. This he opened, and had just closed again, when the cattle were close upon them, but no one had eyes to see whether the cattle were little or big.

"Now there is no more danger!" cried Otto, as soon as he had well closed the gate; but the ladies still fled on, passing among the trees until they reached the spot where the Kammerjunker and his two ladies awaited them with ringing laughter.

Sophie was obliged to support herself against a tree through all the amusement. It had been a most remarkable spectacle, this flight; Eva at the head, and Mr. Thostrup rushing past them to open the gate. Louise was pale as death, and her whole body trembled; the friend supported her arm and forehead on a tree, and drew a long breath.

"Bah!" again cried Sophie, and laughed.

"But where is Eva?" asked Otto, and shouted her name.

"She ran here before me!" said Louise; "she is doubtless leaning against a tree, and recovering her strength."

"Eva!" cried Sophie. "Where is my hero: 'I want a hero!'" [Author's Note: Byron's Don Juan.]

Otto returned to seek her. At this moment Wilhelm arrived.

The Kammerjunker regretted that he had not seen the race with them, and related the whole history to him.

"O come! come!" they heard Otto shout. They found him kneeling in the high grass. Eva lay stretched out on the ground; she was as pale as death; her head rested in Otto's lap.

"God in heaven!" cried Wilhelm, and flung himself down before her. "Eva! Eva! O, she is dead! and thou art to blame for it, Sophie! Thou hast killed her!" Reproachfully he fixed his eyes on his sister. She burst into tears, and concealed her face in her hands.

Otto ran to the peasant's cottage and brought water. Peter Cripple himself hopped like a mountain-elf behind him through the high nettles and burdocks, which closed above and behind him again.

The Kammerjunker took Eva in his strong arms and carried her to the cottage. Wilhelm did not leave hold of her hand. The others followed in silence.

"Try and get her home," said Wilhelm; "I myself will fetch the physician!" He rushed forth, and hastened through the wood to the ball, where he ordered the men to bring out a sedan-chair for the invalid; then had horses put into one of the lightest carriages, seated himself in it as coachman, and drove away to Nyborg, the nearest town, which, however, was distant almost twenty miles.

Sophie was inconsolable. "It is my fault!" she said, and wept.

Otto found her sitting before the house, under an elder-tree. She could not endure to see Eva's paleness.

"You are innocent," said Otto. "Believe me, to-morrow Eva will be completely restored! She herself," added he, in an assuaging tone, "behaved in an imprudent manner. I warned her not to run. Her own terror is to blame for all."

"No, no," returned Sophie; "my folly, my extravagance, has caused the whole misfortune!"

"Now it is much better," said the Kammerjunker, coming out of the house. "She must be devilish tender to fly before a few calves! I really must laugh when I think of it, although it did come to such an end!"

The men now arrived whom Wilhelm had sent with the sedan-chair.

Eva thought she could walk, if she might lean upon some one; but it would be better, her friends thought, if she were carried.

"Dost thou feel any pain?" asked Louise, and gave her a sisterly kiss on the brow.

"No, none at all," replied Eva. "Do not scold me for having frightened you so. I am so fearful, and the bullock were close behind us."

"They were, God help me, only calves!" answered the Kammerjunker; "they wished to play, and only ran because you ran!"

"It was a foolish joke of mine!" said Sophie, and seized Eva's hand. "I am very unhappy about it!"

"O no!" said Eva, and smiled so pensively, yet happily. "To-morrow I shall be quite well again!" Her eye seemed to seek some one.

Otto understood the glance. "The physician is sent for. Wilhelm has himself driven over for him."

Toward the middle of the wood the mother herself approached them; she was almost as pale as Eva.

All sought to calm her; Eva bowed her head to kiss the good lady's hand. The Kammerjunker told the story to her, and she shook her head. "What an imprudent, foolish joke!" said she; "here you see the consequences!"

Not before late in the afternoon did Wilhelm return with the physician; he found his patient out of all danger, but prescribed what should still be done. Quiet and the warm summer air would do the most for her.

"See," said Otto, when, toward evening he met Sophie in the garden, "to-day Wilhelm did not conceal his feelings!"

"I fear that you are right!" returned Sophie. "He loves Eva, and that is very unfortunate. Tell me what you know about it."

"I know almost nothing!" said Otto, and told about little Jonas and the first meeting with Eva.

"Yes, that he has told us already himself! But do you know nothing more?" Her voice became soft, and her eyes gazed full of confidence into Otto's.

He related to her the short conversation which he had had last autumn with Wilhelm, how angry he had been with his candid warning, and how since then they had never spoken about Eva.

"I must confide my fear to our mother!" said Sophie. "I almost now am glad that he will travel in two months, although we shall then lose you also!"

And Otto's heart beat; the secret of his heart pressed to his lips; every moment he would speak it. But Sophie had always still another question about her brother; they were already out of the garden, already in the court-yard, and yet Otto had said nothing.

Therefore was he so quiet when, late in the evening, he and Wilhelm entered their chamber. Wilhelm also spoke no word, but his eye repeatedly rested expectantly on Otto, as if waiting for him to break the silence. Wilhelm stepped to the open window and drank in the fresh air, suddenly he turned round, flung his arms round Otto, and exclaimed, "I can no longer endure it! I must say it to some one! I love her, and will never give her up, let every one be opposed! I have now silently concealed my feelings for some months; I can do so no longer, or I shall become ill, and for that I am not made!"

"Does she know this?" asked Otto.

"No, and yes! I do not know what I should answer! Here at home I have never spoken alone with her. The last time when Weyse played on the organ at Roeskelde I had bought a pretty silk handkerchief, and this I took with me for her; I know not, but I wished to give her pleasure. There came a woman past with lovely stocks; I stood at the open window; she offered me a bouquet, and I bought it. 'Those are lovely flowers!' said Eva, when she entered. 'They will fade with me!' said I; 'put them in water and keep there for yourself!' She wished only to have a few, but I obliged her to take them all: she blushed, and her eyes gazed strangely down into my soul. I know not what sort of a creature I became, but it was impossible for me to give her the handkerchief; it seemed to me that this would almost be an offense. Eva went away with the flowers, but the next morning it seemed to me that she was uneasy; I fancied I saw her color come and go when I bade her adieu! She must have read the thoughts in my soul!"

"And the handkerchief?" interrupted Otto.

"I gave it to my sister Sophie," said Wilhelm.

CHAPTER XXXV

"Tell me
What would my heart?
My heart's with thee,
With thee would have a part."
GOETHE'S *West-östlicher Divan.*

"There stands the man again—
The man with gloomy mien."
Memories of Travel, by B. C. INGEMANN.

Several days passed; the fine crimson again returned to Eva's cheeks. The first occasion of her going out with the others was to see the rape-stalks burned. These were piled together in two immense stacks. In the morning, at the appointed hour, which had been announced through the neighborhood that no one might mistake it for a conflagration, the stalks were set fire to. This took place in the nearest field, close beside the hall, where the rape-seed was threshed upon an out-spread sail.

The landscape-painter, Dahl, has given us a picture of the burning Vesuvius, where the red lava pours down the side of the mountain; in the background one sees across the bay as far as Naples and Ischia: it is a piece full of great effect. Such a splendid landscape is not to be found in flat Denmark, where there are no great natural scenes, and yet this morning presented even there a picture with the same brilliant coloring. We will study it. In the foreground there is a hedge of hazels, the nuts hang in great clusters, and contrast strongly with their bright green against the dark leaves; the blue chicory-flower and the blood-red poppy grew on the side of the ditch, upon which are some tall rails, over which the ladies have to climb: the delicate sylph-like figure is Eva. In the field, where nothing remains but the yellow stubble, stand Otto and Wilhelm; two magnificent hounds wag their tails beside them. To the left is a little lake, thickly overgrown with reeds and water-lilies, with the yellow trollius for its border. In the front, where the wood retreats, lie, like a great stack, the piled-together rape-stalks: the man has struck fire, has kindled the outer side of them, and with a rapidity like that of the descending lava the red fire flashes up the gigantic pile. It crackles and roars within it. In a moment it is all a burning mound; the red flames flash aloft into the blue air, high above the wood which is now no longer visible. A thick black smoke ascends up into the clear air, where it rests like a cloud. Out of the flames, and even out of the smoke, the wind carries away large masses of fire, which, crackling and cracking, are borne on to the wood, and which fill the spectator with apprehension of their falling upon the nearest trees and burning up leaf and branch.

"Let us go further off," said Sophie; "the heat is too great here."

They withdrew to the ditch.

"O, how many nuts!" exclaimed Wilhelm; "and I do not get one of them! I shall go after them if they be ripe."

"But you have grapes and other beautiful fruit!" said Eva smiling. "We have our beautiful things at home!"

"Yes, it is beautiful, very beautiful at home!" exclaimed Wilhelm; "glorious flowers, wild nuts; and there we have Vesuvius before us!" He pointed to the burning pile.

"No," said Sophie; "it seems to me much more like the pile upon which the Hindoo widow lays herself alive to be burned! That must be horrible!"

"One should certainly be very quickly dead!" said Eva.

"Would you actually allow yourself to be burned to death, if you were a Hindoo widow—after, for instance, Mr. Thostrup, or after Wilhelm," said she, with a slight embarrassment, "if he lay dead in the fire?"

"If it were the custom of the country, and I really had lost the only support which I had in the world—yes, so I would!"

"O, no, no!" said Louise.

"In fact it is brilliant!" exclaimed Sophie.

"Burning is not, perhaps, the most painful of deaths!" said Otto, and plucked in an absent manner the nuts from the hedge. "I know a story about a true conflagration."

"What is it like?" asked Wilhelm.

"Yet it is not a story to tell in a large company; it can only be heard when two and two are together. When I have an opportunity, I shall tell it!"

"O, I know it!" said Wilhelm. "You can relate it to one of my sisters there, whichever you like best! Then I shall—yes, I must relate it to Eva!"

"It is too early in the day to hear stories told!" said Louise; "let us rather sing a song!"

"No, then we shall have to weep in the evening," replied Wilhelm. And they had neither the song nor the story.

Mamma came wandering with Vasserine, the old, faithful hound: they two also wished to see how beautiful the burning looked. It succeeded excellently with the rape-stalks; but the other burning, of which the story was to be told, it did not yet arrive at an outbreak! It might be expected, however, any hour in the day.

In the evening Otto walked alone through the great chestnut avenue. The moon shone brightly between the tree-branches. When he entered the interior court Wilhelm and Sophie skipped toward him, but softly, very softly. They lifted their hands as if to impress silence.

"Come and see!" said Sophie; "it is a scene which might be painted! it goes on merrily in the servants' hall; one can see charmingly through the window!"

"Yes, come!" said Wilhelm.

Otto stole softly forward. The lights shone forth.

Within there was laughter and loud talking; one struck upon the table, another sung,—

"And I will away to Prussia land,
Hurrah!
And when I am come to Prussia land,
Hurrah!" [Note: People's song.]

Otto looked in through the window.

Several men and maids sat within at the long wooden table at the end of this stood Sidsel in a bent attitude, her countenance was of a deep crimson; she spoke a loud oath and laughed—no one imagined that they were observed. All eyes were riveted upon a great fellow who, with his shirt-sleeves rolled up, and a pewter tankard in his hand, was standing there. It was the German Heinrich, who was exhibiting to them his conjuring tricks. Otto turned pale; had the dead arisen from the bier before him it could not have shocked him more.

"Hocus-pocus Larifari!" cried Heinrich within, and gave the tankard to a half-grown fellow, of the age between boy and man.

"If thou hast already a sweetheart," said he; "then the corn which is within it will be turned to flour; but if thou art still only a young cuckoo, then it will remain only groats."

"Nay, Anders Peersen!" said all the girls laughing, "now we shall see whether thou art a regular fellow!"

Sophie stole away.

The echoing laughter and clapping of hands announced the result.

"Is it not the same person who was playing conjuring tricks in the park?" inquired Wilhelm.

"Yes, certainly," replied Otto; "he is to me quite repulsive!" And so saying, he followed Sophie.

Late in the evening, when all had betaken themselves to rest, Wilhelm proposed to Otto that they should make a little tour, as he called it.

"I fancy Meg Merrilies, as my sister calls Sidsel," said he, "has made a conquest of the conjuror, although he might be her father. They have been walking together down the avenue; they have been whispering a deal together; probably he will to-night sleep in one of the barns. I must go and look after him; he will be lying there and smoking his pipe, and may set our whole place on fire. Shall we go down together? We can take Vasserine and Fingel with us."

"Let him sleep!" said Otto; "he will not be so mad as to smoke tobacco in the straw! To speak candidly, I do not wish to be seen by him. He was several times at my grandfather's house. I have spoken with him, and now that I dislike him I do not wish to see him!"

"Then I will go alone!" said Wilhelm.

Otto's heart beat violently; he stood at the open window and looked out over the dark wood, which was lit up by the moon. Below in the court he heard Wilhelm enticing the dogs out. He heard yet another voice, it was that of the steward, and then all was again silent. Otto thought upon the German Heinrich and upon Sophie, his life's good and bad angels; and he pictured to himself how it would be if she extended to him her hand—was his bride! and Heinrich called forth before her the recollections which made his blood curdle.

It seemed to him as if something evil impended over him this night. "I feel a forewarning of it!" said he aloud.

Wilhelm came not yet back.

Almost an hour passed thus. Wilhelm entered, both dogs were with him; they were miry to their very sides.

"Did you meet any one?" inquired Otto.

"Yes, there was some one," said Wilhelm, "but not in the barn. The stupid dogs seemed to lose their nature; it was as if there was a somebody stealing along the wall, and through the reeds in the moat. The hounds followed in there; you can see how they look!—but they came the next moment back again, whined, and hung down their ears and tails. I could not make them go in again. Then the steward was superstitious! But, however, it could only be either the juggler, or one of the servant-men who had stilts. How otherwise any one could go in among the reeds without getting up to their necks, I cannot conceive!"

All was again perfectly still without. The two friends went to the open window, threw their arms over each other's shoulders, and looked out into the silent night.

CHAPTER XXXVI

"Bring' häusliche Hülfe

Incubus! incubus.

Tritt herhor und mache den Schluss."

GOETHE's Faust.

"Es giebt so bange Zeiten,

Es giebt so trüben Muth!" —NOVALIS.

The next morning Wilhelm related his evening adventure at the breakfast-table; the sisters laughed at it. The mother, on the contrary, was silent, left the room, and after some time returned.

"There have been thieves here!" said she, "and one might almost imagine that they were persons in the household itself. They have been at the press where the table-linen is kept, and have not been sparing in their levies. The beautiful old silver tankard, which I inherited from my grandmother, is also missing. I would much sooner have given the value of the silver than have lost that piece!"

"Will not the lady let it be tried by the sieve?" asked the old servant: "that is a pretty sure way!"

"That is nothing but superstition," answered she; "in that way the innocent may so easily be suspected."

"As the lady pleases!" said the servant, and shook his head.

In the mean time a search through the house was instituted. The boxes of the domestics were examined, but nothing was discovered.

"If you would only let the sieve be tried!" said the old servant.

In the afternoon Otto went into the garden; he fell into discourse with the gardener, and they spoke of the theft which had occurred.

"It vexes every one of us," said he, "because we think much of the lady, and of the whole family. And some one must, nevertheless, be suspected. We believe that it was Sidsel, for she was a good-for-nothing person! We folks tried among ourselves with the sieve, but however, at the mention of her name, if it did not move out of its place. We had set it upon the point of a knife, and mentioned the name of every person about the place, but it stood as if it were nailed quite fast. But there was really something to see, which not one of us would have believed. I'll say no more about it, although we had every one of us our own thoughts. I would have taken my oath of it."

Otto pressed him to mention the person who was suspected.

"Yes, to you perhaps, I may mention it," replied he; "but you will not say anything about it? As we were standing today, at noon, around the sieve, and it did not move at Sidsel's name, she became angry, because a word bad been let fall which could not be agreeable to her if she were innocent. She drew herself up as if in a passion, and said to us, 'But there are also in the hall a many people besides us, who may slip and slide! There are strangers here, and the fine Mamsell, and the farmers. Yes, I suspect no one, but every one ought to be named!'

"And so we did it. Yes, we mentioned even your name, Mr. Thostrup, although we knew very well that you were guiltless of the charge; but we would not excuse any one. The sieve stood quite entirely still until we mentioned Eva's name, and then it moved. Not one of us actually could believe it, and the servant Peter said also that it was because of the draught from the chimney. We mentioned yet once more all the names, and the sieve stood still until we came to Eva's, and then we perceived very plainly a movement. The servant Peter at the same moment gave a great blow to the sieve, so that it fell to the ground, and he swore that it was a lie, and that he would answer for Eva. I would have done so too; but yet it was very extraordinary with the sieve! Most of the folks, however, have their own thoughts, but no one venture to express them to the gentry who think so much of her. I cannot, however, rightly reconcile it to myself!"

"She is innocent!" said Otto; and it amazed him that any one should cast the slightest suspicion on Eva. He thought of German Heinrich and Sidsel, who alone appeared to him suspicious. There then occurred to him an experiment of which he had heard from Rosalie. It now seemed to him available, and, physiologically considered, much more certain than that with the sieve.

"Probably it may lead to a discovery," said he, after he had communicated his whole plan to Sophie and the steward.

"Yes, we mast try it!" said she; "it is excellent! I also will be put to the proof, although I am initiated into the mystery."

"Yes, you, your sister, Wilhelm, Eva, we all of us must," said Otto. "Only I will not do the speaking: that the steward must do."

"That is proper, very proper!" replied she: "it shall be tried this evening when it is dark."

The time came; the steward assembled the people.

"Now I know," said he, "how we shall find the thief!"

All were to remain in the first room: within a side-room, which was quite dark, there stood in a corner on the right hand a copper kettle; to this every person as they came in, one by one, were to go and lay their hand down on the flat bottom of the kettle. The hand of every one who was innocent would be brought out again white and pure, but the hand of the criminal would be severely burned, and would become black as a coal.

"He who now," said the steward, addressing them, "has a good conscience, may go with this and our Lord into the innermost room, lay his hand upon the bottom of the kettle, and show it to me. Now I go to receive you all!"

The daughters went, the friends, Eva, and all the household. The steward questioned them as they came in: "Answer me, upon thy conscience, did thy hand touch the flat bottom of the kettle?"

All replied, "Yes!"

"Then show me your hand!" said he; and they showed them, and all were black: Sidsel's alone was white.

"Thou art the thief!" said the steward. "Thy evil conscience has condemned thee. Thou hast not touched the kettle; hast not laid thy hand upon it, or it would have become as black as that of the others. The kettle was blackened inside with turpentine smoke; they who came with a good conscience, knowing that their hands would remain pure like their consciences, touched the kettle fearlessly and their hands became black! Thou hast condemned thyself! Confess, or it will go worse with thee!"

Sidsel, uttered a horrible cry and fell down upon her knees.

"O God, help me!" said she, and confessed that she was the thief.

A chamber high up in the roof was prepared as a prison; here the delinquent was secured until the affair, on the following day, should be announced to the magistrate.

"Thou shalt be sent to Odense, and work upon the treadmill!" said Wilhelm: "to that thou belongest!"

The family assembled at the tea-table. Sophie joked about the day's adventure.

"Poor Sidsel!" said Eva.

"In England she would be hanged," said Wilhelm; "that would be a fine thing to see!"

"Horrible!" replied Louise; "they must die of terror in going to the gallows."

"Nay, it is very merry," said Wilhelm. "Now you shall hear what glorious music has been set to it by Rossini!" And he played the march from "Gazza Ladra," where a young girl is led to the gallows.

"Is it not merry?" asked he. "Yes, he is a composer!"

"To me it seems precisely characteristic," answered Otto. "They are not the feelings of the girl which the composer wished to express; it is the joy of the rude rabble in witnessing an execution—to them a charming spectacle, which is expressed in these joyous tones: it is a tragic opera, and therefore he chose exactly this character of expression!"

"It is difficult to say anything against that," replied Wilhelm; "yet what you assert I have not heard from any other person."

"When a soldier is executed they play some lively air," said Otto; "the contrast in this case brings forth the strongest effect!"

The servant now entered, and said with a smile that Peter Cripple, the "new-married man," as he called him, was without and wished to speak to the Baron Wilhelm.

"It is about a waltz," said he, "which the Baron had promised to him!"

"It is late for him to come into the court!" said Sophie "the peasants generally go to bed with the sun."

In the lobby stood the announced Peter in his stocking-feet, with his hat in one hand and a great stick in the other. He knew, he said, that it was still daytime with the gentlefolks; he was just coming past the hall and thought that he could, perhaps, have that Copenhagen Waltz which the Baron had promised him: he should want it to-morrow night to play at a wedding, and, therefore, he wished to have it now that he might practice it first of all.

Sophie inquired after his young wife, and said something merry. Louise gave him a cup of tea, which he drank in the lobby. Otto looked at him through the open door; he made comical grimaces, and looked almost as if he wished to speak with him. Otto approached him, and Peter thrust a piece of paper into his hand, making at the same time a significant gesture indicative of silence.

Otto stepped aside and examined the dirty piece of paper, which was folded together like a powder and sealed with a lump of wax. On the outside stood, in scarcely legible characters,

"*TotH' WeL-borne,*

Mr. Odto Tustraab."

He endeavored, in the first place, to read it in the moonlight; but that was scarcely possible.

After considerable labor he made out the meaning of this letter, written, as it was in a half-German, half-Danish gibberish, of the orthography of which we have given a specimen in the direction. The letter was from the German Heinrich. He besought Otto to meet him this evening in the wood near Peter Cripple's house, and he would give to him an explanation which should be worth the trouble of the walk. It would occasion, he said, much trouble and much misery to Mr Thostrup if he did not go.

A strange anxiety penetrated Otto. How could he steal away without being missed? and yet go he both must and should. An extraordinary anxiety drove him forth.

"Yes, the sooner the better!" said he, hastening down the steps and leaping in haste over the low garden-fence lest the gate should, perhaps, make a noise. He was very soon in the wood: he heard the beating of his own heart.

"Eternal Father!" said he, "strengthen my soul! Release me from this anxiety which overpowers me! Let all be for the best!"

He had now reached Peter Cripple's house. A figure leaned against the wall; Otto paused, measured it with his eye to ascertain who it was, and recognized German Heinrich.

"What do you want with me?" inquired Otto.

Heinrich raised his hand in token of silence, beckoned him forward, and opened a little gate which led to the back of the house. Otto mechanically followed him.

"It goes on badly at the hall," said Heinrich. "Sidsel is really put in prison, and will be taken to-morrow to Odense, to the red house by the river."

"It is what she has deserved!" said Otto. "I did not bring it about."

"O no!" answered Heinrich; "in a certain way we bring nothing about; but you can put in a good word for her. You must see that this punishment does not befall her."

"But the punishment is merited!" replied Otto; "and how can I mix myself up in the affair? What is it that you have to say to me?"

"Yet, the good gentleman must not get angry!" began Heinrich again; "but I am grieved about the girl. I can very well believe that he does not know her, and therefore it gives him no trouble; but if I were now to whisper a little word in his ear? She is your own sister, Mr. Thostrup!"

All grew dark before Otto's eyes; a chill as of death went through his blood; his hands held firmly by the cold wall, or he must have sunk to the earth; not a sound escaped his lips.

German Heinrich laid his hand in a confidential manner upon his shoulder, and continued in a jeering, agitated tone, "Yes, it is hard for you to hear! I also struggled a long time with myself before I could make up my mind to tell you. But a little trouble is preferable to a great one. I had some talk with her yesterday, but I did not mention you, although it seemed queer to me at my heart that the brother should sit at the first table with the young ladies, and the sister be farm swine-maiden. Now they have put her in prison! I am very sorry for her and you too, Mr. Thostrup, for it is disagreeable! If the magistrate come to-morrow morning, and she fall into the claws of the red angel, it will not be so easy to set her at liberty again! But yet you could, perhaps, help her; as, for instance, to-night! I could make an opportunity—I would be in the great avenue beyond the hall. If she could get thus far she would be safe; I would then conduct her out of this part of the country. I may as well tell you that we were yesterday half-betrothed! She goes with me; and you can persuade the gracious lady at the hall to let the bird fly!"

"But how can I? how can I?" exclaimed Otto.

"She is, however, always your sister!" said Heinrich, and they both remained silent for a moment. "Then I will," said Heinrich, "if all be still at the hall, wait in the avenue as the bell goes twelve."

"I must!" exclaimed Otto; "I must! God help me!"

"Jesu, Maria, help!" said Heinrich, and Otto left him.

"She is my sister! she, the most horrible of all!" sighed he; his knees trembled, and he leaned against a tree for support: his countenance was like that of the dead; cold sweat-drops stood upon his brow. All around him lay the dark night-like wood; only to the left glimmered, between the bushes, the moonlight reflected from the lake.

"Within its depths," sighed he, "all would be forgotten—my grief would be over! Yet, what is my sin? Had I an existence before I was born upon this globe? Must I here be punished for sins which I then committed?"

His dark eye stared lifelessly out of his pale countenance. Thus sit the dead upon their graves in the silent night; thus gazes the somnambulist upon the living world around him.

"I have felt this moment before—this moment which now is here; it was the well-spring whence poison was poured over my youthful days! She is my sister! She? unhappy one that I am!"

Tears streamed from his eyes, it was a convulsive weeping; he cried aloud, it was impossible to him to suppress his voice; he sank half down by the tree and wept, for it was night in his soul: silent, bitter tears flowed, as the blood flows when the heart is transpierced. Who could breathe to him consolation? There lay no balsam in the gentle airs of the clear summer night, in the fragrance of the wood, in the holy, silent spirit of nature. Poor Otto!

"*Weep, only weep! it gives repose,*
A world is every tear that flows,—
A world of anguish and unrest,
That rolleth from the troubled breast.

"*And hast thou wept whilst tears can flow,*
A tranquil peace thy heart will know;
For sorrow, trivial or severe,
Hath had its seat in every tear.

"*Think'st thou that He, whose love beholds*
The worm the smallest leaf enfolds,—
That He, whose power sustains the whole
Forgets a world—thy human soul?"

CHAPTER XXXVII

"Mourir! c'est un instant de supplice: mais vivre?"
—*FRÉDÉRIC SOULIE.*

The physician from Nyborg, who had been on a visit to a sick person in the neighborhood, took this opportunity of calling on the family and inquiring after Eva's health. They had prayed him to stay over the night there, and rather to drive hone in the early morning than so late in the evening. He allowed himself to be persuaded. Otto, on his return, found him and the family in deep conversation. They were talking of the "Letters of a Wandering Ghost."

"Where have you been?" asked Sophie, as Otto entered.

"You look so pale!" said Louise; "are you ill?"

"I do not feel well!" replied Otto; "I went therefore down into the garden a little. Now I am perfectly recovered." And he took part in the conversation.

The overwhelming sorrow had dissolved itself in tears. His mind had raised itself up again from its stupefaction, and sought for a point of light on which to attach itself. They were talking of the immense caves of Maastricht, how they stretch themselves out into deep passages and vast squares, in which sound is lost, and where the light, which cannot reach the nearest object, only glimmers like a point of fire. In order to comprehend this vacuity and this darkness, the travellers let the guide extinguish his torch, and all is night; they are penetrated, as it were, with darkness; the hand feels after a wall, in order to have some restraint, some thought on which to repose itself: the eye sees nothing; the ear hears nothing. Horror seizes on the strongest mind: the same darkness, the same desolate emotion, had Heinrich's words breathed into Otto's soul; therefore he sank like the traveller to the earth: but as the traveller's whole soul rivets itself by the eye upon the first spark which glimmers, to kindle again the torch which is to lead him forth from this grave, so did Otto attach himself to the first awakening thought of help. "Wilhelm? his soul is noble and good, him will I initiate into my painful secret, which chance had once almost revealed to him."

But this was again extinguished, as the first spark is extinguished which the steel gives birth to. He could not confide himself to Wilhelm;

the understanding which this very confidence would give birth to between them, must separate them from each other. It was humiliating, it was annihilating. But for Sophie? No, how could he, after that, declare the love of his heart? how far below her should he be placed, as the child of poverty and shame! But the mother of the family? Yes, she was gentle and kind; with a maternal sentiment she extended to him her hand, and looked upon him as on a near relation. His thoughts raised themselves on high, his hands folded themselves to prayer; "The will of the Lord alone be done!" trembled involuntarily from his lips. Courage returned refreshingly to his heart. The help of man was like the spark which was soon extinguished; God was an eternal torch, which illumined the darkness and could guide him through it.

"Almighty God! thou alone canst and willest!" said he; "to thou who knowest the heart, do thou alone help and lead me!"

This determination was firmly taken; to no human being would he confide himself; alone would he release the prisoner, and give her up to Heinrich. He thought upon the future, and yet darker and heavier than hitherto it stood before him. But he who confides in God can never despair the only thing that was now to be done was to obtain the key of the chamber where Sidsel was confined, and then when all in the house were asleep he would dare that which must be done.

Courage and tranquillity return into every powerful soul when it once sees the possibility of accomplishing its work. With a constrained vivacity Otto mingled in the conversation, no one imagining what a struggle his soul had passed through.

The disputation continued. Wilhelm was in one of his eloquent moods. The doctor regarded the "Letters of the Wandering Ghost" as one of the most perfect books in the Danish literature. Once Sophie had been of the same opinion, now she preferred Cooper's novels to this and all other books.

"People so easily forget the good for the new," said Wilhelm; "if the new is only somewhat astonishing, the many regard the author as the first of writers. The nation is, aesthetically considered, now in its period of development. Every really cultivated person, who stands among the best spirits of his age, obtains, whilst he observes his own advance in the intellectual kingdom, clearness with regard to the development of his nation. This has, like himself, its distinct periods; in him some important event in life, in it some agitating world convulsion, may advance them suddenly a great leap forward. The public favor is unsteady; to-day it strews palm-branches, to-morrow it cries, 'Crucify him!' But I regard that as a moment of development. You will permit me to make use of an image to elucidate my idea. The botanist goes wandering through field and wood, he collects flowers and plants; every one of these had, while he gathered it, his entire interest, his whole thought—but the impression which it made faded before that of its successor: nor is it till after a longer time that he is able to enjoy the whole of his treasures, and arrange them according to their worth and their rareness. The public seizes alike upon flowers and herbs; we hear its assiduous occupation with the object of the moment, but it is not yet come into possession of the whole. At one time, that which was sentimental was the foremost in favor, and that poet was called the greatest who best knew how to touch this string; then it passed over to the peppered style of writing, and nothing pleased but histories of knights and robbers. Now people find pleasure in prosaic life, and Schröder and Iffland are the acknowledged idols. For us the strength of the North opened heroes and gods, a new and significant scene. Then tragedy stood uppermost with us. Latterly we have begun to feel that this is not the flesh and blood of the present times. Then the fluttering little bird, the vaudeville, came out to us from the dark wood, and enticed us into our own chambers, where all is warm and comfortable, where one has leave to laugh, and to laugh is now a necessity for the Danes. One must not, like the crowd, inconsiderately place that as foremost which swims upon the waters, but treasure the good of every time, and arrange them side by side, as the botanist arranges his plants. Every people must, under the poetical sunshine, have their sentimental period, their berserker rage, their enjoyment of domestic life, and their giddy flights beyond it; it must merge itself in individuality before it can embrace the beauty of the whole. It is unfortunate for the poet who believes himself to be the wheel of his age; and yet he, with his whole crowd of admirers, is, as Menzel says, only a single wheel in the great machine—a little link in the infinite chain of beauty."

"You speak like a Plato!" said Sophie.

"If we could accord as well in music as we do in poetry," said Otto, "then we should be entirely united in our estimation of the arts. I love that music best which goes through the ear to the heart, and carries me away with it; on the contrary, if it is to be admired by the understanding, it is foreign to me."

"Yes, that is your false estimation of the subject, dear friend!" said Wilhelm: "in aesthetics you come at once to the pure and true; but in music you are far away in the outer court, where the crowd is dancing, with cymbals and trumpets, around the musical golden calf!"

And now the aesthetic unity brought them into a musical disunity. On such occasions, Otto was not one to be driven back from his position; he very well knew how to bear down his assailant by striking and original observations: but Otto, this evening, although he was animated enough—excited, one might almost say—did not exhibit the calmness, the decision in his thoughts and words, which otherwise would have given him the victory.

It was a long hour, and one yet longer and more full of anxiety, which commenced with supper. The conversation turned to the events of the day. Otto mingled in it, and endeavored therefrom to derive advantage; it was a martyrdom of the soul. Sophie praised highly his discovery.

"If Mr. Thostrup had not been here," said she, "then we should hardly have discovered the thief. We must thank Mr. Thostrup for it, and really for a merry, amusing spectacle."

They joked about it alai laughed, and Otto was obliged to laugh also.

"And now she sits up there, like a captive, in the roof!" said he; "it must be an uncomfortable night to her!"

"Oh, she sleeps, perhaps, better than some of us others!" said Wilhelm: "that will not annoy her!"

"She is confined in the gable chamber, out in the court, is she not?" inquired Otto: "there she has not any moonlight."

"Yes, surely she has!" answered Sophie; "it is in the gable to the right, hooking toward the wood, that she is confined. We have placed her as near to the moon as we could. The gable on the uppermost floor is our keep."

"But is it securely locked?" inquired Otto.

"There is a padlock and a great bar outside the door; those she cannot force, and no one about the place will do such a piece of service for her. They dislike her, every one of them."

They rose up from the table; the bell was just on the stroke of eleven.

"But the Baron must play us a little piece!" said the physician.

"Then Mr. Thostrup will sing us the pretty Jutlandish song by Steen-Blicher!" exclaimed Louise.

"O yes!" said the mother, and clapped Otto on the shoulder.

Wilhelm played.

"Do sing!" said Wilhelm; all besought him to do so, and Otto sang the Jutlandish song for them.

"See, you sang that with the proper humor," said Sophie, and clapped her hands in applause. With that all arose, offered to him their hands, and Wilhelm whispered to him, yet so that the sisters heard it, "This evening you have been right amiable!"

Otto and Wilhelm went to their sleeping-room.

"But, my good friend," said Wilhelm, "what did you really go into the garden for? Be so good as to confess to me: you were not unwell! You did not go only into the garden! you went into the wood, and you remained a long time there! I saw it! You made a little visit to the handsome woman while the fiddler was here, did you not? I do not trust you so entirely!"

"You are joking!" answered Otto.

"Yes, yes," continued Wilhelm, "she is a pretty little woman. Do you not remember how, last year at the mowing-feast, I threw roses at her? Now she is Peter Cripple's wife. When she comes with her husband then we have, bodily, 'Beauty and the Beast.'"

That which Otto desired was, that Wilhelm should now soon go to sleep, and, therefore, he would not contradict him; he confessed even that the young wife was handsome, but added that she, as Peter Cripple's wife, was to him like a beautiful flower upon which a toad had set itself,—it would be disgusting to him to press the flower to his lips.

The friends were soon in bed. They bade each other good night, and seemed both of them to sleep; and with Wilhelm this was the case.

Otto lay awake; his pulse throbbed violently.

Now the great hall clock struck twelve. All was still, quite still; but Otto did not yet dare to raise himself. It struck a quarter past the hour. He raised himself slowly, and glanced toward the bed where Wilhelm lay. Otto arose and dressed himself, suppressing the while his very breathing. A hunting-knife which hung upon the wall, and which belonged to Wilhelm, he put in his pocket; and lifted up, to take with him, the fire-tongs, with which he intended to break the iron staple that held the padlock. Yet once more he looked toward Wilhelm, who slept soundly. He opened the door, and went out without his shoes.

He looked out from the passage-windows to see if lights were visible from any part of the building. All was still; all was in repose. That which he now feared most was, that one of the dogs might be lying in the lobby, and should begin to bark. But there was not one. He mounted up the steps, and went into the upper story.

Only once before had he been there; now all was in darkness. He felt with his hands before him as he went.

At length he found a narrow flight of stairs which led into a yet higher story. The opening at the top was closed, and he was obliged to use his whole strength to open it. At length it gave way with a loud noise. This was not the proper entrance; that lay on the opposite side of the story, and had he gone there he would have found it open, whereas this one had not been opened for a long time.

The violent efforts which he had made caused him great pain, both in his neck and shoulders; but he was now at the very top of the building, close before the door he sought, and the moonlight shone in through the opening in the roof.

By the help of the hunting-knife and the fire-tongs he succeeded in forcing the door, and that without any very considerable noise. He looked into a small, low room, upon the floor of which some dirty coverlets were thrown.

Sidsel slept deeply and soundly with open mouth. A thick mass of hair escaped from beneath her cap, upon her brow; the moonlight fell, through the window-pane in the roof, upon her face. Otto bowed himself over her and examined the coarse, unpleasing features. The thick, black eyebrows appeared only like one irregular streak.

"She is my sister!" was the thought which penetrated him. "She lay upon the same bosom that I did! The blood in these limbs has kinship with that in mine! She was the repelled one, the rejected one!"

He trembled with pain and anguish; but it was only for a short time.

"Stand up!" cried he, and touched the sleeper.

"Ih, jane dou! [Author's Note: An exclamation among the common people of Funen, expressive of terror.] what is it?" cried she, half terrified, and fixed her unpleasant eyes wildly upon him.

"Come with me!" said Otto, and his voice trembled as he spoke. "German Heinrich waits in the avenue! I will help you out! Hence; to-morrow it will be too late!"

"What do you say?" asked she, and still looked at him with a bewildered mien.

Otto repeated his words.

"Do you think that I can get away?" asked she, and seized him by the arm, as she hastily sprang up.

"Only silently and circumspectly!" said Otto.

"I should not have expected theft from you!" said she. "But tell me why you do it?"

Otto trembled; it was impossible for him to tell her his reasons, or to express the word,—"Thou art my sister!"

His lips were silent.

"To many a fellow," said she, "have I been kinder than I ought to have been, but see whether any of them think about Sidsel! And you do it! You who are so fine and so genteel!"

Otto pressed together his eyelids; he heard her speak; an animal coarseness mingled itself with a sort of confidential manner which was annihilating to him.

"She is my sister!" resounded in his soul.

"Come now! come now!" and, descending the steps, she followed after him.

"I know a better way!" said she, as they came to the lowest story. She seized his arm and they again descended a flight of steps.

Suddenly a door opened itself, and Louise, still dressed, stepped forth with a light. She uttered a faint cry, and her eye riveted itself upon the two forms before her.

But still more terribly and more powerfully did this encounter operate upon Otto. His feet seemed to fail him, and, for a moment, every object moved before his eyes in bright colors. It was the moment of his severest suffering. He sprang forth toward Louise, seized her hand, and, pale as death, with lifeless, staring eyes, half kneeling, besought of her, with an agitated voice:—

"For God's sake, tell no one of that which you have seen! I am compelled to serve her—she is my sister! If you betray my secret I am lost to this world—I must die! It was not until this evening that I knew this to be the case! I will tell you all, but do not betray me! And do you prevent tomorrow any pursuit after her! O Louise! by the happiness of your own soul feel for the misery of mine! I shall destroy myself if you betray me!"

"O God!" stammered Louise. "I will do all—all! I will be silent! Conduct her hence, quick, that you may meet with no one!"

She seized Otto's hand; he sank upon his knee before her, and looked like a marble image which expressed manly beauty and sorrow.

Louise bent herself with sisterly affection over him; tears flowed down her cheeks; her voice trembled, but it was tranquillizing, like the consolation of a good angel. With a glance full of confidence in her, Otto tore himself away. Sidsel followed him and said not a word.

He led her to the lowest story and opened for her, silently, a window, through which she could descend to the garden, and thence easily reach the avenue where German Heinrich waited for her. To have accompanied her any further was unnecessary; it would have been venturing too much without any adequate cause. She stood now upon the window-sill—Otto put a little money into her hand.

"The Lord is above us!" said he, in a solemn voice. "Never forget Him and endeavor to amend your life! All may yet be well!" He involuntarily pressed her hand in his. "Have God always in your thoughts!" said he.

"I shall get safely away, however," said she, and descended into the garden; she nodded, and vanished behind the hedge.

Otto stood for a while and listened whether any noise was heard, or whether any dog barked. He feared for her safety. All was still.

Just as sometimes an old melody will suddenly awake in our remembrance and sound in our ear, so awoke now a holy text to his thoughts. "Lord, if I should take the wings of the morning, and should fly to the uttermost parts of the sea, thither thou wouldst lead me, and thy right hand would hold me fast! Thou art near to us! Thou canst accomplish and thou willest our well-being! Thou alone canst help us!"

In silence he breathed his prayer.

He returned to his chamber more composed in mind. Wilhelm seemed to sleep; but as Otto approached his bed he suddenly raised himself, and looked, inquiringly, around him.

"Who is there?" exclaimed he; "you are dressed! where have you been?" He was urgent in his inquiry.

Otto gave a joking reason.

"Let me have your hand!" said he. Otto gave it to him, he felt his pulse.

"Yes, quite correct!" said he; "the blood is yet in commotion. One sees plain enough that there is no concealing things! Here was I sleeping in all innocence, and you were running after adventures. You wicked bird!"

The thoughts worked rapidly in Otto's soul. If Louise would only be silent, no one would dream of the possibility of his having part in Sidsel's flight. He must allow Wilhelm quietly to have his joke.

"Was not I right?" asked Wilhelm.

"And if now you were so," replied Otto, "will you tell it to any one?"

"Do you think that I could do such a thing?" replied Wilhelm; "we are all of us only mortal creatures!"

Otto gave him his hand. "Be silent!" he said.

"Yes, certainly," said Wilhelm; and, according to his custom, strengthened it with an oath. "Now I have sworn it," said he; "but when there is an opportunity you must tell me more about it!"

"Yes, certainly," said Otto, with a deep sigh. Before his friend he no longer stood pure and guiltless.

They slept. Otto's sleep was only a hateful dream.

CHAPTER XXXVIII

"...Wie entzückend
Und süss es ist, in einer schönen Seele,
Verherrlicht uns zu fühlen, es zu wissen,
Das uns're Fruede fremde Wangen röthet,
Und uns're Angst in fremdem Busen zittert,
Das uns're Leiden fremde Augen nässen."
SCHILLER.

"How pale!" said Wilhelm the next morning to Otto. "Do you see, that is what people get by night-wandering?"

"How so?" inquired Otto.

Wilhelm made a jest of it.

"You have been dreaming that!" said Otto.

"How do you mean?" replied Wilhelm; "will you make me fancy that I have imagined it? I was really quite awake! we really talked about it; I was initiated in it. Actually I have a good mind to give you a moral lecture. If it had been me, how you would have preached!"

They were summoned to breakfast. Otto's heart was ready to burst. What might he not have to hear? What must he say?

Sophie was much excited.

"Did you, gentlemen, hear anything last night?" she inquired. "Have you both slept?"

"Yes, certainly," replied Wilhelm, and looked involuntarily at Otto.

"The bird is flown, however!" said she; "it has made its escape out of the dove-cote."

"What bird?" asked Wilhelm.

"Sidsel!" replied she; "and, what is oddest in the whole affair is, that Louise has loosed her wings. Louise is quite up to the romantic. Think only! she went up in the night to the topmost story, unlocked the prison-tower, gave a moral lecture to Sidsel, and after that let her go! Then in the morning comes Louise to mamma, relates the whole affair, and says a many affecting things!"

"Yes, I do not understand it," said the mother, addressing Louise. "How you could have had the courage to go up so late at night, and go up to *her*! But it was very beautiful of you! Let her escape! it is, as you say, best that she should. We should all of us have thought of that last evening!"

"I was so sorry for her!" said Louise; "and by chance it happened that I had a great many things to arrange after you were all in bed. Everything was so still in the house, it seemed to me as if I could hear Sidsel sigh; certainly it was only my own imagination, but I could do no other than pity her! she was so unfortunate! Thus I let her escape!"

"Are you gone mad?" inquired Wilhelm; "what a history is this? Did you go in the night up to the top of the house? That is an unseasonable compassion!"

"It was beautiful!" said Otto, bending himself involuntarily, and kissing Louise's hand.

"Yes, that is water to his mill!" exclaimed Wilhelm. "I think nothing of such things!"

"We will not talk about it to anyone," said the mother. "The steward shall not proceed any further in it. We have recovered the old silver tankard, and the losing that was my greatest trouble. We will thank God that we are well rid of her! Poor thing! she will come to an unfortunate end!"

"Are you still unwell, Mr. Thostrup?" said Sophie, and looked at him.

"I am a little feverish," replied he. "I will take a very long walk, and then I shall be better."

"You should take a few drops," said the lady.

"O, he will come to himself yet!" said Wilhelm; "he must take exercise! His is not a dangerous illness."

Otto went into the wood. It was to him a temple of God; his heart poured forth a hymn of thanksgiving. Louise had been his good angel. He felt of a truth that she would never betray his secret. His thoughts clung to her with confidence. "Are you still unwell?" Sophie had said. The tones of her voice alone had been like the fragrance of healing herbs; in her eye he had felt sympathy and—love. "O Sophie!" sighed he. Both sisters were so dear to him.

He entered the garden and went along the great avenue; here he met Louise. One might almost have imagined that she had sought for him: there was no one but her to be seen in the whole avenue.

Otto pressed her hand to his lips. "You have saved my life!" said he.

"Dear Thostrup!" answered she, "do not betray yourself. Yon have come happily out of the affair! Thank God! my little part in it has concealed the whole. For the rest I have a suspicion. Yes, I cannot avoid it. May not the whole be an error? It is possible that she is that which you said! Tell me all that you can let me know. From this seat we can see everybody who comes into the avenue. No one can hear us!"

"Yes, to you alone I can confide it!" said Otto; "to you will I tell it."

He now related that which we know about the manufactory, which he called the house, in which German Heinrich had first seen him, and had tattooed his initials upon his shoulder; their later meeting in the park, and afterwards by St. Ander's Cross.

Louise trembled; her glance rested sympathizingly upon Otto's pale and handsome countenance. He showed her the letter which had been brought to him the last evening, and related to her what Heinrich had told him.

"It may be so," said Louise; "but yet I have not been able to lose the idea all the morning that you have been deceived. Not one of her features resembles yours. Can brother and sister be so different as you and she? Yet, be the truth as it may, promise me not to think too much about it. There is a good Ruler above who can turn all things for the best."

"These horrible circumstances," said Otto, "have robbed me of the cheerfulness of my youth. They thrust themselves disturbingly into my whole future. Not to Wilhelm—no, not to any one have I been able to confide them. You know all! God knows that you were compelled to learn them. I leave myself entirely in your hands!"

He pressed her hand silently, and with the earnest glance of confidence and truth they looked at each other.

"I shall speedily leave my native country," said Otto. "It may be forever. I should return with sorrow to a home where no happiness awaited me. I stand so entirely alone in the world!"

"But you have friends," said Louise; "sincere friends. You must think with pleasure of returning home to Denmark. My mother loves you as if she were your own mother. Wilhelm and Sophie—yes, we will consider you as a brother."

"And Sophie?" exclaimed Otto.

"Yes, can you doubt it?" inquired Louise.

"She knows me not as you know me; and if she did?"—He pressed his hands before his eyes and burst into tears. "You know all: you know more than I could tell her," sighed he. "I am more unfortunate than you can believe. Never can I forget her—never!"

"For Heaven's sake compose yourself!" said Louise rising. "Some one might come, and you would not be able to conceal your emotion. All may yet be well! Confide only in God in heaven!"

"Do not tell your sister that which I have told you. Do not tell any one. I have revealed to you every secret which my soul contains."

"I will be to you a good sister," said Louise, and pressed his hand.

They silently walked down the avenue.

The sisters slept in the same room.

At night, after Sophie had been an hour in bed, Louise entered the chamber.

"Thou art become a spirit of the night," said Sophie. "Where hast thou been? Thou art not going up into the loft again to-night, thou strange girl? Had it been Wilhelm, Thostrup, or myself who had undertaken such a thing, it would have been quite natural; but thou"—

"Am I, then, so very different to you all?" inquired Louise. "I should resemble my sister less than even Mr. Thostrup resembles her. You two are so very different!"

"In our views, in our impulses, we very much resemble each other!" said Sophie.

"He is certainly not happy," exclaimed Louise. "We can read it in his eyes."

"Yes, but it is precisely that which makes him interesting!" said Sophie; "he is thus a handsome shadow-piece in everyday life."

"Thou speakest about it so calmly," said Louise, and bent over her sister, "I would almost believe that it was love."

"Love!" exclaimed Sophie, raising herself up in bed, for now Louise's words had become interesting to her; "whom dost thou think that he loves?"

"Thyself," replied Louise, and seized her sister's hand.

"Perhaps?" returned Sophie. "I also made fun of him! It certainly went on better when our cousin was here. Poor Thostrup!"

"And thou, Sophie," inquired Louise, "dost thou return his love?"

"It is a regular confession that thou desirest," replied she. "He is in love—that all young men are. Our cousin, I can tell thee, said many pretty things to me. Even the Kammerjunker flatters as well as he can, the good soul! I have now resolved with myself to be a reasonable girl. Believe me, however, Thostrup is in an ill humor!"

"If the Kammerjunker were to pay his addresses to you, would you accept him?" asked Louise, and seated herself upon her sister's bed.

"What can make you think of such a thing?" inquired she. "Hast thou heard anything?—Thou makest me anxious! O Louise! I joke, I talk a deal; but for all that, believe me, I am not happy!"

They talked about the Kammerjunker, about Otto, and about the French cousin. It was late in the night. Large tears stood in Sophie's eyes, but she laughed for all that, and ended with a quotation from Jean Paul.

Half an hour afterward she slept and dreamed; her round white arm lay upon the coverlet, and her lips moved with these words:

"*With a smile as if an angel*

Had just then kissed her mouth." [Note: Christian Winther.]

Louise pressed her countenance on the soft pillow, and wept.

CHAPTER XXXIX

"A swarm of colors, noise and screaming,
Music and sights, past any dreaming,
The rattle of wheels going late and early, —
All draw the looker-on into the hurly-burly."
TH. OVERSKOU.

A few days passed on. Otto heard nothing of German Heinrich or of his sister. Peter Cripple seemed not to be in their confidence. All that he knew was, that the letter which he had conveyed to Otto was to be unknown to any one beside. As regarded German Heinrich, he believed that he was now in another part of tire country; but that at St. Knud's fair, in Odense, he would certainly find him.

In Otto's soul there was an extraordinary combating. Louise's words, that he had been deceived, gave birth to hopes, which, insignificant as the grain of mustard-seed, shot forth green leaves.

"May not," thought he, "German Heinrich, to further his own plans, have made use of my fear? I must speak with him; he shall swear to me the truth."

He compared in thought the unpleasing, coarse features of Sidsel, with the image which his memory faintly retained of his little sister. She seemed to him as a delicate creature with large eyes. He had not forgotten that the people about them had spoken of her as of "a kitten that they could hardly keep alive." How then could she now be this square-built, singularly plain being, with the eyebrows growing together? "I must speak with Heinrich," resolved he; "she cannot be my sister! so heavily as that God will not try me."

By such thoughts as these his mind became much calmer. There were moments when the star of love mirrored itself in his life's sea.

His love for Sophie was no longer a caged bird within his breast; its wings were at liberty; Louise saw its release; it was about to fly to its goal.

St. Knud's fair was at hand, and on that account the family was about to set out for Odense. Eva was the only one who was to remain at home. It was her wish to do so.

"Odense is not worth the trouble of thy going to see," said Sophie; "but in this way thou wilt never increase thy geographical knowledge. In the mean time, however, I shall bring thee a fairing—a husband of honey cake, ornamented with almonds."

Wilhelm thought that she should enjoy the passing pleasure, and go with them; but Eva prayed to stay, and she had her will.

"There is a deal of pleasure in the world," said Wilhelm, "if people will only enjoy it. If one day in Paris is a brilliant flower, a day at Odense fair is also a flower. It is a merry, charming world that we live in! I am almost ready to say with King Valdemar, that if I might keep—yes, I will say, the earth, then our Lord might willingly for me keep heaven: there it is much better than we deserve; and God knows whether we may not, in the other world, have longings after the old world down here!"

"After Odense fair?" asked Sophie ironically.

Otto stood wrapped in his own thoughts. This day, he felt, would be one of the most remarkable in his life. German Heinrich must give him an explanation. Sophie must do so likewise Could he indeed meet with success from them both? Would not sorrow and pain be his fairings?

The carriage rolled away.

From the various cross-roads came driving up the carriages of the gentry and the peasants; the one drove past the other; and as the French and English Channel collects ships from the Atlantic Ocean, so did the King's Road those who drove in carriages, those who rode on horseback, and those who went on foot.

Behind most of the peasant-vehicles were tied a few horses, that went trotting on with them. Mamsells from the farms sat with large gloves on their red arms and hands. They held their umbrellas before their faces on account of the dust and the sun.

"The Kammerjunker's people must have set off earlier than we," said Sophie, "otherwise they would have called for us."

Otto looked inquiringly at her. She thought on the Kammerjunker!

"We shall draw up by Faugde church," said Sophie. "Mr. Thostrup can see Kingo's [Author's Note: The Bishop of Funen, who died in 1703.] grave—can see where the sacred poet lies. Some true trumpeting angels, in whom one can rightly see how heavy the marble is, fly with the Bishop's staff and hat within the chapel."

Otto smiled, and she thought also about giving him pleasure.

The church was seen, the grave visited, and they rapidly rolled along the King's Road toward Odense, the lofty tower of whose cathedral had hailed them at some miles' distance.

We do not require alone from the portrait-painter that he should represent the person, but that he should represent him in his happiest moment. To the plain as well as to the inexpressive countenance must the painter give every beauty which it possesses. Every human being has moments in which something intellectual or characteristic presents itself. Nature, too, when we are presented only with the most barren landscape, has the same moments; light and shadow produce these effects. The poet must be like the painter; he must seize upon these moments in human life as the other in nature.

If the reader were a child who lived in Odense, it would require nothing more from him than that he should say the words, "St. Knud's fair;" and this, illumined by the beams of the imagination of childhood, would stand before him in the most brilliant colors. Our description will be only a shadow; it will be that, perhaps, which the many will find it to be.

Already in the suburbs the crowd of people, and the outspread earthenware of the potters, which entirely covered the trottoir, announced that the fair was in full operation.

The carriage drove down from the bridge across the Odense River.

"See, how beautiful it is here!" exclaimed Wilhelm.

Between the gardens of the city and a space occupied as a bleaching ground lay the river. The magnificent church of St. Knud, with its lofty tower, terminated the view.

"What red house was that?" inquired Otto, when they had lost sight of it.

"That is the nunnery!" replied Louise, knowing what thought it was which had arisen in his mind.

"There stood in the ancient times the old bishop's palace, where Beldenak lived!" said Sophie. "Just opposite to the river is the bell-well, where a bell flew out of St. Albani's tower. The well is unfathomable. Whenever rich people in Odense die, it rings down below the water!"

"It is not a pleasant thought," said Otto, "that it rings in the well when they must die."

"One must not take it in that way now!" said Sophie, laughing, and turned the subject. "Odense has many lions," continued she, "from a king's garden with swans in it to a great theatre, which has this in common with La Scala and many Italian ones, that it is built upon the ruins of a convent. [Note: That of the Black Brothers.]

"In Odense, aristocracy and democracy held out the longest," said Wilhelm, smiling; "yet I remember, in my childhood, that when the nobles and the citizens met on the king's birthday at the town-house ball, that we danced by ourselves."

"Were not, then, the citizens strong enough to throw the giddy nobles out of the window?" inquired Otto.

"You forget, Mr. Thostrup, that you yourself are noble!" said Sophie. "I was really the goddess of fate who gave to you your genealogical tree."

"You still remember that evening?" said Otto, with a gentle voice, and the thoughts floated as gayly in his mind as the crowd of people floated up and down in the streets through which they drove.

Somewhere about the middle of the city five streets met; and this point, which widens itself out into a little square, is called the Cross Street: here lay the hotel to which the family drove.

"Two hours and a quarter too late!" said the Kammerjunker, who came out to meet them on the steps. "Good weather for the fair, and good horses! I have already been out at the West-gate, and have bought two magnificent mares. One of them kicked out behind, and had nearly given me a blow on the breast, so that I might have said I had had my fairing! Jakoba is paying visits, drinking chocolate, and eating biscuits. Mamsell is out taking a view of things. Now you know our story."

The ladies went to their chamber, the gentlemen remained in the saloon.

"Yes, here you shall see a city and a fair, Mr. Thostrup!" said the Kammerjunker, and slapped Otto on the shoulder.

"Odense was at one time my principal chief-city," said Wilhelm; "and still St. Knud's Church is the most magnificent I know. God knows whether St. Peter's in Rome would make upon me, now that I am older, the impression which this made upon me as a child!"

"In St. Knud's Church lies the Mamsell with the cats," said the Kammerjunker.

"The bishop's lady, you should say," returned Wilhelm. "The legend relates, that there was a lady of a Bishop Mus who loved her cats to that degree that she left orders that they should be laid with her in the grave. [Author's Note: The remains of the body, as well as the skeletons of the cats, are still to be seen in a chapel on the western aisle of the church.] We will afterward go and see them."

"Yes, both the bishop's lady and the cats," said the Kammerjunker, "look like dried fish! Then you must also see the nunnery and the military library."

"The Hospital and the House of Correction!" added Wilhelm.

The beating of a drum in the street drew them to the window. The city crier, in striped linsey-woolsey jacket and breeches, and with a yellow band across his shoulders, stood there, beat upon his drum, and proclaimed aloud from a written paper many wonderful things which were to be seen in the city.

"He beats a good drum," said the Kammerjunker.

"It would certainly delight Rossini and Spontini to hear the fellow!" said Wilhelm. "In fact Odense would be, at New Year's time, a city for these two composers. You must know that at that season drums and fifes are in their glory. They drum the New Year in. Seven or eight little drummers and fifers go from door to door, attended by children and old women; at that time they beat both the tattoo and the reveille. For this they get a few pence. When the New Year is drummed-in in the city they wander out into the country, and drum there for bacon and groats. The New Year's drumming in lasts until about Easter."

"And then we have new pastimes," said the Kammerjunker.

"Then come the fishers from Stige, [Author's Note: A fishing village in Odense Fjord.] with a complete band, and carrying a boat upon their shoulders ornamented with a variety of flags. After that they lay a board between two boats, and upon this two of the youngest and the strongest have a wrestling-match, until one of them falls into the water. The last years they both have allowed themselves to tumble in. And this has been done in consequence of one young man who fell in being so stung by the jeers which his fall had occasioned that he left, that same day, the fishing village, after which no one saw him. But all the fun is gone now! In my boyhood the merriment was quite another thing. It was a fine sight when the corporation paraded with their ensign and harlequin on the top! And at Easter, when the butchers led about a bullock ornamented with ribbons and Easter-twigs, on the back of which was seated a little winged boy in a shirt. They had Turkish music, and carried flagons with them! See! all that have I outlived, and yet I am not so old. Baron Wilhelm must have seen the ornamented ox. Now all that is past and gone; people are got so refined! Neither is St. Knud's fair that which it used to be."

"For all that, I rejoice that it is not so!" said Wilhelm. "But we will go into the market and visit the Jutlanders, who are sitting there among the heath with their earthenware. You will stand a chance there, Mr. Thostrup, of meeting with an old acquaintance; only you must not have home-sickness when you smell the heather and hear the ringing of the clattering pots!"

The ladies now entered. Before paying any visits they determined upon making the round of the market. The Kammerjunker offered his arm to the mother. Otto saw this with secret gladness, and approached Sophie. She accepted him willingly as an attendant; they must indeed get into the throng.

As in the Middle Ages the various professions had their distinct streets and quarters, so had they also here. The street which led to the market place, and which in every-day life was called the "Shoemaker Street," answered perfectly to its name. The shoemakers had ranged their tables side by side. These, and the rails which had been erected for the purpose, were hung over with all kinds of articles for the feet; the tables themselves were laden with heavy shoes and thick-soled boots. Behind these stood the skillful workman in his long Sunday coat, and with his well-brushed felt-hat upon his head.

Where the shoemakers' quarter ended that of the hatters' began, and with this one was in the middle of the great market-place, where tents and booths formed many parallel streets. The booth of galanterie wares, the goldsmith's, and the confectioner's, most of them constructed of canvas, some few of them of wood, were points of great attraction. Round about fluttered ribbons and handkerchiefs; round about were noise and bustle. Peasant-girls out of the same village went always in a row, seven or eight inseparables, with their hands fast locked in each other; it was impossible to break the chain; and if people tried to press through them, the whole flock rolled together in a heap.

Behind the booths there lay a great space filled with wooden shoes, coarse earthenware, turners' and saddlers' work. Upon tables were spread out toys, generally rudely made and coarsely painted. All around the children assayed their little trumpets, and turned about their playthings. The peasant-girls twirled and twisted both the work-boxes and themselves many a time before the bargain was completed. The air was heavy with all kinds of odors, and was spiced with the fragrance of honey-cake.

Here acquaintances met each other-some peasant-maidens, perhaps, who had been born in the same village, but since then had been separated.

"Good day!" exclaimed they, took each other by the hand, gave their arms a swing, and laughed.

"Farewell!"

That was the whole conversation: such a one went on in many places.

"That is the heather!" exclaimed Otto, as he approached the quarter where the Jutland potters had their station; "how refreshing is the odor!" said he, and stooping down seized a twig fresh and green, as if it had been plucked only yesterday.

"Aye, my Jesus though! is not that Mr. Otto!" exclaimed a female voice just beside him, and a young Jutland peasantwoman skipped across the pottery toward him. Otto knew her. It was the little Maria, the eelman's daughter, who, as we may remember at Otto's visit to the fisher's, had removed to Ringkjoebing, and had hired herself for the hay and cornharvest—the brisk Maria, "the girl," as her father called her. She had been betrothed in Ringkjoebing, and married to the rich earthenware dealer, and now had come across the salt-water to Odense fair, where she should meet with Mr. Otto.

"Her parents lived on my grandfather's estate," said Otto to Sophie, who observed with a smile the young wife's delight in meeting with an acquaintance of her childhood. The husband was busily employed in selling his wares; he heard nothing of it.

"Nay, but how elegant and handsome you are become!" said the young wife: "but see, I knew you again for all that! Grandmother, you may believe me, thinks a deal about you! The old body, she is so brisk and lively; it does not trouble her a bit that she cannot see! You are the second acquaintance that I have met with in the fair. It's wonderful how people come here from all parts of the world! The players are here too! You still remember the German Heinrich? Over there in the gray house, at the corner of the market, he is acting his comedy in the gateway."

"I am glad that I have seen you!" said Otto, and nodded kindly. "Greet them at home, and the grandmother, for me!"

"Greet them also from me!" said Sophie smiling. "You, Mr. Thostrup, must for old acquaintance sake buy something. You ought also to give me a fairing: I wish for that great jug there!"

"Where are you staying!" cried Wilhelm, and came back, whilst the rest went forward.

"We would buy some earthenware," said Sophie. "Souvenir de Jutland. The one there has a splendid picture on it!"

"You shall have it!" said Otto. "But if I requested a fairing from you, I beseech of you, might I say" —

"That it possibly might obtain its worth from my hand," said Sophie, smiling. "I understand you very well—a sprig of heather? I shall steal!" said she to the young wife, as she took a little sprig of heath and stuck it into his buttonhole. "Greet the grandmother for me!"

Otto and Sophie went.

"That's a very laughing body!" said the woman half aloud, as she looked after them; her glance followed Otto, she folded her hands—she was thinking, perhaps, on the days of her childhood.

At St. Knud's church-yard Otto and Sophie overtook the others. They were going into the church. On the fair days this and all the tombs within it were open to the public.

From whichever side this church is contemplated from without, the magnificent old building has, especially from its lofty tower and spire, something imposing about it; the interior produces the same, nay, perhaps a greater effect. But as the principal entrance is through the armory, and the lesser one is from the side of the church, its full impression is not felt on entering it; nor is it until you arrive at the end of the great aisle that you are aware rightly of its grandeur. All there is great, beautiful, and light. The whole interior is white with gilding. Aloft on the high-vaulted roof there shine, and that from the old time, many golden stars. On both sides, high up, higher than the side-aisles of the church, are large Gothic windows, from which the light streams down. The side-aisles are adorned with old paintings, which represent whole families, women and children, all clad in canonicals, in long robes and large ruffs. In an ordinary way, the figures are all ranged according to age, the oldest first, and then down to the very least child, and stand with folded hands, and look piously with downcast eyes and faces all in one direction, until by length of time the colors have all faded away.

Just opposite to the entrance of the church may be seen, built into the wall, a stone, on which is a bas-relief, and before it a grave. This attracted Otto's attention.

"It is the grave of King John and of Queen Christina, of Prince Francesco and of Christian the Second," said Wilhelm; "they lie together in a small vault!" [Author's Note: On the removal of the church of the Grey Brothers, the remains of these royal parents and two of their children were collected in a coffin and placed here in St. Knud's Church. The memorial stone, of which we have spoken, was erected afterwards.]

"Christian the Second!" exclaimed Otto. "Denmark's wisest and dearest king!"

"Christian the Bad!" said the Kammerjunker, amazed at the tone of enthusiasm in which Otto had spoken.

"Christian the Bad!" repeated Otto; "yes, it is now the mode to speak of him thus, but we should not do so. We ought to remember how the Swedish and Danish nobles behaved themselves, what cruelties they perpetrated, and that we have the history of Christian the Second from one of the offended party. Writers flatter the reigning powers. A prince must have committed crimes, or have lost his power, if his errors are to be rightly presented to future generations. People forget that which was good in Christian, and have painted the dark side of his character, to the formation of which the age lent its part."

The Kammerjunker could not forget the Swedish bloodbath, the execution of Torben Oxe, and all that can be said against the unfortunate king.

Otto drove him completely out of the field, in part from his enthusiasm for Christian the Second, but still more because it was the Kammerjunker with whom he was contending. Sophie took Otto's side, her eye sparkled applause, and the victory could not be other than his.

"What is it that the poet said of the fate of a king?" said Sophie.

"Woe's me for him
Who to the world shows more of ill than good!
The good each man ascribes unto himself,
Whilst on him only rest the crimes o' th' age."

"Had Christian been so fortunate as to have subdued the rebellious nobles," continued Otto, "could he have carried out his bold plans, then they would have called him Christian the Great: it is not the active mind, but the failure in any design, which the world condemns."

Louise nevertheless took the side of the Kammerjunker, and therefore these two went together up the aisle toward the tomb of the Glorup family. Wilhelm and his mother were already gone out of the church.

"I envy you your eloquence!" said Sophie, and looked with an expression of love into Otto's face; she bent herself over the railing around the tomb, and looked thoughtfully upon the stone. Thoughts of love were animated in Otto's soul.

"Intellect and heart!" exclaimed he, "must admire that which is great: you possess both these!" He seized her hand.

A faint crimson passed over Sophie's cheeks. "The others are gone out!" she said; "come, let us go up to the chancel."

"Up to the altar!" said Otto; "that is a bold course for one's whole life!"

Sophie looked jestingly at him. "Do you see the monument there within the pillars?" asked she after a short pause; "the lady with the crossed arms and the colored countenance? In one night she danced twelve knights to death, the thirteenth, whom she had invited for her partner, cut her girdle in two in the dance and she fell dead to the earth!" [Author's Note: In Thiele's Danish Popular Tradition it is related that she was one Margrethe Skofgaard of Sanderumgaard, and that she died at a ball, where she had danced to death twelve knights. The people relate it with a variation as above; it is probable that it is mingled with a second tradition, for example, that of the blood-spots at Koldinghuus, which relates that an old king was so angry with his daughter that he resolved to kill her, and ordered that his knights should dance with her one after another until the breath was out of her. Nine had danced with her, and then came up the king himself as the tenth, and when he became weary he cut her girdle in two, on which the blood streamed from her mouth and she died.]

"She was a northern Turandot!" said Otto; "the stony heart itself was forced to break and bleed. There is really a jest in having the marble painted. She stands before future ages as if she lived—a stone image, white and red, only a mask of beauty. She is a warning to young ladies!"

"Yes, against dancing!" said Sophie, smiling at Otto's extraordinary gravity.

"And yet it must be a blessed thing," exclaimed he, "a very blessed thing, amid pealing music, arm-in-arm with one's beloved, to be able to dance life away, and to sink bleeding before her feet!"

"And yet only to see that she would dance with a new one!" said Sophie.

"No, no!" exclaimed Otto, "that you could not do! that you will not do! O Sophie, if you knew!"—He approached her still nearer, bent his head toward her, and his eye had twofold fire and expression in it.

"You must come with us and see the cats!" said the Kammerjunker, and sprang in between them.

"Yes, it is charming!" said Sophie. "You will have an opportunity, Mr. Thostrup, of moralizing over the perishableness of female beauty!"

"In the evening, when we drive home together," thought Otto to himself consolingly, "in the mild summer-evening no Kammerjunker will disturb me. It must, it shall be decided! Misfortune might subject the wildness of childhood, but it gave me confidence, it never destroyed my independence; Love has made me timid,—has made me weak. May I thereby win a bride?"

Gravely and with a dark glance he followed after Sophie and her guide.

CHAPTER XL

"In vain his beet endeavors were;
Dull was the evening, and duller grew." —LUDOLF SCHLEF.

"Seest thou how its little life
The bird hides in the wood?
Wilt thou be my little wife—
Then do it soon. Good!
—A bridegroom am I." —Arion.

Close beside St. Knud's Church, where once the convent stood, is now the dwelling of a private man. [Author's Note: See Oehlenschläger's Jorney to Funen.] The excellent hostess here, who once charmed the public on the Danish stage as Ida Munster, awaited the family to dinner.

After dinner they wandered up and down the garden, which extended to the Odense River.

In the dusk of evening Otto went to visit the German Heinrich; he had mentioned it to Louise, and she promised to divert attention from him whilst he was away.

The company took coffee in the garden-house; Otto walked in deep thought in the avenue by the side of the river. The beautiful scene before him riveted his eye. Close beside lay a water-mill, over the two great wheels of which poured the river white as milk. Behind this was thrown a bridge, over which people walked and drove. The journeyman-miller stood upon the balcony, and whistled an air. It was such a picture as Christian Winther and Uhland give in their picturesque poems. On the other side of the mill arose tall poplars half-buried in the green meadow, in which stood the nunnery; a nun had once drowned herself where now the red daisies grow.

A strong sunlight lit up the whole scene. All was repose and summer warmth. Suddenly Otto's ear caught the deep and powerful tones of an organ; he turned himself round. The tones, which went to his heart, came from St. Knud's Church, which lay close beside the garden. The sunshine of the landscape, and the strength of the music, gave, as it were, to him light and strength for the darkness toward which he was so soon to go.

The sun set; and Otto went alone across the market-place toward the old corner house, where German Heinrich practiced his arts. Upon this place stood St. Albani's Church, where St. Knud, betrayed by his servant Blake, [Author's Note: Whence has arisen the popular expression of "being a false Blake."] was killed by the tumultuous rebels. The common people believe that from one of the deep cellars under this house proceeds a subterranean passage to the so-called "Nun's Hill." At midnight the neighboring inhabitants still hear a roaring under the marketplace, as if of the sudden falling of a cascade. The better informed explain it as being a concealed natural water-course, which has a connection with the neighboring river. In our time the old house is become a manufactory; the broken windows, the gaps of which are repaired either with slips of wood or with paper, the quantity of human bones which are found in the garden, and which remain from the time when this was a church-yard, give to the whole place a peculiar interest to the common people of Odense.

Entering the house at the front, it is on the same level as the market-place; the back of the house, on the contrary, descends precipitously into the garden, where there are thick old walls and foundations. The situation is thus quite romantic; just beside it is the old nunnery, with its dentated gables, and not far off the ruins, in whose depths the common people believe that there resides an evil being, "the river-man," who annually demands his human sacrifice, which he announces the night before. Behind this lie meadows, villas, and green woods.

On the other side of the court, in a back gate-way, German Heinrich had set up his theatre. The entrance cost eight skillings; people of condition paid according to their own will.

Otto entered during the representation. A cloth constituted the whole scenic arrangement. In the middle of the floor sat a horrible goblin, with a coal-black Moorish countenance and crispy hair upon its head. An old bed-cover concealed the figure, yet one saw that it was that of a woman.

The audience consisted of peasants and street boys. Otto kept himself in the background, and remained unobserved by Heinrich.

The representation was soon at an end, and the crowd dispersed. It was then that Otto first came forward.

"We must speak a few words together!" said he. "Heinrich, you have not acted honestly by me! The girl is not that which you represented her to be; you have deceived me: I demand an explanation!"

German Heinrich stood silent, but every feature eloquently expressed first amazement, and then slyness and cunning; his knavish, malicious eye, measured Otto from top to toe.

"Nay; so then, Mr. Thostrup, you are convinced, are you, that I have been cheating you?" said he. "If so, why do you come to me? In that case there needs no explanation. Ask herself there!" And so saying he pointed to the black-painted figure.

"Do not be too proud, Otto!" said she, smiling; "thou couldst yet recognize thy sister, although she has a little black paint on her face!"

Otto riveted a dark, indignant glance upon her, pressed his lips together, and tried to collect himself. "It is my firm determination to have the whole affair searched into," said he, with constrained calmness.

"Yes, but it will bring you some disagreeables!" said Heinrich, and laughed scornfully.

"Do not laugh in that manner when I speak to you!" said Otto, with flushing cheeks.

Heinrich leaned himself calmly against the door which led into the garden.

"I am acquainted with the head of the police," said Otto, "and I might leave the whole business in his hands. But I have chosen a milder way; I am come myself. I shall very soon leave Denmark; I shall go many hundred miles hence shall, probably, never return; and thus you see the principal ground for my coming to you is a whim: I will know wherefore you have deceived me; I will know what is the connection between you and her."

"Nay; so, then, it is *that* that you want to know?" said Heinrich, with a malicious glance. "Yes, see you, she is my best beloved; she shall be my wife: but your sister she is for all that, and that remains so!"

"Thou couldst easily give me a little before thou settest off on thy journey!" said Sidsel, who seemed excited by Heinrich's words, and put forth her painted face.

Otto glanced at her with contracted eyebrows.

"Yes," said she, "I say 'thou' to thee: thou must accustom thyself to that! A sister may have, however, that little bit of pleasure!"

"Yes, you should give her your hand!" said Heinrich, and laughed.

"Wretch!" exclaimed Otto, "she is not that which you say! I will find out my real sister! I will have proof in hand of the truth! I will show myself as a brother; I will care for her future! Bring to me her baptismal register; bring to me one only attestation of its reality—and that before eight days are past! Here is my address, it is the envelope of a letter; inclose in it the testimonial which I require, and send it to me without delay. But prove it, or you are a greater villain than I took you for."

"Let us say a few rational words!" said Heinrich, with a constrained, fawning voice. "If you will give to me fifty rix-dollars, then you shall never have any more annoyance with us! See, that would be a great deal more convenient."

"I abide by that which I have said!" answered Otto; "we will not have any more conversation together!" And so saying, he turned him round to go out.

Heinrich seized him by the coat.

"What do you want?" inquired Otto.

"I mean," said Heinrich, "whether you are not going to think about the fifty rix-dollars?"

"Villain!" cried Otto, and, with the veins swelling in his forehead, he thrust Heinrich from him with such force, that he fell against the worm eaten door which led into the garden; the panel of the door fell out, and had not Heinrich seized fast hold on some firm object with both his hands, he must have gone the same way. Otto stood for a moment silent, with flashing eyes, and threw the envelope, on which his address was, at Heinrich's feet, and went out.

When Otto returned to the hotel, he found the horses ready to be put to the carriage.

"Have you had good intelligence?" whispered Louise.

"I have in reality obtained no more than I had before!" replied he; "only my own feelings more strongly convince me than ever that I have been deceived by him."

He related to her the short conversation which had taken place.

The Kammerjunker's carriage was now also brought out; in this was more than sufficient room for two, whereas in the other carriage they had been crowded. The Kammerjunker, therefore, besought that they would avail themselves of the more convenient seat which he could offer; and Otto saw Sophie and her mother enter the Kammerjunker's carriage. This arrangement would shortly before have confounded Otto, now it had much less effect upon him. His mind was so much occupied by his visit to German Heinrich, his soul was filled with a bitterness, which for the moment repelled the impulse which he had felt to express his great love for Sophie.

"I have been made Heinrich's plaything—his tool!" thought he. "Now he ridicules me, and I am compelled to bear it! That horrible being is not my sister!—she cannot be so!"

The street was now quiet. They mounted into the carriage. In the corner house just opposite there was a great company; light streamed through the long curtains, a low tenor voice and a high ringing soprano mingled together in Mozart's "Audiam, audiam, mio bene."

"The bird may not flutter from my heart!" sighed Otto, and seated himself by the side of Louise. The carriage rolled away.

The full moon shone; the wild spiraea sent forth its odor from the road side; steam ascended from the moor-lands; and the white mist floated over the meadows like the daughters of the elfin king.

Louise sat silent and embarrassed; trouble weighed down her heart. Otto was also silent.

The Kammerjunker drove in first, cracked his whip, and struck up a wild halloo.

Wilhelm began to sing, "Charming the summer night," and the Kammerjunker joined in with him.

"Sing with us man," cried Wilhelm to the silent Otto, and quickly the two companies were one singing caravan.

It was late when they reached the hall.

CHAPTER XLI

*"Destiny often pulls off leaves, as we treat the vine, that
its fruits may be earlier brought to maturity."* —*JEAN PAUL.*

It was not until toward morning that Otto fell into sleep. Wilhelm and
he were allowed to take their own time in rising, and thus it was late in the
day before these two gentlemen made their appearance at the breakfast-
table; the Kammerjunker was already come over to the hall, and now was
more adorned than common.

"Mr. Thostrup shall be one of the initiated!" said the mother. "It will be
time enough this evening for strangers to know of it. The Kammerjunker
and my Sophie are betrothed."

"See, it was in the bright moonlight, Mr. Thostrup, that I became such
a happy man!" said the Kammerjunker, and kissed the tips of Sophie's
fingers. He offered his other hand to Otto.

Otto's countenance remained unchanged, a smile played upon his lips.
"I congratulate you!" said he; "it is indeed a joyful day! If I were a poet, I
would give you an ode!"

Louise looked at him with an extraordinary expression of pain in her
countenance.

Wilhelm called the Kammerjunker brother-in-law, and smiling shook
both his hands.

Otto was unusually gay, jested, and laughed. The ladies went to their
toilet, Otto into the garden.

He had been so convinced in his own mind that Sophie returned
his passion. With what pleasure had she listened to him! with what an
expression had her eye rested upon him! Her little jests had been to him such
convincing proofs that the hope which he nourished was no self-delusion.
She was the light around which his thoughts had circled. Love to her was to
him a good angel, which sung to him consolation and life's gladness in his
dark moments.

Now, all was suddenly over. It was as if the angel had left him; the flame
of love which had so entirely filled his soul, was in a moment extinguished
to its last spark. Sophie was become a stranger to him; her intellectual eye,

which smiled in love on the Kammerjunker, seemed to him the soulless eye of the automaton. A stupefying indifference went through him, deadly as poison that is infused into the human blood.

"The vain girl! she thought to make herself more important by repelling from her a faithful heart! She should only see how changed her image is in my soul. All the weaknesses which my love for her made me pass over, now step forth with repulsive features! Not a word which she spoke fell to the ground. The diamond has lost its lustre; I feel only its sharp corners!"

Sophie had given the preference to a man who, in respect of intellect, stood far below Otto! Sophie, who seemed to be enthusiastic for art and beauty, for everything glorious in the kingdom of mind, could thus have deceived him!

We will now see the sisters in their chamber.

Louise seemed pensive, she sat silently looking before her.

Sophie stood thoughtfully with a smile upon her lips.

"The Kammerjunker is very handsome, however!" exclaimed she: "he looks so manly!"

"You ought to find him love-worthy!" said Louise.

"Yes," replied her sister, "I have always admired these strong countenances! He is an Axel—a northern blackbearded savage. Faces such as Wilhelm's look like ladies'! And he is so good! He has said, that immediately after our marriage we shall make a tour to Hamburg. What dress do you think I should wear?"

"When you make the journey to Hamburg?" inquired Louise.

"O no, child! to-day I mean. Thostrup was indeed very polite! he congratulated me! I felt, however, rather curious when it was told to him. I had quite expected a scene! I was almost ready to beg of you to tell him first of all. He ought to have been prepared. But he was, however, very rational! I should not have expected it from him. I really wish him all good, but he is an extraordinary character! so melancholy! Do you think that he will take my betrothal to heart? I noticed that when I was kissed he turned himself suddenly round to the window and played with the flowers. I wish that he would soon go! The journey into foreign countries will do him good—there he will soon forget his heart's troubles. To-morrow I will write to Cousin Joachim; he will also be surprised!"

Late in the afternoon came Jakoba, the Mamsell, the preacher, and yet a few other guests.

In the evening the table was arranged festively. The betrothed sat together, and Otto had the place of honor—he sat on the other side of Sophie. The preacher had written a song to the tune of "Be thou our social guardian-goddess;" this was sung. Otto's voice sounded beautifully and strong; he rang his glass with the betrothed pair, and the Kammerjunker said that now Mr. Thostrup must speedily seek out a bride for himself.

"She is found," answered Otto; "but now that is yet a secret."

"Health to the bride!" said Sophie, and rung her glass; but soon again her intellectual eye rested upon the Kammerjunker, who was talking about asparagus and stall-feeding with clover, yet her glance brought him back again to the happiness of his love.

It was a very lively evening. Late in the night the party broke up. The friends went to their chamber.

"My dear, faithful Otto!" said Wilhelm, and laid his hand on his shoulder; "you were very lively and good-humored this evening. Continue always thus!"

"I hope to do so," answered Otto: "may we only always have as happy an evening as this!"

"Extraordinary man!" said Wilhelm, and shook his head. "Now we will soon set out on our journey, and catch for ourselves the happiness of the glorious gold bird!"

"And not let it escape again!" exclaimed Otto. "Formerly I used to say, To-morrow! to-morrow! now I say, To-day, and all day long! Away with fancies and complainings. I now comprehend that which you once said to me, that is. Man *can* be happy if he only *will* be so."

Wilhelm took his hand, and looked into his face with a half-melancholy expression.

"Are you sentimental?" inquired Otto.

"I only affect that which I am not!" answered Wilhelm; and with that, suddenly throwing off the natural gravity of the moment, returned to his customary gayety.

The following days were spent in visiting and in receiving visitors. On every post-day Otto sought through the leathern bag of the postman, but he found no letter from German Heinrich, and heard nothing from him. "I have been deceived," said he, "and I feel myself glad about it! She, the horrible one, is not my sister!"

There was a necessity for him to go away, far from home, and yet he felt no longing after the mountains of Switzerland or the luxuriant beauty of the south.

"Nature will only weaken me! I will not seek after it. Man it is that I require: these egotistical, false beings—these lords of everything! How we flatter our weaknesses and admire our virtues! Whatever serves to advance our own wishes we find to be excellent. To those who love us, we give our love in return. At the bottom, whom do I love except myself? Wilhelm? My friendship for him is built upon the foundation,—I cannot do without thee! Friendship is to me a necessity. Was I not once convinced that I adored Sophie, and that I never could bear it if she were lost to me? and yet there needed the conviction 'She loves thee not,' and my strong feeling was dead. Sophie even seems to me less beautiful; I see faults where I formerly could only discover amiabilities! Now, she is to me almost wholly a stranger. As I am, so are all. Who is there that feels right lovingly, right faithfully for me, without his own interest leading him to do so? Rosalie? My old, honest Rosalie? I grew up before her eyes like a plant which she loved. I am dear to her as it! When her canary-bird one morning lay dead in its cage, she wept bitterly and long; she should never more hear it sing, she should never more look after its cage and its food. It was the loss of it which made her weep. She missed that which had been interesting to her. I also interested her. Interest is the name for that which the world calls love. Louise?" He almost spoke the name aloud, and his thoughts dwelt, from a strong combination of circumstances, upon it. "She appears to me true, and capable of making sacrifices! but is not she also very different from all the others? How often have I not heard Sophie laugh at her for it—look down upon her!" And Otto's better feeling sought in vain for a shadow of self-love in Louise, a single selfish motive for her noble conduct.

"Away from Denmark! to new people! Happy he who can always be on the wing, making new friendships, and speedily breaking them off! At the first meeting people wear their intellectual Sunday apparel; every point of light is brought forth; but soon and the festival-day is over, and the bright points have vanished."

"We will set off next week!" said Wilhelm, "and then it shall be—

'Over the rushing blue waters away!*
We will speed along shores that are verdant and gay!'

Away over the moors, up the Rhine, through the land of champagne to the city of cities, the life-animating Paris!"

CHAPTER XLII

"A maiden stood musing, gentle and mild. I grasped the hand
of the friendly child, but the lovely fawn shyly
disappeared.... From the Rhine to the Danish Belt,
beautiful and lovely maidens are found in palaces and tents;
yet nobody pleases me." —SCHMIDT VON LÜBECK.

The last day at home was Sophie's birthday. In the afternoon the whole family was invited to the Kammerjunker's, where Jakoba and the Mamsell were to be quite brilliant in their cookery.

A table filled with presents, all from the Kammerjunker, awaited Miss Sophie; it was the first time that he had ever presented to her a birthday gift, and he had now, either out of his own head or somebody's else, fallen on the very good idea of making her a present for every year which she had lived. Every present was suited to the age for which it was intended, and thus he began with a paper of sugar-plums and ended with silk and magnificent fur; but between beginning and end there were things, of which more than the half could be called solid: gold ear-rings, a boa, French gloves, and a riding-horse. This last, of course, could not stand upon the table. It was a joy and a happiness; people walked about, and separated themselves by degrees into groups.

The only one who was not there was Eva. She always preferred remaining at home; and yet, perhaps, to-day she might have allowed herself to have been overpersuaded, had she not found herself so extremely weak.

Silently and alone she now sat at home in the great empty parlor. It was in the twilight; she had laid down her work, and her beautiful, thoughtful eyes looked straight before her: thoughts which we may not unveil were agitating her breast.

Suddenly the door opened, and Wilhelm stood before her. Whilst the others were walking he had stolen away. He knew that Eva was alone at home; nobody would know that he visited her, nobody would dream of their conversation.

"You here!" exclaimed Eva, when she saw him.

"I was compelled to come," answered he. "I have slipped away from the others; no one knows that I am here. I must speak with you, Eva. To-morrow I set off; but I cannot leave home calmly and happily without knowing—what this moment must decide."

Eva rose, her checks crimsoned, she cast down her eyes.

"Baron Wilhelm!" stammered she, "it is not proper that I should remain here!" She was about to leave the room.

"Eva!" said Wilhelm, and seized her hand, "you know that I love you! My feelings are honorable! Say Yes, and it shall be holy to me as an oath. Then I shall begin my journey glad at heart, as one should do. Your assent shall stand in my breast, shall sound in my ear, whenever sin and temptation assail me! It will preserve me in an upright course, it will bring me back good and unspoiled. My wife must you be! You have soul, and with it nobility! Eva! in God's name, do not make a feeble, life-weary, disheartened being of me!"

"O Heavens!" exclaimed she, and burst into tears, "I cannot, and—will not! You forget that I am only a poor girl, who am indebted for everything to your mother! My assent would displease her, and some time or other you would repent of it! I cannot!—I do not love you!" added she, in a tremulous voice.

Wilhelm stood speechless.

Eva suddenly rang the bell.

"What are you doing?" exclaimed he.

The servant entered.

"Bring in lights!" said she; "but first of all you must assist me with these flowers down into the garden. It will do them good to stand in the dew."

The servant did as she bade; she herself carried down one of the pots, and left the room.

"I do not love you!" repeated Wilhelm to himself, and returned to the company which he had left, and where he found all gayety and happiness.

The supper-table was spread in the garden; lights burned in the open air with a steady flame; it was a summer-evening beautiful as the October of the South; the reseda sent forth its fragrance; and when Sophie's health was drunk cannon were fired among the lofty fir-trees, the pines of the North.

The next morning those countenances were dejected which the evening before had been so gay. The carriage drew up to the door. The dear mother and sisters wept; they kissed Wilhelm, and extended their hands to Otto.

"Farewell!" said Louise; "do not forget us!" and her tearful glance rested upon Otto. Eva stood silent and pale.

"You will not forget me!" whispered Otto, as he seized Louise's hand. "I will forget your sister!"

The carriage rolled away; Wilhelm threw himself back into a corner. Otto looked back once more; they all stood at the door, and waved their white handkerchiefs.

CHAPTER XLIII

"In one short speaking silence all conveys —
And looks a sigh, and weeps without a tear."
MRS. BROWNING.

"Forgive us our debts as we
The debts of others forgive;
And lead us not in tempting ways;
Apart from evil let us live."
A. VON CHAMISSO.

We will not accompany the friends, but will remain behind in Funen, where we will make a bolder journey than they, namely, we will go back one-and-twenty years. We will allow the circumstances of Otto's birth again to come before us. It is a leap backward that we take from 1830 to 1810. We are in Odense, that old city, which takes its name from Odin.

The common people there have still a legend about the origin of the name of the city. Upon Naesbyhoved's Hill [Author's Note: Not far from the city, by the Odense Channel; it is described in Wedel Simonsen's City Ruins.] there once stood a castle; here lived King Odin and his wife: Odense city was not then in existence, but the first building of it was then begun. [Author's Note: The place is given as being that of the now so-called Cross Street.] The court was undecided as to the name which should be given to the city. After long indecision it was at last agreed that the first word which either King or Queen should speak the next morning should be the name given to it. In the early morning the Queen awoke and looked out from her window over the wood. The first house in the city was erected to the roof, and the builders had hung up a great garland, glittering with tinsel, upon the rooftree. "Odin, see!" exclaimed the Queen; and thenceforward the city was called Odensee, which name, since then, has been changed by daily speech to Odense.

When people ask the children in Copenhagen whence they have come, they reply, out of the Peblingsöe. The little children of Odense, who know nothing about the Peblingsöe, say that they are fetched out of Rosenbaek, a little brook which has only been ennobled within the few last years, just as in Copenhagen is the case with Krystal Street, which formerly had an unpleasant name. This brook runs through Odense, and must, in former times, when united with the Odense River, have formed an island where the city at that time stood; hence some people derive the name of Odense from Odins Ei, or Odins Ö, that is, Odin's Island. Be it then as it might, the brook flows now, and in 1810, when the so-called Willow-dam, by the West Gate, was not filled up, it stood, especially in spring, low and watery. It often overflowed its banks, and in so doing overflowed the little gardens which lay on either side. It thus ran concealed through the city until near the North Gate, where it made its appearance for a moment and then dived again in the same street, and, like a little river, flowed through the cellars of the old justice-room, which was built by the renowned Oluf Bagger. [Author's Note: He was so rich that once, when Frederick the Second visited him, he had the room heated with cinnamon chips. Much may be found about this remarkable man in the second collection of Thiele's Popular Danish Legends. His descendants still live in Odense, namely, the family of the printer Ch. Iversen, who has preserved many curiosities which belonged to him.]

It was an afternoon in the summer of 1810; the water was high in the brook, yet two washerwomen were busily employed in it; reed-matting was fast bound round their bodies, and they beat with wooden staves the clothes upon their washing-stools. They were in deep conversation, and yet their labor went on uninterruptedly.

"Yes," said one of them, "better a little with honor, than much with dishonor. She is sentenced; to-morrow she is to go about in the pillory. That is sure and certain! I know it from the trumpeter's Karen, and from the beggar-king's [Author's Note: Overseer of the poor.] wife: neither of them go about with lies."

"Ih, my Jesus!" exclaimed the other, and let her wooden beater fall, "is Johanne Marie to go in the pillory, the handsome girl? she that looked so clever and dressed herself so well?"

"Yes, it is a misfortune!" said the first; "a great misfortune it must be! No, let every one keep his own! say I every day to my children. After the sweet claw comes the bitter smart. One had much better work till the blood starts from the finger-ends."

"Ih, see though!" said the other; "there goes the old fellow, Johanne Marie's father. He is an honest man; he was so pleased with his daughter, and to-morrow he must himself bind her to the pillory! But can she really have stolen?"

"She has herself confessed," returned she; "and the Colonel is severe. I fancy the Gevaldiger is going there."

"The Colonel should put the bridle on his own son. He is a bad fellow! Not long ago, when I was washing yarn there, and was merry, as I always am, he called me 'wench.' If he had said 'woman,' I should not have troubled myself about it, for it has another meaning; but 'wench,' that is rude! Ei, there sails the whole affair!" screamed she suddenly, as the sheet which she had wound round the washing-stool got loose and floated down the stream: she ran after it, and the conversation was broken off.

The old man whom they had seen and compassionated, went into a great house close by, where the Colonel lived. His eyes were cast upon the ground; a deep, silent suffering lay in his wrinkled face; he gently pulled at the bell, and bowed himself deeply before the black-appareled lady who opened to him the door.

We know her—it was the old Rosalie, then twenty years younger than when we saw her upon the western coast of Jutland.

"Good old man!" said she, and laid her hand kindly on his shoulder. "Colonel Thostrup is severe, but he is not, however, inhuman; and that he would be if he let you tomorrow do your office. The Colonel has said that the Gevaldiger should stay at home."

"No!" said the old man, "our Lord will give me strength. God be thanked that Johanne Marie's mother has closed her eyes: she will not see the misery! We are not guilty of it!"

"Honest man!" said Rosalie. "Johanne was always so good and clever; and now"—she shook her head—"I would have sworn for her, but she has confessed it herself!"

"The law must have its course!" said the old man, and tears streamed down his cheeks.

At that moment the door opened, and Colonel Thostrup, a tall, thin man, with a keen eye, stood before them. Rosalie left the room.

"Gevaldiger," said the Colonel, "to-morrow you will not be required to act in your office."

"Colonel," returned the old man, "it is my duty to be there, and, if I may say a few words, people would speak ill of me if I kept away."

On the following forenoon, from the early morning, the square where lay the council-house and head-watch, was filled with people; they were come to see the handsome girl led forth in the pillory. The time began to appear long to them, and yet no sign was seen of that which they expected. The sentinel, who went with measured step backward and forward before the sentry-box, could give no intelligence. The door of the council-house was closed, and everything gave occasion to the report which suddenly was put into circulation, that the handsome Johanne Marie had been for a whole hour in the pillory within the council-house, and thus they should have nothing at all to see. Although it is entirely opposed to sound reason that punishment should be inflicted publicly, it met with much support, and great dissatisfaction was excited.

"That is shabby!" said a simple woman, in whom we may recognize one of the washerwomen; "it is shabby thus to treat the folks as if they were fools! Yesterday I slaved like a horse, and here one has stood two whole hours by the clock, till I am stiff in the legs, without seeing anything at all!"

"That is what I expected," said another woman; "a fair face has many friends! She has known how to win the great people to her side!"

"Do not you believe," inquired a third, "that she has been good friends with the Colonels son?"

"Yes; formerly I would have said No, because she always looked so steady, and against her parents there is not a word to be said; but as she has stolen, as we know she has, she may also have been unsteady. The Colonel's son is a wild bird; riots and drinks does he in secret! We others know more than his father does: he had held too tight a hand over him. Too great severity causes bad blood!"

"God help me, now it begins!" interrupted another woman, as a detachment of soldiers marched out of the guard-house, and at some little distance one from the other inclosed an open space. The door of the council-house now opened, and two officers of police, together with some of the guard, conducted out the condemned, who was placed in the pillory. This was a sort of wooden yoke laid across the shoulders of the delinquent; a piece of wood came forward from this into which her hands were secured: above all stood two iron bars, to the first of which was fastened a little bell; to the other a long fox's tail, which hung down the lack of the condemned.

The girl seemed hardly more than nineteen, and was of an unusually beautiful figure; her countenance was nobly and delicately formed, but pale as death: yet there was no expression either of suffering or shame,—she seemed like the image of a penitent, who meekly accomplishes the imposed penance.

Her aged father, the Gevaldiger, followed her slowly; his eye was determined; no feature expressed that which went forward in his soul: he silently took his place beside one of the pillars before the guard house.

A loud murmur arose among the crowd when they saw the beautiful girl and the poor old father, who must himself see his daughter's disgrace.

A spotted dog sprang into the open space; the girl's monotonous tread, as she advanced into the middle of the square, the ringing of the little bell, and the fox-tail which moved in the wind, excited the dog, which began to bark, and wanted to bite the fox's tail. The guards drove the dog away, but it soon came back again, although it did not venture again into the circle, but thrust itself forward, and never ceased barking.

Many of those who already had been moved to compassion by the beauty of the girl and the sight of the old father, were thrown again by this incident into a merry humor; they laughed and found the whole thing very amusing.

The hour was past, and the girl was now to be released. The Gevaldiger approached her, but whilst he raised his hand to the yoke the old man tottered, and sank, in the same moment, back upon the hard stone pavement.

A shriek arose from those who stood around; the young girl alone stood silent and immovable; her thoughts seemed to be far away. Yet some people fancied they saw how she closed her eyes, but that was only for a moment. A policeman released her from the pillory, her old father was carried into the guard-house, and two policemen led her into the council-house.

"See, now it is over!" said an old glover, who was among the spectators; "the next time she'll get into the House of Correction."

"O, it is not so bad there," answered another; "they sing and are merry there the whole day long, and have no need to trouble themselves about victuals."

"Yes, but that is prison fare."

"It is not so bad—many a poor body would thank God for it; and Johanne Marie would get the best of it. Her aunt is the head-cook, and the cook and the inspector they hang together. It's my opinion, however, that this affair will take the life out of the old man. He got a right good bump as he fell on the stone-pavement; one could hear how it rung again."

The crowd separated.

The last malicious voice had prophesied truth.

Three weeks afterward six soldiers bore a woven, yellow straw coffin from a poor house in East Street. The old Gevaldiger lay, with closed eyes and folded hands, in the coffin. Within the chamber, upon the bedstead, sat Johanne Marie, with a countenance pale as that of the dead which had been carried away. A compassionate neighbor took her hand, and mentioned her name several times before she heard her.

"Johanne, come in with me; eat a mouthful of pease and keep life in you; if not for your own sake, at least for that of the child which lies under your heart."

The girl heaved a wonderfully deep sigh. "No, no!" said she, and closed her eyes.

Full of pity, the good neighbor took her home with her.

A few days passed on, and then one morning two policemen entered the poor room in which the Gevaldiger had died. Johanne Marie was again summoned before the judge.

A fresh robbery had taken place at the Colonel's. Rosalie said that it was a long time since she had first missed that which was gone, but that she thought it best to try to forget it. The Colonel's violent temper and his exasperation against Johanne Marie, who, as he asserted, by her bad conduct, had brought her old, excellent father to the grave, insisted on summoning her before the tribunal, that the affair might be more narrowly inquired into.

Rosalie, who had been captivated by the beauty of the girl and by her modest demeanor, and who was very fond of her, was this time quite calm, feeling quite sure that she would deny everything, because, in fact, the theft had only occurred within the last few days. The public became aware of this before long, and the opinion was that Johanne Marie could not possibly have been an actor in it; but, to the astonishment of the greater number, she confessed that she was the guilty person, and that with such calmness as amazed every one. Her noble, beautifully formed countenance seemed bloodless; her dark-blue eyes beamed with a brilliancy which seemed like that of delirium; her beauty, her calmness, and yet this obduracy in crime, produced an extraordinary impression upon the spectators.

She was sentenced to the House of Correction in Odense. Despised and repulsed by the better class of her fellow-beings, she went to her punishment. No one had dreamed that under so fair a form so corrupt a soul could have been found. She was set to the spinning-wheel; silent and introverted, she accomplished the tasks that were assigned her. In the coarse merriment of the other prisoners she took no part.

"Don't let your heart sink within you, Johanne Marie," said German Heinrich, who sat at the loom; "sing with us till the iron bars rattle!"

"Johanne, you brought your old father to the grave," said her relation, the head-cook; "how could you have taken such bad courses?"

Johanne Marie was silent; the large, dark eyes looked straight before her, whilst she kept turning the wheel.

Five months went on, and then she became ill—ill to death, and gave birth to twins, a boy and a girl—two beautiful and well-formed children, excepting that the girl was as small and delicate as if its life hung on a thread.

The dying mother kissed the little ones and wept; it was the first time that the people within the prison had seen her weep. Her relation the cook sat alone with her upon the bed.

"Withdraw not your hand from the innocent children," said Johanne Marie; "if they live to grow up, tell them some time that their mother was innocent. My eternal Saviour knows that I have never stolen! Innocent am I, and innocent was I when I went out a spectacle of public derision, and now when I sit here!"

"Ih, Jesus though! What do you say?" exclaimed the woman.

"The truth!" answered the dying one. "God be gracious to me!—my children!"

She sank back upon the couch, and was dead.

CHAPTER XLIV

"Ah! wonderfully beautiful is God's earth, and worthy it is to live contented." —HÖLTY.

We now return to the hall in Funen, to the family which we left there; but autumn and winter are gone whilst we have been lingering on the past. Otto and Wilhelm have been two months away. It is the autumn of 1832.

The marriage of the Kammerjunker and Sophie was deferred, according to her wish, until the second of April, because this day is immortal in the annals of Denmark. In the house, where there now were only the mother, Louise, and Eva, all was quiet. Through the whole winter Eva had become weaker; yet she did not resemble the flowers which wither; there was no expression of illness about her—it was much more as if the spiritual nature overpowered the bodily; she resembled an astral lamp which, filled with light, seems almost resembled be an ethereal existence. The dark-blue eyes had an expression of soul and feeling which attracted even the simple domestics at the hall. The physician assured them that her chest was sound, and that her malady was to him a riddle. A beautiful summer, he thought, would work beneficially upon her.

Wilhelm and Otto wrote alternately. It was a festival-day whenever a letter came; then were maps and plans of the great cities fetched out, and Louise and Eva made the journey with them.

"To-day they are here, to-morrow they will be there," cried they.

"How I envy them both, to see all these glorious things!" said Louise.

"The charming Switzerland!" sighed Eva. "How refreshing the air must be to breathe! How well one must feel one's self there!"

"If you could only go there, Eva," said Louise, "then you would certainly get better."

"Here all are so kind to me; here I am so happy!" answered she. "I am right thankful to God for it. How could I have hoped for such a home as this? God reward you and your good mother for your kindness to me. Once I was so unhappy; but now I have had a double repayment for all my sorrow, and all the neglect I have suffered. I am so happy, and therefore I would so willingly live!"

"Yes, and you shall live!" said Louise. "How came you now to think about dying? In the summer you will perfectly recover, the physician says. Can you hide from me any sorrow? Eva, I know that my brother loves you!"

"He will forget that abroad!" said Eva. "He must forget it! Could I be ungrateful? But we are not suited for each other!" She spoke of her childhood, of long-passed, sorrowful days. Louise laid her arm upon her shoulder: they talked till late in the evening, and tears stood in Louise's eyes.

"Only to you could I tell it!" said Eva. "It is to me like a sin, and yet I am innocent. My mother was so too—my poor mother! Her sin was love. She sacrificed all; more than a woman should sacrifice. The old Colonel was stern and violent. His wrath often became a sort of frenzy, in which he knew not what he did. The son was young and dissipated; my mother a poor girl, but very handsome, I have heard. He seduced her. She had become an unfortunate being, and that she herself felt. The Colonel's son robbed his father and an old woman who lived in the family: that which had been taken was missed. The father would have murdered the son, had he discovered the truth; the son, therefore, sought in his need help from my poor mother. He persuaded her to save him by taking the guilt on herself. The whole affair as regarded her was, he intended, only to come from the domestics. She thought that with her honor all was lost. She, indeed, had already given him the best of which she was possessed. In anguish of heart, and overpowered by his prayers, she said, 'Yes; my father has been angry and undone already.'"

Eva burst into tears.

"Thou dear, good girl!" said Louise, and kissed her forehead.

"My poor mother," continued Eva, "was condemned to an undeserved punishment. I cannot mention it. For that reason I have never had a desire to go to Odense. The old lady in the Colonel's family concealed, out of kindness, her loss; but by accident it was discovered. The Colonel was greatly embittered. My mother was overwhelmed by shame and misfortune: the first error had plunged her into all this. She was taken to the House of Correction in Odense. The Colonel's son shortly afterward went away in a vessel. My unhappy mother was dispirited: nobody knew that she had endured, out of despair and love, a disgrace which she had not deserved. It was not until she lay upon her death-bed, when I and my brother were born, that she told a relation that she was innocent. Like a criminal, in the early morning she was carried to the grave in a coffin of plaited straw. A great and a noble heart was carried unacknowledged to the dead!"

"You had a brother?" inquired Louise, and her heart beat violently. "Did he die? and where did you, poor children, remain?"

"The cook in the house kept us with her. I was small and weak; my brother, on the contrary, was strong, and full of life. He lived mostly among the prisoners. I sat in a little room with my doll. When we were in our seventh year, we were sent for to the old Colonel. His son died abroad; but before his death he had written to the old man, confessing to him his crime, my mother's innocence, and that we were his children! I resembled my father greatly. The old gentleman, as soon as he saw me, was very angry, and said, 'I will not have her!' I remained with my foster-mother. I never saw my brother after that time. The Colonel left the city, and took him with him."

"O God!" cried Louise; "you have still some papers on this subject? Do you not know your brother? It is impossible that it should be otherwise! You are Otto's sister!"

"O Heavens!" exclaimed Eva; her hands trembled, and she became as pale as a corpse.

"You are fainting!" cried Louise, throwing her arm around her waist and kissing her eyes and her cheeks. "Eva! he is your brother! the dear, good Otto! O, he will be so happy with you! Yes, your eyes are like his! Eva, you beloved girl!"

Louise related to her all that Otto had confided to her. She told her about German Heinrich, and how Otto had assisted Sidsel away, and how they had met.

Eva burst into tears. "My brother! O Father in heaven, that I may but live! live and see him! Life is so beautiful! I must not die!"

"Happiness will make you strong! There is no doubt but that he is your brother! We must tell it to mamma. O Heavens! how delighted she will be! and Otto will no longer suffer and be unhappy! He may be proud of you, and happy in you! O, come, come!"

She led Eva out with her to her mother, who was already in bed; but how could Louise wait till next morning?

"May the Lord bless thee, my good child!" said the lady, and pressed a kiss upon her forehead.

Eva related now how the Colonel had, given a considerable sum to her foster-mother; but that was all she was to receive, he had said. Afterward, when the foster-mother died, Eva had still two hundred rix-dollars; and on consideration of this the sister of the deceased had taken Eva to live with her. With her she came to Copenhagen and to Nyboder, and at that time she was ten years old. There she had to nurse a little child—her brother she called it—and that was the little Jonas. As she grew older, people told her that she was handsome. It was now four years since she was followed one evening by two young men, one of whom we know—our moral Hans Peter. One morning her foster-mother came to her with a proposal which drove her to despair. The merchant had seen her, and wished to purchase the beautiful flower. Upon this Eva left her home, and came to the excellent people at Roeskelde; and from that day God had been very good to her.

She sank down upon her knees before the elderly lady's bed. She was not among strangers: a mother and a sister wept with the happy one.

"O that I might live!" besought Eva, in the depths of her heart. As a glorified one she stood before them. Her joy beamed through tears.

The next morning she felt herself singularly unwell. Her feet trembled; her cheeks were like marble. She seated herself in the warm sunshine which came in through the window. Outside stood the trees with large, half-bursting buds. A few mild nights would make the wood green. But summer was already in Eva's heart; there was life's joy and gladness. Her large, thoughtful eyes raised themselves thankfully to heaven.

"Let me not die yet, good God!" prayed she; and her lips moved to a low melody, soft as if breezes passed over the outstretched chords:—

> *"The sunshine warm, the odorous flowers,*
> *Of these do not bereave me!*
> *I breathe with joy the morning hours,*
> *Let not the grave receive me!*
> *There can no pleasant sunbeams fall,*
> *No human voice come near me;*
> *There should I miss the flow'rets small,*
> *There have no friends to cheer me.*
>
> *Now, how to value life I know—*
> *I hold it as a treasure;*
> *There is no love i' th' grave below,*
> *No music, warmth, or pleasure.*
> *On it the heavy earth is flung,*
> *The coffin-lid shuts tightly!*

My blood is warm, my soul is young!

Life smiles — life shines so brightly!"

She folded her hands: all became like flowers and gold before her eyes. Afar off was the sound of music: she reeled and sank down upon the sofa which was near her. Life flowed forth from her heart, but the sensation was one of bliss; a repose, as when the weary bow down their heads for sleep.

"Here is a letter!" cried Louise, full of joy, and found her white and cold. Terrified, she called for help, and bent over her.

Eva was dead.

CHAPTER XLV

*"Knowest thou the mountain and its cloudy paths? where the
mule is seeking its misty way." —GOETHE.*

The letter was from Wilhelm; every line breathed life's joy and gladness.

"MIA CARA SORELLA!

"Does it not sound beautifully? It is Italian! Now then, I am in that so-often-sung-of Paradise, but of the so much-talked-about blue air, I have as yet seen nothing of consequence. Here it is gray, gray as in Denmark. To be sure Otto says that it is beautiful, that we have the heaven of home above us, but I am not so poetical. The eating is good, and the filth of the people strikes one horribly after being in Switzerland, the enchanting Switzerland! Yes, there is nature! We have made a crusade through it, you may think. But now you shall hear about the journey, and the entrance into 'la bella Italia,' which is yet below all my expectations. I cannot at all bear these feeble people; I cannot endure this monk-odor and untruthfulness. We are come direct from the scenery of Switzerland, from clouds and glaciers, from greatness and power. We travelled somewhat hastily through the valley of the Rhone; the weather was gray, but the whole obtained therefrom a peculiar character. The woods in the lofty ridges looked like heather; the valley itself seemed like a garden filled with vegetables, vineyards, and green meadows. The clouds over and under one another, but the snow-covered mountains peeped forth gloriously from among them, It was a riven cloud-world which drove past,—the wild chase with which the daylight had disguised itself. It kissed in its flight Pissevache, a waterfall by no means to be despised. In Brieg we rested some time, but at two o'clock in the morning began again our journey over the Simplon. This is the journey which I will describe to you. Otto and I sat in the coupée. Fancy us in white blouses, shawl-caps, and with green morocco slippers, for the devil may travel in slippers—they are painful to the feet.

"We both of us have mustaches! I have seduced Otto. They become us uncommonly well, and give us a very imposing air; and that is very good now that we are come into the land of banditti, where we must endeavor to awe the robbers. Thus travelled we. It was a dark night, and still as death, as in the moment when the overture begins to an opera. Soon, indeed, was the great Simplon curtain to be rolled up, and we to behold the land of music. Immediately on leaving the city, the road began to ascend; we could not see a hand before us; around us tumbled and roared the water-courses,—it was as if we heard the pulse of Nature beat. Close above the carriage passed the white clouds; they seemed like transparent marble slabs which were slid over us. We had the gray dawn with us, whilst deep in the valley lay yet the darkness of night; in an hour's time it began to show itself there among the little wooden houses.

"It is a road hewn out of the rocks. The giant Napoleon carried it through the backbone of the earth. The eagle, Napoleon's bird, flew like a living armorial crest over the gigantic work of the master. There it was cold and gray; the clouds above us, the clouds below us, and in the middle space steep rocky walls.

"At regular distances houses (relais) are erected for the travellers; in one of these we drank our coffee. The passengers sat on benches and tables around the great fire-place, where the pine logs crackled. More than a thousand names were written on the walls. I amused myself by writing mamma's, yours, Sophie's, and Eva's; now they stand there, and people will fancy that you have been on the Simplon. In the lobby I scratched in that of Mamsell, and added 'Without her workbox.' Otto was thinking about you. We talked in our, what the rest would call 'outlandish speech,' when I all at once exclaimed, 'It is really Eva's birthday!' I remembered it first. In Simplon town we determined to drink her health.

"We set off again. Wherever the glaciers might fall and destroy the road the rocks have been sprung, and formed into great galleries, through which one drives without any danger. One waterfall succeeds another. There is no balustrade along the road, only the dark, deep abyss where the pine-trees raise themselves to an immense height, and yet only look like rafters on the mighty wall of rock. Before we had advanced much further, we came to where trees no longer grew. The great hospice lay in snow and cloud. We came into a valley. What solitude! what desolation! only naked crags! They seemed metallic, and all had a green hue. The utmost variety of mosses grew there; before us towered up an immense glacier, which looked like green bottle-glass ornamented with snow. It was bitterly cold here, and in Simplon the stoves were lighted; the champagne foamed, Eva's health was drunk, and, only think! at that very moment an avalanche was so gallant as to fall. That was a cannonade; a pealing among the mountains! It must have rung in Eva's ears. Ask her about it. I can see how she smiles.

"We now advanced toward Italy, but cold was it, and cold it remained. The landscape became savage; we drove between steep crags. Only fancy, on both sides a block of granite several miles long, and almost as high, and the road not wider than for two carriages to pass, and there you have a picture of it. If one wanted to see the sky, one was obliged to put one's head out of the carriage and look up, and then it was as if one looked up from the bottom of the deepest well, dark and narrow. Every moment I kept thinking, 'Nay, if these two walls should come together!' We with carriage and horses were only like ants on a pebble. We drove through the ribs of the earth! The water roared; the clouds hung like fleeces on the gray, craggy walls. In a valley we saw boys and girls dressed in sheep-skins, who looked as wild as if they had been brought up among beasts.

"Suddenly the air became wondrously mild. We saw the first fig-tree by the road-side. Chestnuts hung over our heads; we were in Isella, the boundary town of Italy. Otto sang, and was wild with delight; I studied the first public-house sign, 'Tabacca e vino.'

"How luxuriant became the landscape! Fields of maize and vineyards! The vine was not trained on frames as in Germany!—no, it hung in luxuriant garlands, in great huts of leaves! Beautiful children bounded along the road, but the heavens were gray, and that I had not expected in Italy. From Domo d'Ossola, I looked back to my beloved Switzerland! Yes, she turns truly the most beautiful side toward Italy. But there was not any time for me to gaze; on we must. In the carriage there sat an old Signorina; she recited poetry, and made: with her eyes 'che bella cosa!'

"About ten o'clock at night we were in Baveno, drank tea, and slept, whilst Lago Maggiore splashed under our window. The lake and the Borromaen island we were to see by daylight.

"'Lord God!' thought I, 'is this all?' A scene as quiet and riant as this we—have at home! Funen after this should be called Isola bella, and the East Sea is quite large enough to be called Lago Maggiore. We went by the steamboat past the holy Borromeus [Author's Note: A colossal statue on the shore of Lago Maggiore.] to Sesto de Calende; we had a priest on board, who was very much astonished at our having come from so far. I showed him a large travelling map which we had with us, where the Lago Maggiore was the most southern, and Hamburg the most northern point. 'Yet still further off,' said I; 'more to the north!' and he struck his hands together when he perceived that we were from beyond the great map. He inquired whether we were Calvinists.

"We sped through glorious scenes. The Alps looked like glass mountains in a fairy tale. They lay behind us. The air was warm as summer, but light as on the high mountains. The women wafted kisses to us; but they were not handsome, the good ladies!

"Tell the Kammerjunker that the Italian pigs have no bristles, but have a coal-black shining skin like a Moor.

"Toward night we arrived at Milan, where we located ourselves with Reichmann, made a good supper, and had excellent beds; but I foresee that this bliss will not last very long. On the other side of the Apennines we shall be up to the ears in dirt, and must eat olives preserved in oil; but let it pass. Otto adapts himself charmingly to all things; he begins to be merry—that is, at times! I, too, have had a sort of vertigo—I am taken with Italian music; but then there is a difference in hearing it on the spot. It has more than melody; it has character. The luxuriance in nature and in the female form; the light, fluttering movement of the people, where even pain is melody, has won my heart and my understanding. Travelling changes people!

"Kiss mamma for me! Tell Eva about the health-drinking on the Simplon, and about the falling avalanche: do not forget that; that is precisely the point in my letter! Tell me too how Eva blushed, and smiled, and said, 'He thought of me!' Yes, in fact it is very noble of me. My sweet Sophie and her Kammerjunker, Jakoba and Mamsell, must have a bouquet of greetings, which you must arrange properly. If you could but see Otto and me with our mustaches! We make an impression, and that is very pleasant. If the days only did not go on so quickly—if life did not pass so rapidly!

"'Questa vita mortale

Che par si bella, a quasi piuma al vento

Che la porta a la perde in un momento,' [Note: Guarini]

as we Italians say. Cannot you understand that?

"Thy affectionate brother,

"WILHELM."

Otto wrote in the margin of the letter, "Italy is a paradise! Here the heavens are three times as lofty as at home. I love the proud pine-trees and the dark-blue mountains. Would hat everybody could see the glorious objects!"

Wilhelm added to this, "What he writes about the Italian heavens is stupid stuff. Ours at home is just as good. He is an odd person, as you very well know!

"'Addic! A rivederci!'"

CHAPTER XLVI

"Thou art master in thy world.

Hast thou thyself, then thou hast all!"

—*WAHLMANN.*

In the summer of 1834 the friends had been absent for two years. In the last year, violet-colored gillyflowers had adorned a grave in the little country church-yard.

"A heart which overflowed with love,

Was gone from earth to love and God,"

were the words which might be read upon the grave-stone.

A withered bouquet of stocks had been found by Louise, with the certificate of Eva's birth and her hymn-book. These were the flowers which Wilhelm had given her that evening at Roeskelde. Among the dry leaves there lay a piece of paper, on which she had written,—"Even like these flowers let the feelings die away in my soul which these flowers inspire it with!"

And now above her grave the flowers which she had loved sent forth their fragrance.

It was Sunday; the sun shone warm; the church-goers, old and young, assembled under the great lime-tree near Eva's grave. They expected their young preacher, who to-day was to preach for the third time.

The gentlefolks would also certainly be there, they thought, because the young Baron was come back out of foreign parts, and with him the other gentleman, who certainly was to have Miss Louise.

"Our new preacher is worth hearing," said one of the peasant women; "such a young man, who actually preaches the old faith! as gentle and as meek in conversation as if he were one of ourselves! And in the pulpit, God help us! it went quite down into my legs the last time about the Day of Judgment!"

"There is Father!" [Note: The general term applied to the preacher by the Danish peasants.] exclaimed the crowd, and the heads of old and young were uncovered. The women courtesied deeply as a young man in priest-robes went into the church-door. His eyes and lips moved to a pious smile, the hair was smooth upon his pale forehead.

"Good day, children!" said he.

It was Hans Peter. He had, indeed, had "the best characters," and thus had received a good living, and now preached effectively about the devil and all his works.

The singing of the community sounded above the grave where the sun shone, where the stocks sent forth their fragrance, and where Eva slept: she whose last wish was to live.

"There is no love i' th' grave below,
No music, warmth, or pleasure."

The earth lay firm and heavy upon her coffin-lid.

During the singing of the second hymn a handsome carriage drove up before the church-yard. The two friends, who were only just returned to their home in Denmark, entered the church, together with the mother and Louise.

Travelling and two years had made Wilhelm appear somewhat older; there was a shadow of sadness in his otherwise open and life-rejoicing countenance. Otto looked handsomer than formerly; the gloomy expression in his face was softened, he looked around cheerfully, yet thoughtfully, and a smile was on his lips when he spoke with Louise.

There was in the sermon some allusion made to those who had returned home; for the rest, it was a flowery discourse interlarded with many texts from the Bible. The community shed tears; the good, wise people, they understood it to mean that their young lord was returned home uninjured from all the perils which abound in foreign lands.

The preacher was invited to dinner at the hall. The Kammerjunker and Sophie came also, but it lasted "seven long and seven wide," as Miss Jakoba expressed herself, before they could get through all the unwrapping and were ready to enter the parlor, for they had with them the little son Fergus, as he was called, after the handsome Scotchman in Sir Walter Scott's "Waverley." That was Sophie's wish. The Kammerjunker turned the name of Fergus to Gusseman, and Jacoba asserted that it was a dog's name.

"Now you shall see my little bumpkin!" said he, and brought in a square-built child, who with fat, red cheeks, and round arms, stared around him. "That is a strong fellow! Here is something to take hold of! Tralla-ralla-ralla!" And he danced him round the room.

Sophie laughed and offered her hand to Otto.

Wilhelm turned to Mamsell. "I have brought something for you," said he, "something which I hope may find a place in the work-box—a man made of very small mussel-shells; it is from Venice."

"Heavens! from all that way off!" said she and courtesied.

After dinner they walked in the garden.

Wilhelm spoke already of going the following year again to Paris.

"Satan!" said the Kammerjunker. "Nay, I can do better with Mr. Thostrup. He is patriotic. He lays out his money in an estate. It is a good bargain which you have made, and in a while will be beautiful; there is hill and dale."

"There my old Rosalie shall live with me," said Otto; "there she will find her Switzerland. The cows shall have bells on their necks."

"Lord God! shall they also be made fools of?" exclaimed Jakoba: "that is just exactly as if it were Sophie."

They went through the avenue where Otto two years before had wept, and had related all his troubles to Louise. He recollected it, and a gentle sigh passed his lips whilst his eyes rested on Louise.

"Now, do you feel yourself happy at home?" asked she; "a lovelier summer's day than this you certainly have not abroad."

"Every country has its own beauties," replied Otto. "Our Denmark is not a step child of Nature. The people here are dearest to me, for I am best acquainted with them. They, and not Nature, it is that makes a land charming. Denmark is a good land; and here also will I look for my happiness." He seized Louise's hand; she blushed, and was silent. Happy hours succeeded.

This circle assembled every Sunday; on the third, their delight was greater, was more festal than on any former occasion.

Nature herself had the same expression. The evening was most beautiful; the full moon shone, magnificent dark-blue clouds raised themselves like mountains on the other side the Belt. Afar off sailed the ships, with every sail set to catch the breeze.

Below the moon floated a coal-black cloud, which foretold a squall.

A little yacht went calmly over the water. At the helm sat a boy—half a child he seemed: it was Jonas, the little singing-bird, as Wilhelm had once called him. Last Whitsuntide he had been confirmed, and with his Confirmation all his singer-dreams were at an end: but that did not trouble him; on the contrary, it had lain very heavy upon his heart that he was not to be a fifer. His highest wish had been to see himself as a regimental fifer, and then he should have gone to his Confirmation in his red uniform, with a sabre at his side, and a feather in his hat half as tall as himself. Thus adorned, he might have gone with the girls into the King's Garden and upon the Round Tower, the usual walk for poor children in Copenhagen. On Confirmation-day they ascend the high tower, just as if it were to gain from it a free view over the world. Little Jonas, however, was confirmed as a sailor, and he now sat at the helm on this quiet night.

Upon the deck lay two persons and slept; a third went tranquilly up and down. Suddenly he shook one of the sleepers, and caught hold on the sail. A squall had arisen with such rapidity and strength, that the vessel in a moment was thrown on her side. Mast and sail were below the water. Little Jonas uttered a shriek. Not a vessel was within sight. The two sleepers had woke in time to cling to the mast. With great force they seized the ropes, but in vain; the sail hung like lead in the water. The ship did not right herself.

"Joseph, Maria!" exclaimed one of them, a man with gray hairs and unpleasing features. "We sink! the water is in the hold!"

All three clambered now toward the hinder part of the vessel, where a little boat floated after. One of them sprang into it.

"My daughter!" cried the elder, and bent himself toward the narrow entrance into the cabin. "Sidsel, save thy life!" and so saying, he sprang into the boat.

"We must have my daughter out," cried he. One of the ship's cabin windows was under water; he burst in the other window.

"We are sinking!" cried he, and a horrible scream was heard within.

The old man was German Heinrich, who was about to come with this vessel from Copenhagen to Jutland: Sidsel was his daughter, and therefore he wished now to save her life a second time.

The water rushed more and more into the ship. Heinrich thrust his arm through the cabin-window, he grasped about in the water within; suddenly he caught hold on a garment, he drew it toward him; but it was only the captain's coat, and not his daughter, as he had hoped.

"The ship sinks!" shrieked the other, and grasped wildly on the rope which held the boat fast: in vain he attempted to divide it with his pocket-knife. The ship whirled round with the boat and all. Air and water boiled within it, and, as if in a whirlpool, the whole sunk into the deep. The sea agitated itself into strong surges over the place, and then was again still. The moon shone tranquilly over the surface of the water as before. No wreck remained to tell any one of the struggle which there had been with death.

The bell tolled a quarter past twelve; and at that moment the last light at the hall was extinguished.

"I will go to Paris," said Wilhelm, "to my glorious Switzerland; here at home one is heavy-hearted; the gillyflowers on the grave have an odor full of melancholy recollections. I must breathe the mountain air; I must mingle in the tumult of men, and it is quite the best in the world."

Otto closed his eyes; he folded his hands.

"Louise loves me," said he. "I am so happy that I fear some great misfortune may soon meet me; thus it used always to be. Whilst German Heinrich lives I cannot assure myself of good! If he were away, I should be perfectly tranquil, perfectly happy!"